The Faiths of the Founding Fathers

The Faiths of the Founding Fathers

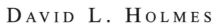

D AVID L. H OLMES

OXFORD
UNIVERSITY PRESS
2006

OXFORD
UNIVERSITY PRESS

Oxford University Press, Inc., publishes works that
further Oxford University's objective of excellence
in research, scholarship, and education.

Oxford   New York
Auckland   Cape Town   Dar es Salaam   Hong Kong   Karachi
Kuala Lumpur   Madrid   Melbourne   Mexico City   Nairobi
New Delhi   Shanghai   Taipei   Toronto

With offices in
Argentina   Austria   Brazil   Chile   Czech Republic   France   Greece
Guatemala   Hungary   Italy   Japan   Poland   Portugal   Singapore
South Korea   Switzerland   Thailand   Turkey   Ukraine   Vietnam

Published by Oxford University Press, Inc.
198 Madison Avenue, New York, NY 10016
www.oup.com

Oxford is a registered trademark of Oxford University Press

Library of Congress Cataloging-in-Publication Data
Holmes, David Lynn.
The faiths of the founding fathers / David L. Holmes
p. cm.   Includes bibliographical references and index.
ISBN-13: 978-0-19-530092-5 (cloth)
ISBN-10: 0-19-530092-0 (cloth)
1. Deism—United States—History—18th century.
2. Statesmen—Religious Life—United States—History—18th century.
3. United States—Religion—To 1800.
I. Title.
BL2747.4.H63 2006   200.973'09033—dc22   2005033077

3 5 7 9 8 6 4 2

Printed in the United States of America
on acid-free paper

To Catesby

The past is a foreign country; they do things differently there.

—L. P. Hartley

Acknowledgments

My thanks to the following alumni and students of the College of William and Mary who assisted in preparing this publication: Meghan K. Cunningham, Nathanael J. C. Nichols, and David C. Williard. Additional thanks go to Jenna P. Abel, to Ash Lawn-Highland: The Home of James Monroe, to the staffs of the libraries of the University of Virginia and of the College of William and Mary, and to Professor David Hein for reading the manuscript.

Contents

1 Religion in the American Colonies in 1770 1
 The Sects 3
 Tolerant Pennsylvania 5
 The Mainline Churches 8
 Religion in New England 9
 Religion in the Middle Colonies 15
 Religion in the Southern Colonies 18
 The Rise of the Evangelical Tradition in America 25

2 The Anglican Tradition and the Virginia
 Founding Fathers 33

3 The Enlightenment Religion of Deism 39

4 The Founding Fathers and Deism 49

5 The Religious Views of Benjamin Franklin 53

6 The Religious Views of George Washington 59

7 The Religious Views of John Adams 73

8 The Religious Views of Thomas Jefferson   79

9 The Religious Views of James Madison   91

10 The Religious Views of James Monroe   99

11 The Wives and Daughters of the Founding Fathers   109
  The Appeal of Christian Orthodoxy to Women   109
  Martha Custis Washington   112
  Eleanor Parke Custis Lewis   115
  Abigail Smith Adams   117
  Martha Wayles Skelton Jefferson   121
  *Jefferson's Daughters: Martha Jefferson Randolph and
      Maria Jefferson Eppes*   122
  Dolley Payne Madison   125

12 A Layperson's Guide to Distinquishing a Deist
  from an Orthodox Christian   133

13 Three Orthodox Christians   143
  Samuel Adams   143
  Elias Boudinot   150
  John Jay   154

14 The Past Is a Foreign Country   161

  Epilogue   165

  Notes   187

  Bibliography   203

  Illustration Credits   211

  Index   215

The Wolf shall dwell with the Lamb, and the Leopard lie down with the Kid—the Cow, and the Bear shall feed; their young ones shall lie down together, and the Lyon shall eat straw like the Ox—none shall then hurt, or destroy; for the earth shall be full of the Knowledge of the Lord.

When this Millennium shall commence, if there shall be any need of Civil Government, indulge me in the fancy that it will be in the republican form, or something better.

—Samuel Adams (The Father of the American Revolution)
to John Adams, 4 October 1790

The Faiths of the Founding Fathers

1

RELIGION IN THE
AMERICAN COLONIES IN 1770

On my arrival in the United States," the famous French traveler Alexis de Tocqueville observed in the early nineteenth century, "the religious aspect of the country was the first thing that struck my attention."[1] If in 1770—six years before the thirteen colonies became the UnitedStates—a different group of foreign visitors had traveled the narrow roads of the colonies, they would have agreed with de Tocqueville's later observance. The travelers would have further noted that the Americans of 1770 were either overwhelmingly Protestant or unchurched. Yet in such ports as Newport, Rhode Island, New York City, Philadelphia, Charleston, and Savannah—places where transatlantic vessels carrying passengers and crew regularly docked—the travelers would have come across not only Christian churches but also Jewish synagogues. As of 1770, some one thousand Jews probably lived in the colonies. In 1790, the first federal census counted 1,243 Jews in a total American population of almost three million. By the end of the century, the new republic had synagogues in Charleston, New York, Newport, Savannah, Philadelphia, and Richmond.

In these and other port cities, the travelers would also have found scattered Roman Catholics. Most of the Roman Catholics lacked churches and priests, but some had "Mass stations"—homes or

Touro Synagogue, Newport, Rhode Island.

buildings where itinerant priests said Mass regularly or occasionally. The travelers would have found most of the approximately thirty
thousand Roman Catholics and virtually all of their churches located
in the colonies of Maryland and Pennsylvania, especially in polyglot
Philadelphia.

When the Continental Congress was meeting, John Adams, George
Washington, and others attended afternoon Mass at St. Mary's Church,
one of Philadelphia's two Roman Catholic Churches. The visit was
apparently Adams's first to a Roman Catholic Church. The lavish
ornamentation and use of Latin (a language the congregation did not
understand) bothered the Puritan soul of Adams, but he also found
the service appealing. "The dress of the priest was rich with lace," he
wrote to his wife, Abigail:

> His pulpit was velvet and gold. The altar piece was very rich—little images
> and crucifixes about wax candles lighted up. But how shall I describe the

picture of our Savior in a frame of marble over the altar at full length Upon the Cross, in the agonies, and the blood dropping and streaming from his wounds?[2]

Both repelled and moved, Adams remained to the end of the Mass, describing the service to Abigail as "aw[e]ful and affecting."[3]

The Sects

In 1770, the visitors would also have seen or heard about a certain number of what in religious history are often called "sects"—groups that remained within the wide spectrum of Christian belief but that broke off into what they considered pure communities of ethics and doctrine based upon their interpretations of Scripture.

And therein lies a story. From approximately the fourth to the sixteenth century, certain practices or doctrines recorded in the New Testament or in the writings of the early church fathers dropped out of use in Christianity. The Protestant Reformation, beginning with Martin Luther's ninety-five theses of 1517, attempted to restore what it viewed as lost central teachings of early Christianity. These teachings included the authority of Scripture, the lack of universal authority of the Pope, the salvation of the individual by grace through faith, the priesthood of all believers, the legitimacy of a married clergy, the use of the vernacular (the language commonly used in a country) for worship, and similar doctrines. In the centuries prior to the Reformation, similar reform movements had broken out sporadically in Europe, but none succeeded because the civil power, in union with the church, had put them down.

During and after the Reformation, however, new movements continually emerged in Christianity. Called by some church historians "the Radical Reformation," they attempted to restore more of the beliefs and rites of original Christianity than the mainline Protestant churches had thought necessary or appropriate. They restricted baptism to converted adults and separated church and state. Additionally, they refused, according to the teachings of Christ, to bear arms or to participate in war (a doctrinal practice called variously "nonresistance" or "pacifism"). These were three of their most radical reforms, though there were many others.

Other groups attempted to restore such practices as speaking in tongues during worship, the "love feast" (a common meal held by early Christians in connection with the Lord's Supper, or Holy Communion), the ritual of foot washing, the communalism depicted in the early chapters of the Book of Acts, the belief that Christ would soon return in majesty and power to judge the world, and other early Christian beliefs and practices. Persecuted in Europe, many of these groups immigrated to America during the colonial period. Following the Revolution and the subsequent separation of church and state, the United States became a fermenting vat of such Christian sects.

Thus while traveling through New England in 1770, the European visitors might have learned of the Sandemanians. Named for the leader who brought them from Scotland to New Hampshire, this small sect lived simply, opposed the accumulation of wealth, and observed a Lord's Supper that included a love feast and the ceremonial washing of feet. Other Sandemanian teachings—such as the dietary obligation of Christians to abstain not only from blood but also from the meat of animals killed by strangulation—returned the group to some of the practices of the earliest Jewish Christians.

Had the visitors traveled through New England one to two decades later, they would have learned of a growing movement of celibate, communal, pacifist Christians who worshiped uniquely and believed in the imminent Second Coming. Formally named the "United Society of Believers in Christ's Second Appearing" and located in the state of New York as well as in New England, the sect was called by others "the Shakers." The travelers might also have encountered some members of the Universalist Church, a Christian group whose name came from their belief in universal salvation. Because God is merciful, Universalists believed, God would ultimately save all humans, not simply save some and consign all others to damnation. Their reading of both the New Testament and early Christian history also caused them to question the Trinity, a doctrine officially defined by church councils beginning in the fourth century.

But the principal "sect" the travelers would have encountered would have been the Quakers, or the Religious Society of Friends. Plain in appearance, believing in an Inner Light that was the presence of Christ within each person, asserting the fundamental equality of all men and women, and opposing not only trained clergy and formal worship but also military service and the swearing of oaths, the Quakers were widely dispersed. Ranking as perhaps the fifth largest of the colonial churches, they existed in substantial numbers in Rhode Island, New York, New Jersey, Maryland, Virginia, North Carolina, and especially in Pennsylvania, a colony founded under Quaker auspices.

Tolerant Pennsylvania

Pennsylvania, in fact, would have been the colony in which the travelers would have encountered the richest mosaic of sects. Because the English Quaker William Penn had founded the colony as a "Holy Experiment" where Quakers and other persecuted religious sects could live and worship freely, Pennsylvania had attracted many small religious groups by 1770. The visitors would have discovered that most of the groups had come from Germany, that all believed that they had restored practices of apostolic Christianity that mainstream Christianity had wrongly abandoned, and that virtually all were pacifistic. Because of the pacifistic views of these sects, Pennsylvania was the only colony that did not have a legally instituted militia system, a situation the citizens had to rectify during the American Revolution.

Inland from Philadelphia, for example, the visitors would have encountered the *Unitas Fratrum*, or Moravian Brethren. Originating prior to the Protestant Reformation from the teachings of the Czech reformer John Huss, the Moravians refocused their teachings after they fled to the German state of Saxony in the eighteenth century. Valuing Christian conduct over the finer points of creeds, they were influenced by both Lutheran and Calvinist teachings. They stressed the inner testimony of the spirit and held to the principle of "in essentials unity; in nonessentials liberty; in both, charity." They celebrated a simple liturgy—or set of forms for public religious worship—marked by the rich use of music, attempted to reproduce the love feasts of early Christianity, and emphasized evangelism at a time when most Protestant churches did not. Pacifists, the Moravians were found not only in Pennsylvania but also in North Carolina and, briefly, in Georgia and elsewhere. In North Carolina they established the town of

Salem; in Pennsylvania they settled Bethlehem, Nazareth, and Lititz. All of these towns were initially exclusively Moravian.

In counties adjacent to Philadelphia, the visitors might also have encountered a small mystical sect historically related to the Moravians. Named after a former follower who came to view Luther as a religious compromiser and called him "Dr. Sit-on-the-fence," the loosely organized, pacifistic, and somewhat mystical Schwenkfelders opposed infant baptism and emphasized inward spirituality over the doctrinal and churchly aspects of Christianity. Though residents of Pennsylvania for some decades by 1770, they had erected neither a meeting house nor a church building.

In colonial Pennsylvania, the visitors would also have encountered the Mennonites, the principal heirs of the radical Anabaptist (or "Rebaptizer") wing of the Reformation. The program of the Mennonites to reproduce biblical Christianity caused them not only to deviate markedly from the norms of contemporary Christian orthodoxy of their day but also to suffer persecution. Rather than baptize infants, the Mennonites baptized only converted, believing adults. Rather than regard baptism as a sacrament that washed away original sin, they viewed it as a symbolic act that ratified an inner change that had already occurred in the converted individual. Instead of viewing Christianity as a religion into which people were born, they taught that churches should be "gathered" out of the world and composed of believing, converted adults who had voluntarily chosen to follow Jesus Christ.

Unlike Eastern Orthodoxy, Roman Catholicism, and such mainline Protestant movements as Lutheranism, Calvinism, and Anglicanism, the Mennonites and all Anabaptists advocated the separation of church and state. Teaching that the true Christian withdrew from the fallen world and rejected its values and amusements, they opposed wearing fashionable clothes, holding public office, using the courts, swearing oaths, and serving in the military. They took the doctrine of the priesthood of all believers so seriously that they selected their leaders by the biblical pattern of drawing lots. Whatever the visitors in 1770 would have thought of the Mennonites, the typical European of the time would have viewed them as akin to gypsies. Executed in Europe by Protestant and Roman Catholic countries alike for their teachings, the Mennonites lived and worshiped openly in tolerant Pennsylvania.

If the visitors had traveled inland to the mountainous areas of Pennsylvania and then down into the valleys of Maryland and Virginia, they would have encountered another group of "plain people" from Germany. Calling themselves by the biblical name of "Brethren" but referred to by others as "Dunkers" or "Tunkers" (from the German verb *tunken*, meaning "to dip"), the Brethren fully immersed (or "dunked") their adult baptizees in water three times face forward, once at the mention of each name of the Trinity. Heeding the instructions given in chapter 5 of the New Testament letter of James ("Is any among you sick? Let him call for the elders of the church, and let them pray over him, anointing him with oil in the name of the Lord"), they anointed the sick with oil. Basing their practice on the New Testament's depiction of the Last Supper, they held their solemn communion service in the evening and accompanied it with footwashing, a love feast, and the "holy kiss" (or kiss of charity) enjoined in the New Testament as a Christian greeting. Like many of the other Pennsylvania sects, they refused to swear oaths, bring civil suits in the courts, or bear arms.

The Ephrata Community of Lancaster County—a strict semi-monastic society noted for its choral music, printing, and illuminated manuscripts—represented a break-off from the Brethren. Besides adopting communal living, the Ephrata Community restored the early Christian practice of commemorating Saturday as the Sabbath. Although the community was in decline by 1770, the foreign travelers might have stopped there, for Ephrata was known for its hospitality and worship. At least two of the founding fathers—Benjamin Franklin, who printed music books for the community and kept copies in his library, and George Washington, who used the Ephrata buildings as a temporary hospital for his wounded after the Battle of Brandywine—were well acquainted with the community.

In their attempt to return to first-century Christianity, all of these interpretations of Christianity differed markedly from those advocated by the mainstream of Christianity. But in colonial Pennsylvania, the Christian sects and the mainstream churches lived side by side. The European visitors would have chanced upon some sects

A solitary sister at Ephrata cloister, depicted in
1745.

and visited or heard about others, not only in Pennsylvania but also
in other colonies. And in the years in which the affairs of the new
nation centered in Philadelphia, the founding fathers of the United
States would have encountered members of many of these sects.

The Mainline Churches

In 1770, sects were only footnotes to the story of religion in America.
In that year the story focused on what were called "established
churches" or "state churches." A concept transplanted to the American colonies from Europe, an established or state church is the official religious organization of a country or colony. The government
supports it financially, legislates for it, and protects it against competition. Russia, Greece, Scandinavia, Germany, Italy, France, Spain,

the Netherlands, England, Scotland, and other European countries all had state churches at one time. Citizens were born into membership in churches just as they were born into citizenship in countries. From the fourth century on, state churches represented the norm in European Christianity. Some European countries, such as England, still have them. Of the thirteen colonies that came to form the United States, nine had established churches during the colonial period.

Religion in New England

As the travelers worked their way down the colonies from north to south, they would have found one tolerant, religiously diverse colony in New England—Rhode Island. Founded by Roger Williams, an exile from Puritan Massachusetts who opposed governmental coercion in religious matters, the "livelie experiment" of Rhode Island had no established church. It guaranteed freedom of belief to all but outspoken atheists and—for some decades—to Roman Catholics. In the words of a critic from adjacent Massachusetts, the colony contained "Antinomians, Anabaptists, Antisabbatarians, Arminians, Socinians, Quakers, Ranters—everything in the world but Roman Catholics and real Christians."[4]

In this diverse colony, the Baptists (English Calvinists whose reading of the New Testament caused them to reject infant baptism and to baptize only believing adults), Quakers, Anglicans, and Congregationalists had the most members. Before he left the ministry and became a "Seeker" after a true Christianity that he never found, Williams had briefly been a Baptist.

By "real Christians," the Puritan critic of course meant his own Congregationalist Church, which was the established church not only in Massachusetts but also in Connecticut and New Hampshire. The largest of four branches of Calvinist Christianity the visitors would have observed in the colonies, Congregationalism arguably emphasized the intellect to a greater extent than any other church in colonial America. In the same way that other groups received their names from certain acts (for example, the Quakers or Baptists) or modes of church governance (for example, the Presbyterians or Episcopalians), the Congregational churches took their name from the belief that early Christian congregations ran their own affairs and were subject to no higher supervision than Christ.

Congregationalism originated in the movement of English Calvinists called "puritans"—a name acquired because of the efforts of its adherents to "purify" the Church of England from certain doctrines and liturgical practices that remained from its Roman Catholic past and were held to be untrue to the New Testament and to early Christian practice. The Puritan movement—both in the British Isles and in the

American colonies—included the Presbyterians, the Baptists, and some Anglicans who decided to remain within England's established church.

In the backcountry of New England and especially in the colonies below it, the travelers would have encountered a third form of Calvinism—Presbyterianism (the name that Calvinism adopted in Scotland). In the area of Boston and especially in the colonies from New York to South Carolina, they would have learned of the Reformed (the name that Calvinism took on the European continent).

Except in two areas, these four groups shared the common heritage of Calvinism and displayed only minor homegrown dissimilarities in terminology and worship. Their principal differences lay in the areas of governance and baptismal practice. In matters of church government (or polity), the Congregationalists and Baptists followed a

First Baptist Church, Providence, Rhode Island, where Brown University still holds commencements.

democratic form. The Presbyterians and Reformed, however (like John Calvin himself), saw the republican form with an ascending hierarchy of synods and assemblies as true to the New Testament and to early Christianity. In matters of baptism, the Baptists believed that early Christians baptized only converted adults, whereas the Congregationalists, Presbyterians, and Reformed believed that the baptism of infants was true to apostolic practice.

Because all four Calvinist traditions gave laypeople significant authority in the government of the churches they insisted on an educated laity. As a result, these churches tended to found colleges wherever they went. As of 1770, two-thirds of the institutions of higher education in the American colonies were of Calvinist origin. Five years later, when Presbyterians founded a final college on the eve of the Revolution, the percentage of American colleges with a Congregationalist, Baptist, Presbyterian, or Reformed origin rose to 70 percent.

Church historians have estimated that over 80 percent of American Christians in the colonial period—from Anglicans on the right-center of the Christian spectrum to Quakers on the left—were significantly influenced by John Calvin's teachings. Only the Roman Catholics, some of the Lutherans, and some of the "sects" remained distinctly free from Calvinist influence. Even the Quakers—on the surface a very un-Calvinistic body—were in reality the "puritans of the Puritans" and emerged in England from the left wing of the Puritan movement.

An interpretation of Christianity that professed less warmth and intimacy with God than Lutheranism or Roman Catholicism, Calvinism was full of awe and homage to what it considered a just and majestic God. Like virtually all of Protestantism, it agreed with the main points of the Lutheran Reformation, but it viewed the Bible as more of an instruction manual for worship, church government, and conduct than Lutheranism did. Roman Catholicism, for example, taught that bishops were descendants of the apostles and were essential to the Christian faith. Luther held that early Christianity displayed a variety of forms of ordained ministry and that true Christianity could exist with or without bishops.

Calvin, however, believed that the New Testament (in such passages as Acts 20:17, 28, and Titus 1:5–7) indicated that bishops and presbyters—or, to use synonyms for the second word, "elders" or "priests"—were originally the same office. In Calvin's view, the separate office of a monarchical bishop (a bishop superior to all presbyters in rank and authority, in the same way that monarchs are superior to all of their subjects) emerged in Christianity only after the apostolic period. Thus Calvin argued that the presbyter-bishops who ministered in his churches—that is, the pastors—were just as much Christian bishops as the Pope of Rome, the Patriarch of Constantinople, or the Archbishop of Canterbury.

The key concept of Calvinism, that God is sovereign in all things, led to its teaching (a standard concept of the Protestant Reformation) that salvation comes entirely from God. Puritans believed that all humans were sinners through Adam's and Eve's Original Sin in the Garden of Eden, which was then transmitted to their descendants. Puritan doctrine asserted that humans could do nothing (in belief or in action) to save themselves, but that God out of his mercy did save some humans (the "elect") while damning others (the "reprobate"). Known as double predestination (the foreordination of individuals not only to heaven but also to hell), the doctrine was modified and ultimately abandoned in later centuries by the main bodies of Calvinism. John Calvin, however, asserted that the doctrine was taught in both the Old and New Testaments. It protected, he declared, the freedom of the all-knowing, all-powerful God.[5] He also observed that the doctrine was taught by many of the early church fathers, especially by Augustine of Hippo, the fourth-century bishop whose thought formed the basis of Western Christian theology.

At its apex the doctrine had a great hold on believers. Its teachings are embedded in the familiar hymn "Rock of Ages," written by an English Calvinist in 1776, six years after the foreign visitors would have toured the American colonies:

> Rock of ages, cleft for me,
> Let me hide myself in thee.
> Let the water and the blood
> From thy wounded side that flowed,
> Be of sin the double cure,
> Cleanse me from its guilt and power.

Should my tears for ever flow,
Should my zeal no langour know;
All for sin could not atone:
Thou must save, and thou alone.
In my hand no price I bring,
Simply to thy cross I cling.

Three years later, another English Calvinist wrote what has become perhaps the best-known hymn in the English language. Its words display not only the sovereignty of an all-powerful God but also the gratitude that predestinarian Calvinists have felt that God's grace might still save them despite all of their sin:

Through many dangers, toils, and snares,
I have already come.
'Tis Grace that brought me safe thus far,
and Grace will lead me home.[6]

That both authors were clergy in the Church of England displays the widespread influence of Calvinism during the formative years of the United States. Anglicanism fused the influences of several Christian traditions and was not, strictly speaking, a Calvinist body. But churches, like political parties, have wings, and the Church of England contained a Calvinist wing.

As the visitors would have observed in New England, Puritans believed in the union of church and state. This teaching emerged from the Calvinist concern that every aspect of life should acknowledge God's sovereignty. In addition, it stemmed from the belief of Calvinists that God worked with humanity, as God had with the Israelites, through solemn agreements, or covenants. Only through the union of church and state, Puritans believed, could humans produce a Christian society conformed to scriptural teaching. Thus the Puritan colonies in New England were strict and intolerant on matters of doctrine and behavior, for their goal was to produce a sober, righteous, and godly Christian society. Although continually challenged by adversaries, the Puritan establishments were strong enough to survive into the early nineteenth century, longer than any other American state churches.

Yale College and Chapel.

Readers can gain a good indication of where religious groups were concentrated in colonial America by looking at its colleges. Because religious groups established all but one of the ten institutions of higher education in the colonies, the schools tended to be located where a denomination had strength.[7] Thus in New England, Harvard, Yale, and Dartmouth were Congregationalist, though Harvard later became Unitarian (a denomination that emerged from the liberal wing of Congregationalism). In Rhode Island, where several churches had strength, Baptists founded the College of Rhode Island (now Brown

University). Since colonial colleges were small, there were probably fewer than one thousand college students in America at any time. The colleges had the primary purposes of producing ministers and educated laity for their denominations, though in time all accepted members of other churches. Although most student bodies were composed of young men from nearby areas, Brown enrolled Baptists from all over the colonies. Because of its reputation for Christian orthodoxy, Princeton attracted a steady stream of students from outside the middle colonies.

Religion in the Middle Colonies

In their travels through New England, the foreign visitors would have seen Anglican churches, for the Church of England began to grow significantly in Connecticut, Massachusetts, and Rhode Island during the eighteenth century. Although the Puritans had previously packed off to England or to more congenial colonies any residents who openly followed Anglican usages, they were obligated (as English citizens) to tolerate Anglicanism after the passage in 1689 of the English Toleration Act. Upon entering the most northern of the middle colonies, New York, the visitors would have learned that the only college in the colony—King's College (now Columbia University)— was an Anglican institution. Its existence testified to the status of the Church of England as the colony's established church, though only in the area of densest population from Staten Island to Westchester County.

Late arrivals in New York, the English seized the colony of New Netherland in 1664 from the original Dutch settlers. Changing its name and its language, they also changed the established church from Dutch Reformed to Anglican. Traces of the original Dutch presence remained not only in such names as "Harlem," "Bronx," "Brooklyn," and "Catskill" but also in the numbers of Reformed churches dotting the length of the Hudson River to Albany and beyond.

Always a minority faith in a colony whose diversity of nationality and religion rivaled that of Pennsylvania, Anglicanism nevertheless attracted many of the most influential families in New York. The principal organization for spreading Anglicanism in New York and elsewhere in the colonies was the London-based Society for the Propagation of the Gospel in Foreign Parts (S.P.G.), which sent more than three hundred missionaries to America through the end of the Revolutionary War. Not only Anglicans and Dutch Reformed but also Lutherans, Presbyterians, and Quakers maintained a significant presence in the colony. In addition, small numbers of Congregationalists, Mennonites, Jews, Roman Catholics, and other religious groups were in the colony from the seventeenth century on. French Reformed (or "Huguenots") fleeing persecution founded two French-speaking communities—New Paltz and New Rochelle—along the Hudson River.

Settled in the 1600s first by the Dutch and then by the Swedes and Finns, New Jersey—like New York—subsequently became an English colony. In the late seventeenth century, Quakers, an affluent and significant presence in the colony, owned a part of it. Thus New Jersey, like Rhode Island, developed into a kind of religious free market. Scattered throughout the colony the foreign visitors would have found Baptist, Lutheran, Anglican, and a substantial number of Dutch Reformed, Quaker, and Presbyterian churches. The latter stemmed from the large numbers of Scots and Scots-Irish (Scots Presbyterians originally sent by the English crown across the Irish Sea to colonize and Protestantize Ireland in the 1600s) who chose to settle in New Jersey.

Along the Delaware River in both New Jersey and Pennsylvania, the visitors would have encountered the Lutheran remnants of Sweden's brief attempt in the seventeenth century to establish a New Sweden in America. The eight "Old Swedes" churches developed close relations with the Church of England and became Episcopalian after the Revolution. In New Jersey, Anglicanism grew slowly but steadily after the colony came under the control of the crown in 1702. The Anglican presence was significant enough to produce an unsuccessful plan to settle a bishop in Burlington, but the legislature, dominated by Quakers and by other dissenters, withstood all efforts to establish the Church of England. The colony's two colleges mirrored New Jersey's heterogeneity. The Dutch Reformed founded Queens College (now Rutgers University); Presbyterians established the College of New Jersey (now Princeton University).

In Pennsylvania the visitors would have come into contact not only with sects (as earlier described) but also with the mainstream Protestant churches. John Adams once wrote that Philadelphia included "Roman Catholics, English Episcopalians, Scotch and American Presbyterians, Methodists, Moravians, Anabaptists, German Lutherans, German Calvinists, Universalists, Arians, Priestleyans, Socinians, Independents, Congregationalists, . . . Deists and Atheists, and 'Protestants qui ne croyent rien.'"[8] So many Germans of Lutheran and Reformed (as well as sectarian) background settled in the fertile farmland of southeastern Pennsylvania that Benjamin Franklin reported the colony's population to be one-third German at the time of the Revolution. Scots-Irish Presbyterians emigrated to Pennsylvania in larger numbers than to any other colony, often squatting on land they did not own. Settling in the valleys in the mountainous central areas, they pushed westward toward Pittsburgh and southward via the Shenandoah Valley.

The foreign travelers would have found Philadelphia to be the metropolis of the thirteen colonies. The second largest city in the British empire by 1770, Penn's "City of Brotherly Love" served as an administrative center both for the Presbyterians and for the Baptists. It also contained the largest concentration of Jews in the colonies. Encompassing not only the congregations established in Pennsylvania by English and Welsh Baptists but also Baptist churches stretching from New England to Virginia, the Philadelphia Baptist Association sent out missionaries to gather new congregations. To produce a ministry for them, it founded the College of Rhode Island, in the colony where Baptists had possessed major strength. By 1770, however, the colonies of Pennsylvania, Virginia, and the Carolinas were surpassing Rhode Island as Baptist centers.

In Pennsylvania, the Church of England was concentrated in the eastern counties. Its influence grew steadily in the eighteenth century as wealthy Quakers, including the heirs of William Penn and the proprietors of the colony, converted to it. Anglicans provided the major influence in the founding of the College of Philadelphia (now the University of Pennsylvania)—though the institution, like the colony, was unaffiliated with any denomination.

The adjacent colony of Delaware went through Swedish, Dutch, and finally English control before its residents reluctantly accepted temporary annexation by William Penn's "radical" colony. Delaware's religious profile resembled that of Pennsylvania, but with a greater percentage of Anglicans, fewer Quakers, and only one Swedish Lutheran church (in Wilmington). Like Philadelphia, New Castle and Lewes became major ports of entry for Scots and Scots-Irish Presbyterians.

Religion in the Southern Colonies

In the border colony of Maryland, the foreign travelers would have encountered a colony with an unusual history. Founded in the 1630s by George Calvert, first Lord Baltimore, as a proprietary colony (a grant of land bestowed by the monarch on an individual or group, who then operated it as a commercial venture), Maryland was largely colonized under the direction of two of his sons. Because the Calverts were Roman Catholic, a principal purpose of the colony was to provide a place where other English Roman Catholics could worship freely. An important secondary purpose was to make money for the family—a necessity that required the Calverts to create conditions that would assure steady immigration to their colony. Ironically, by 1770 Maryland had passed through periods of Roman Catholic and Puritan control and had become a colony not only with an Anglican established church but also with laws that imposed severe restrictions against Roman Catholics.

Yet in 1770 the visitors would have found Maryland largely populated by persons who were neither Roman Catholic nor Anglican. The colony contained Irish and Scottish Presbyterians, Quakers, some Baptists, and members of a miscellany of other Protestant churches. So many German Lutherans and Reformed had spilled over from Pennsylvania or landed in Baltimore and relocated that western Maryland resembled the German areas of Pennsylvania. Despite being a minority, Anglicans were highly influential in the colony. By 1770 Maryland's eastern counties were full of Anglican churches whose rectors received such high salaries that clerical applicants for vacancies needed to place their names on a waiting list.

P. Andreas Vitus, S.J. Angl₉, in Anglia et Marilan-
dia Americæ Provincia, Apostolicis laboribus clarus.
Obijt in Anglia prope octogenarius. A° 1655.

Jesuit Father Andrew White baptizing Native Americans in seventeenth-century Maryland.

In 1770 the foreign travelers would have found that the Roman Catholics composed approximately 10 percent of the colony's population. They would also have noted that Roman Catholics worshiped in churches designed to look like houses. Served by circuit-riding Jesuit priests who often traveled hundreds of miles a week to celebrate private Masses, the houses had living quarters at one end and chapels at the other end. The Jesuits themselves owned large tracts of land in the colony, lived and dressed as bachelor gentry, had slaves and indentured servants working on their plantations, and possessed considerable influence.

As for the Roman Catholic laity, they were denied the right to vote or to hold public office during most of the eighteenth century. They had to send their children abroad in "educational convoys" to be educated at Roman Catholic schools. Meanwhile, though they considered it a heretical church, they paid taxes to support the colony's established Church of England.

Yet Roman Catholics continued to rank among Maryland's leading landowners throughout the colonial period. Except for religion, many were identical in outlook, lifestyle, and even English surnames to the Anglican gentry across the Potomac who composed the First Families of Virginia. Two of these Maryland Roman Catholic gentlemen planters—Charles Carroll (whose fortune was estimated at over £2,000,000) and Daniel Carroll—signed the Declaration of Independence and the Constitution, respectively. It is no surprise that two of the oldest Roman Catholic colleges in the nation —Mount St. Mary's and Georgetown—are located in Maryland or in the part of the District of Columbia that was once a part of the colony of Maryland.

The foreign visitors probably would have seen the religious history of Maryland in a more accurate perspective than some Americans have in the centuries since. At some point in the twentieth century, many Americans came to believe that Maryland was a Roman Catholic colony in inception and population, that it generously offered religious freedom to non-Catholics, and that the famous "Act Concerning Religion" passed by its legislature in 1649 was the world's pioneering act of religious freedom. Ann Landers's columns, letters to the editors, and textbooks of American history used in parochial and public schools have lent support to these assertions.

In fact, this interpretation of Maryland's history is largely inaccurate. George Calvert established Maryland not only as a place where his fellow Roman Catholics could worship freely but also as a business venture. As an English citizen he was obligated to include Anglicans in the venture. He received his charter from an Anglican king (Charles I) and kept it at the pleasure of an Anglican parliament. "One can scarcely speak of tolerating in English territory," two church historians write, "a church whose 'supreme governor' was the English monarch."⁹ The colony's charter, in fact, presupposed that the Church of England would be Maryland's established church. Although they held the proprietorship, Roman Catholics were dominant in the colony only for a short period. Anglicans were in the majority even on the two ships that carried the first colonists. In the middle of the seventeenth century, Puritans gained substantial control, and the percentage of Roman Catholics steadily decreased as the colony grew.

As the travelers might have learned, the "Act Concerning Religion" of 1649 was passed by a legislature composed of a Protestant majority. It was an act not of religious freedom but of religious toleration— hence its alternate name, the "Maryland Toleration Act." *Religious freedom* means that citizens are free to worship in any way or not at all—and that the state protects that freedom. *Religious toleration* means that the state allows a group to exist and to worship, but retains the right to withdraw or limit that permission at any time. From 1654 to 1661 and from 1692 to the end of the Revolutionary period, Maryland, in fact, nullified its Toleration Act.

Granting religious rights only to Trinitarian Christians, Maryland's act provided for the execution or forfeiture of all lands of any resident who blasphemed or denied the doctrines of the Trinity and the divinity of Christ. It imposed fines, whipping, or imprisonment for any resident who spoke disparagingly of the Virgin Mary, the apostles, or Evangelists. Yet the act strictly enforced tolerance (as long as the act was in force) by punishing any person who dared to offend a Maryland subject by calling him or her, in a judgmental manner, a host of offensive religious terms, including "heritick, Scismatick, Idolator, puritan, Independent, Prespiterian, popish priest, Jesuite, Jesuited papist, Lutheran, Calvenist, Anabaptist, Brownist, Antinomian, Barrowist, Roundhead, Separatist, or any other name or term in a reproachfull manner relating to matter of Religion."[10] The punishment was ten shillings or public whipping and imprisonment until such time as the aggrieved party was satisfied with the repentance of the offender. Any person who was "willfully to wrong disturbe trouble or molest any person . . . professing to believe in Jesus Christ" was also strictly punished.[11] Non-Christians were not protected at all.

Despite its limitations and shortcomings, the act represented a major advance for the time. In addition, it reflected a policy that the Calverts

had followed from the colony's beginning. As the colonists boarded ships for the voyage to America, George Calvert's instructions included a caveat not to abuse each other about religion. When the colonists arrived in Maryland, Protestants and Roman Catholics initially shared a chapel in St. Mary's City, the colony's first capital.[12]

Thus the Maryland Toleration Act was a pioneering piece of legislation. It came decades before England's own Toleration Act or William Penn's Holy Experiment. Religious toleration generally arose from the Enlightenment, and Maryland's policy of toleration antedates the Enlightenment. But it was an act of limited religious toleration only, and for most of Maryland's colonial history it was not in force. Genuine religious free-

Charles Calvert, third Lord Baltimore and second proprietor of Maryland.

dom did not come to the United States until the late 1780s. And when it did come, it emerged from the religion of the founding fathers.

When the travelers reached Virginia, they would have entered a colony that contained Quakers and Lutherans and small but growing numbers of Presbyterians, Baptists, and Methodists. Directly across the Potomac from Maryland, Virginia also contained a Roman Catholic Mass station and burial ground in Stafford County. But the Church of England was the colony's established church, and in 1770 it was still the church with which most Virginians identified. Thus the College of William and Mary—the first of two colleges established in Virginia in the colonial period—was Anglican. Not until 1775 did the Scots-Irish Presbyterians who settled the Shenandoah Valley found Hampden-Sydney College. Because Anglicanism is so intimately connected with the lives of four of the founding fathers included in this study, its doctrines and church life are discussed in detail in the next chapter.

For right or wrong, North Carolina had the reputation as the most irreligious of the American colonies. In the 1730s William Byrd of Virginia declared that North Carolinians had "the least Superstition of any People living. They do not know Sunday from any other day."[13] Several decades prior to Byrd's comment, one of a series of frustrated Anglican missionaries declared that North Carolina contained four kinds of people:

> First the Quakers. . . . Second . . . a great many who have no religion, but would be Quakers, if by that they were not obliged to lead a more moral life. . . . A third sort . . . preach and baptize through the country, without any manner of orders from any sect or pretended Church. A fourth sort, who are really zealous for the interest of the Church [of England], are the fewest in number, but are the better sort of people.[14]

During their travels in 1770, the foreign travelers might have found North Carolina somewhat less irreligious. German Lutherans, German Reformed, and Scots-Irish Presbyterians from Pennsylvania had come down the Shenandoah Valley and settled in the west. The Moravians had established a flourishing center at Salem. Scots Presbyterians and smaller groups of French, Swiss, and Welsh Protestants had immigrated to the eastern part of the colony. The Quakers, who had religion virtually to themselves in North Carolina in the seventeenth century, were declining in prominence but still a significant feature of the religious landscape.

Starting in the 1750s, North Carolina had also become a center of the fervent Separate Baptist movement. A revivalistic and zealous form of Baptists from New England who preached the need for an emotional conversion to Christ, the Separate Baptists used farmer-preachers, itinerant evangelists, and extensive lay witnessing to gather churches throughout the Carolinas and Virginia. Merging with the older forms of the Baptist tradition present in the colonies, they planted the foundation for much of later southern Baptist life and thought. All of these developments should have increased the number of what the Anglican missionary termed "the better sort of people" in North Carolina. Yet Anglicanism itself, though it became the colony's established church in the early eighteenth century, remained a small church whose parishes existed largely on paper.

In South Carolina, the experience of the foreign travelers would have differed. There they would have found an Anglican established church that was in a healthy condition, even though non-Anglicans by 1770 had come to outnumber Anglicans in the colony. Strong and effective lay support and a disarming policy of moderation toward other churches (including Jews) represent two of the reasons the established church remained dominant. Anglicanism was also strengthened by the accession of most of the French Reformed (or Huguenots) who fled to South Carolina and rose to influential positions in its affairs. Other significant religious groups in the colony included the Presbyterians, Lutherans, Quakers, and increasingly the Baptists. All were present from an early date in the cosmopolitan city of Charleston.

Had the visitors left the plantation-centered Low Country and entered the colony's vast backcountry, they would have experienced a situation that more closely resembled that of North Carolina. Settlers poured into this frontier area of South Carolina's piedmont after 1750. But many of its residents were unchurched, the established Anglican church was almost nonexistent, and the level of literacy and refinement was low. Even settlements in the backcountry that desired organized religion—such as the several dozen of Presbyterian origin—lacked pastors and had to depend upon the services of occasional missionaries. The one religious group that did well in the backcountry were the Separate Baptists.

In Georgia, the foreign travelers would have visited the most sparsely populated and least prosperous of the thirteen colonies. A product of political necessity and humanitarian idealism, the colony was founded in 1733 as a military buffer zone between Spanish Florida and South Carolina. It was also intended as a haven for the English

George Whitefield, less impressive
in physical appearance than in
preaching ability.

poor. In its first decades it attracted not only debtors but also
members of religious groups
persecuted in Europe, including Jews.
In the middle of the eighteenth century, when this initially experimental colony came
under the control of the crown,
its Assembly established the Church of England. But like its counterpart in North Carolina, the Anglican establishment in Georgia existed
largely on paper. By 1770 Presbyterians, Quakers, Lutherans, other
religious groups, and the many irreligious substantially outnumbered
Anglicans. In addition, the Separate Baptists were in the wings, ready
to flourish in the decades after the Revolution. In an otherwise unre-
markable religious history, colonial Georgia stands out for its relationship to three fathers of American evangelicalism—John Wesley, Charles
Wesley, and George Whitefield.

The Rise of the Evangelical Tradition in America

"Do you know Jesus Christ?" a Moravian bishop asked Oxford don
John Wesley while he and his younger brother Charles were serving
as missionaries to Georgia for the Society for the Propagation of the
Gospel in the 1730s. An inflexible Anglican whose religion—like
that of most Christians of his time—was based upon creeds, sacraments, and good works, Wesley replied that he knew that Christ was
the savior of the world. "True," replied the bishop, "but do you know
he has saved you?" The Oxford-educated, Greek-reading Wesley had
to admit that this was a piece of knowledge he did not possess. "Do
you know yourself?" the bishop then added as a final question.

Returning to England after two months and viewing himself (as Charles also regarded himself) as a failure in gaining the sympathy of those to whom he preached, John Wesley underwent a conversion experience in London one evening in 1738. In his words, he felt on that definitive occasion "my heart strangely warmed. I felt I did believe in Christ, in Christ alone for salvation; and an assurance was given me that He had taken away my sins, even mine, and saved me from the law of sin and death."

A few days earlier, his brother Charles had experienced a similar conversion. The two Wesleys now formed the Methodist movement—a highly disciplined, conversion-centered, and largely lay movement in the Church of England. It took its name from the methodically pious "Holy Club" founded by the then high-church Wesleys while they were at Oxford. John Wesley hoped that "the people called Methodists" would act as an evangelical yeast to lift not only the established church but also all of the British Isles to "vital, practical religion" and to the practice of "Scriptural holiness."

John was the movement's principal organizer and preacher. Charles supported it by writing thousands of hymns. Whitefield, a protégé of the Wesleys at Oxford who had followed them to Georgia, became one of the most dramatic and effective evangelists in the history of Christianity. Making seven trips to colonial America, preaching in fields as well as churches, often preaching thirty days a month and four times a Sunday, he attracted huge crowds that would stand in rapt silence to hear his sermons. A farmer's account of a visit of Whitefield to Connecticut in 1740 illustrates the great excitement that the young evangelical's preaching created:

> One morning . . . there came a messenger and said Mr. Whitfeld . . . is to preach at Middletown this morning at 10 o clock. I was in my field at work [and] I dropt my tool . . . and run home . . . and bade my wife to get ready quick to goo and hear Mr. Whitfeld I brought my hors home and soon mounted and took my wife up and went forward as fast as I thought the hors could bear. . . . We improved every moment to get along as if we was fleeing for our lives, all this while fearing we should be too late to hear the Sarmon, for we had twelve miles to ride double in littel more than an hour. . . .
>
> I saw before me a Cloud or fog rising—I first thought—off from the great river. But as I came nearer the road I heard a noise, something like a

low rumbling thunder, and I presently found it was the rumbling of horses feet coming down the road and this Cloud was a Cloud of dust made by the running of horses feet. . . . And when I came nearer it was like a stedy streem of horses and their riders. . . . Every hors semed to go with all his might to carry his rider to hear the news from heaven for the saving of their Souls. It made me trembel to see the Sight. . . . I herd no man speak a word all the way . . . but evry one presing forward in great haste.

And when we gat down to the old meating house, thare was a great multitude. It was said to be 3 or 4000 people assembled together. . . . I turned and looked toward the great river and saw the fery boats running swift . . . bringing over loads of people. . . . Everything—men, horses and boats—all seamed to be struglin for life. The land and the banks over the river looked black with people and horse all along the 12 miles. I see no man at work in his field, but all seamed to be gone.

Mr. Whitfeld . . . looked almost angellical—a young, slim, slender youth before some thousands of people, and with a bold, undaunted countenance. And my hearing how God was with him everywhere . . . it solomnized my mind, and put me in a trembling fear before he began to preach, for he looked as if he was Cloathed with authority from the great God . . . and my hearing him preach gave me a heart wound, by god's blessing. My old foundation was broken up and I saw that my righteousness would not save me. Then I was convinced of the doctrine of Election . . . because all that I could do would not save me, and he [God] had decreed from Eternity who should be saved and who not.[15]

An Anglican Calvinist, Whitefield preached an eloquent but simple message—that his listeners must confront the terrifying realization that they deserve damnation and can be saved from Hell only through the grace and forgiveness of God. In gratitude for God's forgiveness, they must be born again, become new men or women in Christ Jesus, and live a reformed life. This was the message of what came to be called "Evangelicalism," an interpretation of Christianity that would sweep across America in later centuries and influence many denominations.

Benjamin Franklin (who not only knew Whitefield but also printed his sermons and journals) held markedly different religious views from those of Whitefield. Yet even Franklin fell under the "Grand Itinerant's" spell when Whitefield appealed in Philadelphia for funds for an orphanage he wished to establish in Georgia but build with materials and workmen from Pennsylvania:

I thought it would have been better to have built the house here, and brought the children to it. This I advis'd; but he . . . rejected my counsel, and I therefore refus'd to contribute. I happened soon after to attend one of his sermons, in the course of which I perceived he intended to finish with a collection, and I silently resolved he should get nothing from me. I had in my pocket a handful of copper money, three or four silver dollars, and five pistoles in gold. As he proceded I began to soften, and concluded to give the coppers. Another stroke of his oratory made me asham'd of that, and determin'd me to give the silver; and he finish'd so admirably, that I empty'd my pocket wholly into the collector's dish, gold and all.[16]

Franklin not only admired Whitefield's oratorical ability but also liked him personally. Franklin accommodated him at his home, profited monetarily from publishing Whitefield's writing, and corresponded with him for more than three decades after their first meeting in Philadelphia. One biographer has counted forty-five descriptions of Whitefield's preaching in the weekly issues of Franklin's *Gazette* as well as eight front pages that included the texts of Whitefield's sermons.[17] Whitefield died in 1770, the year in which the foreign visitors came to the colonies.

Along with Congregationalist minister Jonathan Edwards, White-field personified the Great Awakening, the wave of religious revivals that swept the American colonies beginning in the 1730s and 1740s and emphasized "the new birth" or personal experience of the grace of God. "Hard to define, being one of those popular movements which have no obvious beginning or end, no pitched battles or legal victories with specific dates, no constitutions or formal leaders, no easily quantifiable statistics and no formal set of beliefs," the Great Awakening was nevertheless the single most transforming event in the religious history of colonial America.[18] It left the legacy of evangelical "born-again" Christianity. Although the awakening affected many churches, the Baptists and Methodists were its greatest heirs.

At the time of the visit of the foreign travelers, Methodism had gained substantial converts and some influence in the British Isles. In the American colonies, however, it was still a small movement. Emotional, conversion-centered, largely lower class in constituency, it taught a message of free will and of the possibility of salvation for all humans (and not just for the elect). It was served by lay preachers sent from England by Wesley, the first of whom had arrived in the colonies only in 1769. Thus until it separated in 1784 from Anglicanism,

The ordination of Francis Asbury in 1784 as "general superintendent" marked the beginning of Methodism as a separate American denomination.

Methodism existed in America as a small ultra-evangelical wing of the Church of England. Yet along with the Baptists, it represented the future of American Protestantism. Below the Mason-Dixon line, the Baptist and Methodist interpretations of Christianity became the folk religion of the American South. And in the rural areas and small towns of nineteenth-century America, the Methodist circuit rider became a familiar figure.

In 1770 Baptist and Methodist Christianity also represented the religious future of African-Americans. To a far greater extent than in the Caribbean or in Roman Catholic Latin America, the forms of religion the slaves brought from Africa were suppressed in the Protestant atmosphere of the American colonies. From the seventeenth century on, various colonial Protestant churches baptized and catechized a small percentage of the colonies' blacks. In contrast to the visible presence of a small minority of blacks in white churches, African-Americans mixed some ancestral practices and beliefs with Christianity in their "Invisible Institution" of secret, unrecorded worship.

The Great Awakening of the 1730s and 1740s, however, caused the widespread evangelization not only of poor whites and Indians but also of enslaved and free blacks. The Awakening's message of the "new birth" resonated with the American experience of blacks as well as with some aspects of their African religious background. Yet the emergence of separate congregations of black Baptists is generally dated to the early 1770s, and the founding of the first black denomination—the African Methodist Episcopal Church—did not occur until the late 1780s. The emergence of the form of religious music called "Spirituals"—in which African-Americans adapted evangelical Protestantism to meet their own needs and to keep alive their hopes for freedom—also occurred largely in the nineteenth century.

Thus the foreign travelers of 1770, as well as the six founding fathers covered in this study, would have had little contact with African-American Christianity. In addition, they would have known relatively little about the Baptists, Methodists, or Roman Catholics— the three religious groups that became so prominent in the United States in the nineteenth century. The founders knew Roman Catholicism in America only through fleeting associations, though most were well aware of its European history. Those like Franklin, Adams,

Jefferson, and Monroe who served the new nation in France experienced Roman Catholicism first hand.

Only the southerners would have had any experience with black religion, and it would have been limited. None of the founding fathers was an evangelical, although Madison attended a moderately evangelical Episcopal church in the last years of his life. In fact, James Monroe was offended by an evangelical sermon during his presidential tour of 1817, and John Adams belonged to the anti-Great Awakening wing of Congregationalism—much of which later became Unitarian.[19]

Finally, none of the founding fathers knew anything of the churches that became so large in the United States in the twentieth century—the Pentecostals (or charismatics) and the nondenominational evangelicals. What the six founding fathers did know were the churches in which they had been raised—and in all cases those churches were the established churches of their colonies. But the founders were also very familiar with a radical religious outlook called Deism, to which this study now turns.

2

THE ANGLICAN TRADITION AND THE VIRGINIA FOUNDING FATHERS

To discuss the religion of the founding fathers means to discuss religion in the United States of their time. Washington, Jefferson, Madison, and Monroe were born and baptized in what Virginians of the time called "the Church," "the Church of England," "the Established Church," or "the Church of Virginia." The independence of the thirteen colonies from the mother country prompted the American members of the Church of England to discard the word "England." In its place they adopted the term "Episcopal" (essentially meaning "we have bishops") and named their denomination "The Protestant Episcopal Church in the United States of America."

The name "Episcopal" traced back to the tumultuous Commonwealth period in English history, when clergy and laity who desired continued rule by bishops employed that term for themselves. To some extent, members of the Church of England used it for their church during the colonial period. In later centuries the term *Anglican* (from the Latin for "English") came into common use to describe churches in any country that held the faith and practice of the Church of England. This book will use the terms *Church of England*, *Established Church*, and *Anglican* interchangeably, but will generally employ the word *Episcopal* when discussing that church following the Revolution.

Throughout the colonial period, the Church of England was the established church of colonial Virginia. Colonial Virginians were born into the Anglican faith just as they were born into the English nation. The Virginia General Assembly legislated for the established church, supported it through taxation, and protected it against competition.

State churches represented the norm in European Christianity beginning in the fourth century. Of the thirteen colonies, nine—almost 70 per cent—had established churches. Congregationalism (or the faith of the Puritans) was established in New Hampshire, Massachusetts, and Connecticut. Anglicanism was established in the lower counties of New York, as well as in Maryland, Virginia, North Carolina, South Carolina, and Georgia. It was strong, however, only in Maryland, Virginia, and South Carolina.

A form of Christianity that claims to blend the best of Christian teachings and practice from the periods of the apostles, the church fathers, and the Reformation, Anglicanism emerged from the English Reformation of the sixteenth and seventeenth centuries. Like Roman Catholicism and Eastern Orthodoxy, it kept a hierarchical ministry of bishops, priests, and deacons and maintained a formal style of worship. Like those churches, its members used a Mass book, or book of prayers and rites. Titled the *Book of Common Prayer*, it was intended to reproduce the worship and teachings of early Christianity.

But like Protestant churches, the Church of England held that Holy Scripture—not the teachings

President James Madison of William and Mary, teacher and pastor of the founding generation and friend and correspondent of Jefferson, Franklin, and others.

of popes or church councils—was the final authority for Christian belief. It accepted the authority of the early General Councils and emphasized the Apostles' Nicene and Athanasian creeds as standards of faith precisely because it believed their teachings were true to Scripture. Like the continental Protestant churches and unlike Roman Catholicism and Eastern Orthodoxy, it believed that churches could err in their teachings. "There was never any thing by the wit of man so well devised, or so sure established, which in continuance of time hath not been corrupted," the preface to the first Book of Common Prayer asserted in 1549.

Anglicanism can best be viewed as what Queen Elizabeth I and her theologians desired it to be. They attempted to make the Church of England a middle way—or *via media*—between Roman Catholicism and Calvinism, the two interpretations of Christianity that contended for control of England in the Reformation period. Anglican theologians asserted that Roman Catholicism had added too much man-made doctrine to Christianity. Conversely, they believed that the teachings of the Swiss Reformer John Calvin, or Calvinism—which had won over Scotland and was embodied in England by the Puritans—had subtracted too much that was important to Christianity. With England divided between these two views, and with many citizens desiring only an end to conflict, Elizabeth and her advisors tried to steer a middle course patterned upon early Christianity.

Finding the middle course is one thing, and keeping to it is another. Thus it was not surprising that the Church of England quickly developed parties, or factions. The *high-church* party wanted the national church to tack more toward Eastern Orthodoxy and Roman Catholicism. The *low-church* party wanted to move Anglican faith and practice closer to Calvinism and Lutheranism. Largely, however, the Church of England remained what it had become during the reign of Elizabeth—a church more Catholic than the continental Protestant churches, but one substantially more Protestant than the Catholic churches centered on Rome and Constantinople. It claimed to be a unique synthesis of Catholicism and Protestantism.

Anglicanism came to Virginia in 1607, first at Jamestown and then in ever-widening settlements along Virginia's rivers and newly created roads. Whenever settlers moved too far from existing courthouses and parishes, the General Assembly of Virginia simply established new counties and new parishes. *Parishes* were geographical districts, perhaps 150 square miles in size, containing two to four Anglican churches, a minister called a *rector*, and a governing body of self-perpetuating laymen called a *vestry* headed by two *churchwardens*. Gradually parishes containing substantial churches of Gothic or Georgian design dotted Virginia. By the start of the American Revolution, Virginia's Established Church had some 250 churches spread over 100 parishes stretching as far west as Kentucky.

This church provided the religious background out of which Washington, Jefferson, Madison, and Monroe—as well as such founding fathers as Patrick Henry, George Mason, and George Wythe—emerged. The earliest religious memories of these men would have revolved around the wood or brick church their families attended on Sundays. Most of their fathers would have served as vestrymen of their parishes. In due time, the founding fathers would have assumed the same position. The parish priest—or parson—would have been a familiar figure to them, and they would have received much of their early education at academies run by Anglican clergy.

Additionally, the words and cadences of the Book of Common Prayer ran in their blood: "Almighty and most merciful Father: we have erred and strayed from thy ways like lost sheep. . . . We thine unworthy servants do give thee most humble and hearty thanks for all thy goodness and loving-kindness to us. . . . Ye that do truly and earnestly repent you of your sins, and are in love and charity with your neighbors . . . draw near with faith, and take this holy Sacrament to your comfort. . . . Fulfill now, O Lord, the desires and petitions of thy servants, as many be most expedient for them; granting us in this world knowledge of thy truth, and in the world to come life everlasting. Amen." Continuing to belong to the Episcopal Church even when at variance with some of its central doctrines did not seem to discomfort Deistically inclined founders such as Jefferson, for they liked its liturgy and the historic cadences of its language.

The Anglican faith of Virginia differed from the New England Puritanism out of which Adams and Franklin emerged. Both Adams and Franklin changed their religious views and embraced a form of Deism. So, too, did Washington, Jefferson, Madison, and Monroe.

But all of these men, except Franklin, continued to worship at least occasionally in the church of their ancestors—and their wives and daughters were usually devout supporters of it. The Virginia founding fathers married under the church's auspices, consigned their children to its care, and were buried by its clergy. The impress of their religious background remained strong, even though their questioning of certain of their church's fundamental doctrines led them to Deism.

3

THE ENLIGHTENMENT
RELIGION OF DEISM

The religion of Deism is superior to the Christian Religion," the radical Deist Thomas Paine declared:

It is free from all those invented and torturing articles that shock our reason . . . with which the Christian religion abounds. Its creed is pure and sublimely simple. It believes in God, and there it rests. It honours Reason as the choicest gift of God to man and the faculty by which he is enabled to contemplate the power, wisdom, and goodness of the Creator displayed in the creation; And reposing itself on his protection, both here and hereafter, it avoids all presumptuous beliefs and rejects, as the fabulous inventions of men, all books pretending to revelation.[1]

"The Deists," an American clergyman wrote,

. . . were never organized into a sect, had no creed or form of worship, recognized no leader, and were constantly shifting their ground . . . so that it is impossible to include them strictly under any definition.

The cleric went on to attempt "as near a definition as possible":

Deism is what is left of Christianity after casting off everything that is peculiar to it. The Deist is one who denies the Divinity, the Incarnation, and the

Atonement of Christ, and the work of the Holy Ghost; who denies the God of Israel, and believes in the God of nature.[2]

From the late seventeenth century on, a school of religious thought called *Deism* existed in England and on the European continent. It emerged from the Enlightenment, a complex movement of ideas marked by an emphasis on human inquiry as well as a self-confident challenge of traditional political, religious, and social ideas. In France the writings of Voltaire (François-Marie Arouët), Jean-Jacques Rousseau, and Denis Diderot personified the movement. In England, the nation that most influenced the American colonies, the scientific and philososophical work of Francis Bacon, Isaac Newton, and John Locke undergirded the Enlightenment.

A philosopher and a lawyer, Bacon insisted that observation and experience—not abstract principles—provided the only true foundations of human knowledge. Applying Bacon's methodology to science, Isaac Newton, the leading physicist of his time, concentrated on discovering and reporting immutable laws of nature. For Bacon a "first cause" created the universe, which operated according to natural laws. Locke, a philosopher and the author of *An Essay Concerning Human Understanding* and *The Reasonableness of Christianity*, argued that human experience and rationality—rather than religious dogma and mystery—determined the validity of human beliefs. Locke's test of truth was whether a belief made sense to human reason.

Bacon, Newton, and Locke were all Anglicans of varying degrees of orthodoxy. But their work and those of other philosophers and scientists provided the foundation for Deism's new understanding of the universe and of human life. "There arose in our society," the historian Crane Brinton wrote, "what seems to me clearly to be a new religion, certainly related to, descended from, and by many reconciled with, Christianity. I call this religion simply Enlightenment, with a capital *E*."[3]

During the eighteenth century and into the nineteenth, Deism had adherents throughout continental Europe, the British Isles, and the American colonies. It became the creed of Holy Roman Emperor Joseph II and of Frederick the Great of Prussia. Because it was guided by individual reason, the movement was neither organized nor uniform. Thus some Deists renounced Christian belief more thoroughly than others.

Personified in England, France, and America by such controversial figures as Anthony Collins, Voltaire, and Thomas Paine, the movement's radical wing viewed Christianity as a barrier to moral improvement and to social justice. In successive books and tracts written early in the eighteenth century, Collins defended the use of reason. He found fraud in one part of the Church of England's statement of faith, attacked clergy of all denominations, argued that the Bible commanded free inquiry, and denied any relationship between Old Testament prophecies and the life of Jesus of Nazareth. The keen-witted Voltaire satirized competing philosophical systems, argued for the use of reason as common sense, and spread Locke's ideas on political and religious tolerance. Perhaps no writer has attacked dogmatic Christianity more effectively.

The son of an English Quaker artisan, Paine immigrated to the American colonies in his late thirties. He became well known for his pamphlets—*Common Sense* and *The Crisis*—supporting the movement for independence from England. When he temporarily moved to France in the 1790s to assist the French Revolution, Paine lived in Paris in the home of James Monroe while Monroe served as minister to France. Like other founding fathers, Monroe had been impressed by Paine's patriotic writings during the Revolutionary War; the pamphleteer had befriended not only Monroe but also Franklin, Jefferson, Adams, and Washington (though Paine later broke with the last two).

Arrested on contrived charges during the French Reign of Terror, Paine was one of many persons released from Paris prisons through Monroe's adroit interventions. Long months in prison had left him in bad health, and the Monroes took him into their residence in Paris to convalesce. For two years (substantially longer than Elizabeth Monroe had probably anticipated), Paine recuperated with the Monroe family and participated in their social circle. He and Monroe formed a close friendship that lasted until Paine's death in 1809. The two men may have discussed religion frequently, and it is not idle to speculate that Monroe's views moved further away from Christian orthodoxy and into Deism during this period.

Written during 1793 and 1794, partially in a French jail and partially at Monroe's home, Paine's *The Age of Reason* (published in 1794–95) helped to popularize Deism in the United States. Paine wrote the second part (which deals with the Bible) using a King James Version borrowed from the Monroes. Because it mercilessly assaulted and lampooned Judeo-Christian beliefs—Paine viewed Christianity as a negative influence on world history—the book alienated many of his previous supporters. "I have now to inform you, why I wrote it and published it at the time I did," Paine later wrote to the disapproving Samuel Adams,

> In the first place, I saw my life in my continual danger. –My friends were falling as fast as the guillotine could cut their heads off, and as I every day expected the same fate, I resolved to begin my work. I appeared to myself to be on my deathbed, for death was on every side of me, and I had no time to lose. . . .
>
> In the second place, the people of France were running headlong into *Atheism*, and I had the work translated and published in their own language, to stop them in that career, and fix them to the first article . . . of every man's Creed who has any creed at all,—"*I believe in God.*"
>
> I endangered my own life, . . . by opposing *Atheism*; and yet some of your priests, cry out, . . .—What an infidel, what a wicked man, is Thomas Paine!—They might as well add, for he believes in God.[4]

Nevertheless, to orthodox American Christians, Paine became a villain and an "infidel." Voltaire had derided organized religion, but Paine's critique went further. *The Age of Reason* denied "that the Almighty ever did communicate anything to man, by any mode of speech, in any language, or by any kind of vision." Paine termed Christianity "a fable, which, for absurdity and extravagance is not exceeded by any thing that is to be found in the mythology of the ancients." He called the book of Psalms (which Jews and Christians traditionally attributed to King David) "a collection, as song-books are nowadays, from different song-writers, who lived at different times." By defining the word *prophet* as "the Bible word for poet" and the word *prophesying* as meaning "the art of making poetry," he placed a new meaning on biblical prophecies.

For readers who had encountered trouble believing some of the biblical narratives —such as the story of Adam, Eve, and the talking

COMMON SENSE;

ADDRESSED TO THE

INHABITANTS

OF

AMERICA,

On the following interesting

SUBJECTS.

I. Of the Origin and Design of Government in general, with concise Remarks on the English Constitution.

II. Of Monarchy and Hereditary Succession.

III. Thoughts on the present State of American Affairs.

IV. Of the present Ability of America, with some miscellaneous Reflections.

WRITTEN BY AN ENGLISHMAN.

THE SECOND EDITION.

Man knows no Master save creating HEAVEN,
Or those whom choice and common good ordain.

THOMSON.

PHILADELPHIA;
Printed, and Sold, by R. BELL, in Third-Street.

MDCCLXXVI.

John Adams's copy of Thomas Paine's *Common Sense*.

snake—Paine offered a simple explanation: they were simply not true. For those who could temporarily disregard their religious belief long enough to see the humor, Paine's choice of words and analogies could be comical. The *Age of Reason*'s hammer-like approach is displayed by its treatment of a passage in the Gospel of Matthew that depicts deceased followers of Jesus rising from their graves and going into Jerusalem after the crucifixion:

> The writer . . . should have told us who the saints were . . . and what became of them afterward . . . whether they came out naked . . . or . . . full dressed, and where they got their dresses; whether they went to their former habitations, and reclaimed their wives, their husbands, and their property, and how they were received; whether they . . . brought actions of *crim. con.* against the rival interlopers; . . . whether they died again, or went back to their graves alive, and buried themselves.[5]

If Paine was a non-Christian Deist, others tried to reconcile Deism with Christianity. Viewing themselves as Christians, they went to church, prayed, and assigned a salvatory role to Jesus. Certain clergy in the Christian churches of France, the British Isles, Germany, America, and other countries held Deistic views in the eighteenth century. Deists were found even in Roman Catholic pews and pulpits in Maryland.

Regardless of where they fell on the Deist spectrum, many Deists continued to respect the moral teachings of Jesus without believing in his divine status. But the tendency of Deism was to emphasize ethical endeavors—hence the concern of most Deists for social justice and their profound opposition to all forms of tyranny. In addition, they replaced the Judeo-Christian explanation of existence with a religion far more oriented to reason and nature than to the Hebrew Bible, Christian Testament, and Christian creeds. In the understanding of the typical Deist, a rational "Supreme Architect"—one of a variety of terms Deists used for the deity—created the earth and human life. This omnipotent and unchangeable creator then withdrew to let events take their course on earth without further interference.

Just as a ticking watch presupposes a watchmaker, so Deists thought that the rational, mechanistic harmony of nature revealed a deity. The Deistic view of nature was so high that men such as Ethan Allen and Paine could write of it as God's revelation. "There is a word of God," Paine declared, "there is a revelation. *The word of God is the creation we behold.*"[6]

Do we want to contemplate his power? We see it in the immensity of the Creation.—Do we want to contemplate his wisdom: We see it in the unchangeable order by which the incomprehensible whole is governed.—Do we want to contemplate his munificence? We see it in the abundance with which he fills the earth.—Do we want to contemplate his mercy? We see it in his not withholding that abundance even from the unthankful.[7]

Whereas, for Deists, the principal revelation for Christianity—the Bible—bore every sign of human counterfeiting or alteration, they saw the magnificent design of nature as revealing a Creator, or what Thomas Jefferson termed "a superattending power." Some Deists even employed rhapsodic terms to describe nature—"All loving and All-lovely, All-divine" or "righteous and immortal."[8] Writing in 1815, an aging American poet of Deistic belief praised nature in similar words:

All that we see, about, abroad,
What is it all, but nature's God?
In meaner works discovered here
No less than in the starry sphere. . . .

In all the attributes divine
Unlimited perfectings shine;
In these enwrapt, in these complete,
All virtues in that centre meet.[9]

To be sure, when citizens of the twenty-first century look at nature, they may see not simply majesty, order, and beauty but also tsunamis, earthquakes, tornadoes, hurricanes, and famine. But at a time when most people thought that the world was thousands rather than millions of years old, Deists could more easily see nature as bearing the impress of a Maker. Governed by reason—which Paine called "the most formidable weapon against errors of every kind"—the human mind possessed the ability to comprehend the natural laws God had initiated.[10]

Though technically not a Deist, Edward Herbert, first Lord Herbert of Cherbury, formulated the classic five points of Deism in the seventeenth century. Herbert stated that (1) there is a God; (2) he ought to be worshiped; (3) virtue is the principal element in this worship; (4) humans should repent of their sins; and (5) there is a life after death, where the evil will be punished, and the good rewarded. Herbert's reduction of the essence of religion to these five points as well as his rejection of revelation causes many historians to view him as the forerunner, or father, of the movement.

This five-point program is far from atheism. For that reason, Theodore Roosevelt's later description of Paine as "a filthy little atheist" was incorrect. Paine was far more certain of the existence of God than some practicing Jews, Christians, or Muslims may be today. He wrote *The Age of Reason* as an antidote to the atheism that was sweeping revolutionary France.

In Paine's mind, Christianity was the infidel, and he was the faithful believer. Declaring *The Age of Reason* his "profession of faith," Paine wrote:

> I believe in one God, and no more; and I hope for happiness beyond this life. I believe in the equality of man and I believe that religious duties consist in doing justice, loving mercy, and endeavoring to make our fellow-creatures happy.[11]

Yet if a reader cannot call Deism "atheistic," it is equally impossible to call the movement "Christian." Deists repeatedly called into question any teaching or belief of Christianity that they could not reconcile with human reason. For them reason was paramount in determining religious truth.

Thus Elihu Palmer, a former Presbyterian minister who became a leading American Deist, not only published a treatise entitled *Reason, the Glory of Our Nature*, but also edited a newspaper called the *Temple of Reason*. In 1784, Ethan Allen, the Revolutionary War hero from Vermont, published *Reason: the Only Oracle of Man*. On this basis many Deists dismissed the doctrines of the Trinity (the teaching that God exists in the three persons of Father, Son, and Holy Spirit), the incarnation (the assertion that God took human nature and form in the person of Jesus of Nazareth), the virgin birth (the belief that the Holy Spirit was the father of Jesus and the Virgin Mary his mother), and the resurrection (the declaration that Jesus physically rose from the grave after his crucifixion and burial). Additionally, they found belief in biblical revelation—the concept that the Bible revealed God and God's will—faulty when subjected to rational analysis. Paine and other left-wing Deists found the Bible a pastiche of magic, superstition, irrationality, pre-scientific thinking, and bloodthirsty ethics. Because they believed that only an imperfect God would suspend his universal laws to perform "irrational" acts, they dismissed the miracles recorded in the Bible. Paine found the doctrine of the atonement—the Christian teaching that Christ died on behalf of sinful humanity—so irrational that he declared he could not fathom how anyone in possession of full faculties could honestly believe in it.

Moreover, most Deists differed from the Judeo-Christian tradition in their concept of God. Judaism and Christianity asserted that a God named YHWH had revealed himself to Moses at Mt. Sinai. This God was the God of Abraham, Isaac, Jacob, Joseph, David, Solomon, the Prophets, John the Baptist, and Jesus of Nazareth. He was a God whom the Bible depicts as acting in history and hearing prayers.

In place of this Hebrew God, Deists postulated a distant deity to whom they referred with terms such as "the First Cause," "the Creator of the Universe," "the Divine Artist," "the Divine Author of All Good," "the Grand Architect," "the God of Nature," "Nature's God," "Divine Providence," and (in a phrase used by Franklin) "the Author and Owner of our System." The Declaration of Independence displays precisely this kind of wording and sense of a distant deity. In its 1,323 words, the Declaration speaks of "Nature's God," "Creator," "Supreme Judge," and "divine Providence."

Thus Deism inevitably undermined the personal religion of the Judeo-Christian tradition. In the worldview of the typical Deist, humans had no need to read the Bible, to pray, to be baptized or circumcised, to receive Holy Communion, to attend church or synagogue, or to heed the words or ministrations of misguided priests, ministers, or rabbis. They did not need to assume that the teaching of Moses came from God. They needed no personal relationship with

Jesus Christ. In his tract *The Religion of Nature Delineated*, the English Deist William Wollaston declared that humans would learn more truths about religion if they studied nature and science rather than the Bible and Christian theology.

But many Deists went further than simply absenting themselves from religious rites. They criticized not only the Judeo-Christian tradition but also all organized religion for fostering divisive sectarianism, for encouraging persecution, and for stifling freedom of thought and speech throughout history. "Persecution is not an original feature in any religion," Paine wrote "but it is always the strongly marked feature of all . . . religions established by law."[12] As the French philosopher Denis Diderot's hyperbolic words—"let us strangle the last king with the guts of the last priest"—indicate, Deists despised political and religious despotism.[13] Their fundamental belief in reason and equality drove them to embrace liberal political ideals. In the eighteenth century, many Deists advocated universal education, freedom of the press, and separation of church and state. These principles are commonplace in the twenty-first century, but they were radical in the eighteenth.

Today some aspects of Deism are continued in the United States in the Masonic order, in the Unitarian-Universalist denomination, in the Ethical Culture movement, in the tradition of free thought, in the historical-critical approach to the Bible that emerged in the late nineteenth century (and that is foreshadowed on some pages of the *Age of Reason*), and to some extent in the Religious Society of Friends (or Quakers). The spirit of rational inquiry, of skepticism about dogma, and of religious toleration that animated Deism continues to influence the religious views of many persons who occupy pews in churches and synagogues.

4

THE FOUNDING FATHERS
AND DEISM

Deism proved influential in the United States from roughly 1725 through the first several decades of the nineteenth century. By the time Thomas Paine died in 1809, the movement was in clear decline. Emphasizing human inquiry, reason, and personal freedom, it catered to American principles of individuality. Paradoxically, the movement also failed in part because of these characteristics. Deism excluded the emotional and mysterious aspects of religion. It ignored the need of many humans for spiritual guidance, worship, and a community of faith. In the wake of the violent French Revolution and Napoleon's reign, the liberal values espoused by such Enlightenment writers as Paine suffered. Here Americans saw the grotesque end to which such thought might lead.

Among educated eighteenth-century Americans, however, the idea of reason as a liberator from the shackles of repressive religion and tyrannical government won widespread acclaim. By the 1750s, orthodox clergy had begun to warn against the movement. Deism became especially fashionable at American colleges in the decades immediately following the Revolution. In those decades Enlightenment rationalism unseated Christian orthodoxy at Yale, Harvard, and other denominational colleges.

In Virginia, the center of Deism was William and Mary, the alma mater of Monroe and Jefferson, and the institution where Washington also served as chancellor. "At the end of the century, the College of William and Mary was regarded as the hotbed of infidelity and of the wild politics of France," an orthodox Episcopalian remembered:

> The intimacy produced between infidel France and our own country, by the union of our arms against the common foe, was most baneful in its influence with our citizens generally, and on none more than those of Virginia. The grain of mustard-seed which was planted at Williamsburg, about the middle of the century, had taken root there and sprung up and spread its branches over the whole State.[1]

Students and young people generally embrace novelty and new ideas. Thus it would be surprising if Deism—which was viewed as cutting-edge thought—had not influenced the founding fathers, for most were young men when the movement began to spread. Washington and Adams were born in the 1730s, Jefferson in the 1740s, and Madison and Monroe in the 1750s. Four of the first five presidents of the United States began their college studies during the formative years of Deism. Adams attended Harvard in the 1750s, Jefferson studied at William and Mary in the 1760s, and Monroe enrolled there in the 1770s. Although Washington never attended college, he moved in the circles of gentry who had been educated at William and Mary and at other colleges.

Only Madison attended a college (the College of New Jersey, later renamed Princeton) known for most of the eighteenth century for its Christian orthodoxy. Yet after Madison returned to Virginia, his religious beliefs clearly moved in a Deistic direction. An orthodox opponent of Deism who knew the disposition of the Madison family attributed the young squire's change to "political associations with those of infidel principles, of whom there were many in his day."[2]

As these words indicate, Deism influenced, in one way or another, most of the political leaders who designed the new American government. Since the founding fathers did not hold identical views on religion, they should not be lumped together. But if census takers trained in Christian theology had set up broad categories in 1790 labeled "Atheism," "Deism and Unitarianism," "Orthodox Protestantism," "Orthodox Roman Catholicism," and "Other," and if they had interviewed Franklin, Washington, Adams, Jefferson, Madison, and Monroe, they would undoubtedly have placed every one of these six founding fathers in some way under the category of "Deism and Unitarianism."

5

The Religious Views of Benjamin Franklin

I ndustrious, temperate but outspoken, possessor of an almost pixyish humor, Benjamin Franklin was the first prominent American Deist and the most universal American of his time. Although Franklin grew up in the ethos of Calvinist New England, his youth coincided with the introduction of British Deistic thought into the colonies.

Franklin's father, a candlemaker, sent his son at age eight to Boston Latin School (where many Puritan divines studied), probably because he intended the young man for the Congregationalist ministry. But no stories from Benjamin's youth depict him as pious or faithful; rather, others described him as "skeptical, puckish . . . and irreverent."[1] Removed after a year by his father from the Latin School and enrolled in a writing and arithmetic academy, Benjamin ultimately educated himself from the age of ten on. Thus he never attended college, though he later received numerous honorary degrees (including the first one awarded by William and Mary). Franklin tried on various theological positions while young, but he came to view theology as a discipline that often focused on petty distinctions rather than on broader truths.

Although young Franklin's voracious reading included defenses of the Calvinist tradition in which he had been raised, he found Deistic authors more persuasive. "Franklin adopted much from deism that would have alienated him from Puritanism," one of his biographers asserted, "but nothing from Puritanism that would be incompatible with deism."[2] By the age of fifteen, he had become a convinced Deist. By seventeen, he had already read such representative Deistic writers as Locke, Collins, Joseph Addison, and Locke's patron, the third Earl of Shaftesbury. By nineteen, during a two-year stay in London, he had published a pamphlet on morality that brought him to the attention of English Deists, though he later repudiated its radicalism.

Franklin's new Deistic views and his absence from church services unsettled not only his parents but also such religious figures as Boston's Puritan patriarch Increase Mather. Some of the aphorisms in *Poor Richard's Almanack*, which Franklin published from 1732 to 1757, display his Deistic concern that good beliefs beget good works. "Sin is not hurtful because it is forbidden," he wrote in the Almanac in 1739, "but it is forbidden because it is hurtful. . . . Nor is a Duty beneficial because it is commanded, but it is commanded, because it is beneficial." In other passages Poor Richard observes in good Deistic fashion: "Many have quarreled about religion that never practiced it." At another point he declares that "serving God is doing good to man, but praying is thought an easier service and therefore is more generally chosen."

Despite his break with orthodoxy, Franklin retained some of the Calvinist views he had been taught. Although his Deistic religion was free from the agonized concern and introspection about salvation that characterized Calvinism, Franklin's diligence, frugality, and dislike of religious pretension can fairly be seen as carryovers from his background. "No man 'er was glorious, who was not laborious," he had Poor Richard opine in 1734 in words that recall the Puritan teaching about calling and work ethic.

Benjamin Franklin, prudent Deist.

Similarly, Calvinists insisted that sin infuses all human thoughts and actions. Thus it is not surprising that Franklin remained skeptical about the claims advanced by Enlightenment writers about the innate goodness and ultimate perfectibility of humanity. Calvinism was sufficiently influential that he chose as his first church home in Philadelphia (where he moved in 1723) the Presbyterian Church, the body closest in doctrine and practice to his inherited Congregationalism. With its apparent affirmation of the resurrection of the body, the epitaph he wrote for himself as a young printer also seems to display his background in orthodox Christianity:

> The body of
> B. Franklin, Printer;
> (like the cover of an old book,
> Its contents worn out,
> and stripped of its lettering and gilding)
> Lies here, food for worms.
> But the work shall not be lost:
> For it will, (as he believed) appear once more,
> In a new and more elegant edition,
> Revised and corrected
> By the Author.

Franklin was also among those Deists who remained open to the possibility of divine intervention or special providence in human affairs. As he wrote in an essay in the 1730s, God "sometimes interferes by His particular providence and sets aside the effects which would otherwise have been produced by . . . causes."[3]

Unlike radical, or anti-Christian Deists, Franklin perceived that organized religion could benefit society by encouraging public virtue as well as by promoting social order. He believed in a benevolent Creator, whom humans should worship through virtuous behavior. Thus Franklin urged his daughter Sarah to "go constantly to church." He himself was an infrequent churchgoer. But because he developed a certain fondness for ceremony and ritual, the church he most frequently attended was Christ Church, one of Philadelphia's three Episcopal churches. He did so despite being at odds with the ruling Penn family, many of whom had become Episcopalian. One of the several reasons Franklin seems to have befriended George Whitefield may have stemmed from the discomfiting effect Whitefield's evangelical preaching had on the stodgy elites of Philadelphia.

Franklin's American protégé Paine (whom he had met in England and persuaded to emigrate to the colonies) became a propagandist for Deism. But Franklin did not. He would satirize, but seldom directly criticize, other religious faiths. Although Franklin privately questioned such Christian doctrinal teachings as the incarnation, the Trinity, and the resurrection, he remained cautious when discussing them publicly. Thus his religious views display not dogmatism but rather tentativeness and ambivalence. Prudent and tolerant, he contributed to the construction budgets not only of every church in Philadelphia but also of the city's one synagogue.

This ambivalence toward dogma fostered Franklin's conviction that no system of thought is wholly right or entirely wrong. As a result, Franklin (like other Deists) came to believe that religious toleration was vital to a free society. When his grandson was unable to marry a young woman in France because her parents opposed her marrying a Protestant, Franklin's view was that religious differences did not matter in marriage, in that all religions were basically the same.

Insatiably curious, ambivalent about religion, prudent in his declarations about it, offended by dogmatism and intolerance, opposed to the highly emotional conversion experiences of the Great Awakening, Franklin made morality primary in his interpretation of religion. Like other Deists, he believed that humans served God best when they performed good works on behalf of humanity and society. "I think vital religion has always suffered," Franklin wrote to his parents shortly after his thirtieth birthday, "when orthodoxy is more regarded than virtues." He once defined "a good Christian" as someone who is "a good Parent, a good Child, a good Husband or Wife, a good Neighbour or Friend, a good Subject or citizen."[4] He wrote a liturgy that emphasized morality, and he worked hard to infuse morality into the common life of Philadelphia.

Five weeks before his death, when he received an inquiry about his religious beliefs from a Congregationalist minister who was president of Yale College, Franklin replied:

> Here is my Creed. I believe in one God, Creator of the Universe: That he governs the World by his Providence. That he ought to be worshiped. That

the most acceptable Service we can render to him, is doing good to his other Children. That the Soul of Man is immortal, and will be treated with Justice in another life, respecting its Conduct in this. These I take to be the fundamental Principles of all sound Religion.

Morality remained primary for Franklin even as he approached death. Jesus had established the best system of morals and religion in the history of the world, Franklin continued, though Christianity itself had undergone some corrupting changes since the time of Jesus. He concluded:

> I have . . . some Doubts as to his Divinity, tho' it is a Question I do not dogmatize upon, having never studied it, & think it needless to busy myself with it now, when I expect soon an Opportunity of knowing the Truth with less Trouble.[5]

Late in the evening of April 17, 1790, Franklin died with a picture of the Day of Judgment by his bedside. Almost twenty thousand citizens observed his solemn funeral procession in Philadelphia. At the front of the cortege marched "the clergymen of the city, all of them, of every faith."[6] He was buried in the cemetery of Christ Church.

6

THE RELIGIOUS VIEWS OF
GEORGE WASHINGTON

Historians have learned much about George Washington's religious practices and beliefs, not only from his own writings but also from the observations and experiences of persons who knew him. In the twenty-first century, Washington's religious views continue to be the subject of controversy.

Washington was baptized and raised in the Established Church of Virginia. His wife, Martha, was a devoted Anglican and regular churchgoer. By the standards of the eighteenth century, Washington was religiously active. As an officer prior to the Revolution, he read services for his soldiers when no chaplain was available and required officers and men not on duty to attend. He scrupulously observed the fast days of the Church of England prescribed for the English Army. He served as a vestryman and churchwarden (a vestryman with special responsibilities) in the Episcopal Church. He is commonly credited with surveying and mapping Virginia's Truro Parish and with persuading its vestry to change the location of Pohick Church, its principal church. From the reports of visitors to Mount Vernon, he occasionally said grace at the table.

During his presidential years, Washington sometimes worshiped in churches of other denominations, but he normally attended Anglican and Episcopal churches. In Virginia his regular churches were

The interior of St. Peter's Church, Philadelphia, where founding fathers often worshiped.

Pohick Church in Fairfax County (where he placed his monogram on the door of his box pew) and, in later years, Christ Church in Alexandria. In New York City, he attended St. Paul's Chapel of Trinity Parish and, less frequently, Trinity Church on Wall Street (the church in which James Monroe was married and from which he was buried). When the nation's capital was in Philadelphia, he attended Christ Church (where other founding fathers worshiped) and, less frequently, St. Peter's Church. Perhaps because of their association with the Father of the Country, five of the six churches he attended—Trinity Church on Wall Street (whose building dates from 1846) is the sole exception—still use their eighteenth-century buildings for regular worship.

Washington's diary indicates that he worshiped more frequently during national crises and periods of residence in cities, where churches were more accessible than they were from Mount Vernon. The assistant rector of Christ Church attested to Washington's "regular attendance" when the capital was in Philadelphia.[1] One memento adds a personal touch to Washington's churchgoing in New York City. "The President of the United States presents his Compliments to Mr. Jay," a note from Washington to John Jay in 1789 declares,

and informs him that the Harness of the President's Carriage was so much injured in coming from Jersey that he will not be able to use it to-day. If Mr. Jay should propose going to Church this morning the President would be obliged to him for a seat in his Carriage.[2]

Despite his record of churchgoing, the fervor and devoutness of Washington's religion has long been the subject of conflicting assertions.

According to the statements of several Revolutionary officers made long after the Revolution, Washington not only was a "constant attendant" at church services but also kept a strict Lord's Day, or Sabbath. But if a contemporaneous source—Washington's diary—is used as an index, he attended church somewhat more than once a month while living at Mount Vernon, and sometimes less. In 1760, the diary indicates that Washington went to church four times during the first five months of the year. In 1768, it records that Washington attended divine services on fifteen Sundays.

In part the discrepancy has to do with the difference between rural Virginia and urban New York or Philadelphia. Weather and its effect on the roads inevitably influenced church attendance in Virginia. By carriage, Pohick Church was a half dozen miles from Mount Vernon, and Christ Church was nine or ten miles in a different direction. In contrast, worshipers could make their way to services of worship in cities with much less difficulty.

Moreover, Washington's diary may not include some of his journeys to church. Nevertheless, the diary indicates that Washington passed up church on many Sundays. Sometimes he visited relatives and friends, received visitors, traveled or went fox-hunting, but most frequently he remained at Mount Vernon "alone all day." According to Nelly Custis, his adopted granddaughter, he generally limited his activities on Sundays.

When Washington did attend church, he was by all testimony a reverent participant. Many who have left descriptions of Washington at worship specifically note that he insisted on standing in his pew for prayers, instead of (as was usual for Anglicans) kneeling. Washington's choice of posture represents a puzzling idiosyncrasy, unless it stemmed from childhood upbringing, from a knowledge that Christians (like Jews) originally stood for prayer, or from his field experience on Sundays in the English Army.

In the fashion of the Deists, however, Washington seems to have remained indifferent to two significant rites of his church. Like many of the founding fathers who were raised Anglican, he was never confirmed. Confirmation was available after the Episcopal Church secured bishops in the 1780s, and by going forward for confirmation Washington would have provided an example to other Episcopalians. At age eighty-four, for example, James Madison's mother was confirmed when an Episcopal bishop finally visited her rural parish.[3] A later chapter will discuss in greater detail the rite of confirmation during the Revolutionary period.

Even more significantly, Washington apparently avoided the sacrament of Holy Communion. According to Eleanor Parke "Nelly" Custis, Washington's adopted granddaughter, Martha Washington was under the clear impression that Washington had regularly received Holy Communion with his mother prior to the Revolution.[4] Because the sacrament would have represented a curiosity to a young adult, no substantial reason exists to doubt the story. Writers continue to debate whether Washington received Holy Communion before or during the Revolutionary War, but the convergence of evidence seems to indicate that he did not receive it after the war. And therein lies a story.

During the eighteenth century, the typical Anglican or Episcopal church celebrated the sacrament of Holy Communion four times a year. On those "Sacrament Sundays," rectors added communion—which all Anglicans were technically supposed to receive at least once a year—to the end of the normal Sunday "Desk and Pulpit service." The latter consisted of Scripture readings, Psalms (which were sung), prayers, and a sermon. In other words (though it contained Christian elements), the service was patterned upon the synagogue worship of Jesus' time. To that synagogue service, Christianity—

originally a Jewish sect—had simply added a reenactment of the Last Supper, which it initially called the "Lord's Supper." This reenactment changed names and became increasingly elaborate as the centuries went on, but in eighteenth-century Anglicanism it was a relatively simple service.

Except during Easter, the percentage of churchgoers who remained for the communion in the eighteenth century was generally low, although some Anglican parishes were exceptions. Yet the sacrament represented a principal way in which Anglicans displayed a commitment to Jesus Christ. To receive the bread and wine, a worshiper (or "communicant") stood up, walked forward from the pew, and knelt at the altar rail in front of the holy table. Anglicanism also taught that Christ was present in the elements of the Holy Communion—a belief that Deists would have seen as superstition.

Much of the evidence that Washington remained on such Sundays for the communion service consists of what a judge would term hearsay. That which is not second-hand raises questions of credibility.[5] Far more persuasive is the account of Nelly Custis that she and Washington always left church at the end of the Desk and Pulpit service on Communion Sundays and then sent the carriage back from Mount Vernon to pick up Martha, who had remained.[6]

Also instructive is the testimony of the gentlemanly William White, Washington's bishop and pastor when the seat of government was in Philadelphia. White was simultaneously bishop of Pennsylvania and rector of the three Episcopal churches in Philadelphia. Late in his life, he answered an inquiry about Washington's attendance at communion services with the following discreet words: "Truth requires me to say, that General Washington never received the communion, in the churches of which I am parochial minister. Mrs. Washington was an habitual communicant."[7]

In an era when Episcopal bishops were dependent upon salaries they received as parish rectors or college presidents, White had the overall charge of the three Episcopal churches in Philadelphia. At each he had an assistant who presided when he was elsewhere. The Reverend James Abercrombie, the assistant at Christ Church, objected so much to the practice of the president of the United States (and others) walking out of church prior to communion that he preached a sermon on public worship. In it he spoke of the "unhappy tendency of . . . those in elevated stations who invariably turned their backs upon the celebration of the Lord's Supper." Although the sermon named no one, Washington correctly assumed that the message was "a very just reproof" directed especially at him. Realizing that he was setting a bad example, he never again attended Christ Church on Sacrament Sundays. This solution was presumably not what the Reverend Mr. Abercrombie had in mind.

Repetitive patterns tell their own story.[8] Washington did not receive communion in Philadelphia or Virginia. For a practicing Christian to refrain from Holy Communion is so surprising that writers continue to propose explanations. "One wonders why," a contemporary historian muses. "Whatever the reason, it must have been a matter of conscience. A less scrupulous political leader would have taken refuge in conformity to have presented an appealing image to his constituents."

The scholar then cites the Apostle Paul's warning in 1 Corinthians 11:25–29 as a potential underlying cause for Washington to avoid communion: "Wherefore whoever shall eat this bread and drink this cup of the Lord, unworthily; shall be guilty of the body and blood of the Lord. But let a man examine himself. . . . For he that eateth and drinketh unworthily, eateth and drinketh damnation to himself."

Above all, two questions about Washington engage the historian:

> Did he question his own worthiness, not because of some strict hidden sin of great magnitude but because of his strict standard of self-judgment? Did he deplore his own lack of humility or his honest but energetic pursuit of riches? He always demanded a tremendous amount of himself.[9]

This attempted explanation is recent, but over the years other historians have conjectured similarly. Yet the problem with such explanations is immense. Only a small percentage of a typical Anglican congregation remained for the administration of Holy Communion during Washington's lifetime. Thus the explanation presupposes that thousands of Anglicans or Episcopalians must have felt themselves unworthy to receive the sacrament. By avoiding Holy Communion, these church members would also have consistently ignored the admonitions of their clergy (admonitions that a cleric could read to them directly from the Book of Common Prayer) that they had a Christian duty to receive the bread and the wine. If this explanation were true, the conscience-stricken would include not only Washington but also three other early presidents of the United States and many members of the Continental and U.S. congresses. A later chapter will discuss in detail the rite of Holy Communion during the Revolutionary period.

If these are the actions (or nonactions) of a Deist, what do Washington's private letters and public statements say about his religious views? His public statements contain the majority of his statements about religion. Aides-de-camp and presidential staff wrote much of this material, and historians have noted that the tone of Washington's addresses became more fervent after the appointment of two particular speech writers. But the staff knew Washington's mind. Additionally, because the original manuscripts display changes made in Washington's hand—such as his substitution of "Great Spirit" for "God" in the draft of a formal letter to an Indian tribe—Washington undoubtedly read most of the statements written for him by others before they were issued.

With only a few exceptions (which may or may not have stemmed from the work of pious assistants), Washington's speeches, orders, official letters, and other public communications on religion give a more or less uniform picture. They seem clearly to display the outlook of a Deist. Their references to religion lack emotion. They omit such words as "Father," "Lord," "Redeemer," and "Savior." In their place, they use such Deistic terms as "Providence," "Heaven," "the Deity," "the Supreme Being," "the Grand Architect," "the Author of all Good," and "the Great Ruler of Events."[10] They refer infrequently to Christianity and rarely to Jesus Christ.

When Washington answers a letter from a German Reformed congregation in 1783, for example, he uses the terms "Supreme Ruler of the Universe" and "Heaven" in his reply. In 1789, when he writes to "the United Baptist Churches of Virginia," he uses "Heaven," "the Deity," and "God" twice. Writing to the General Assembly of the Presbyterian Church in 1789, he speaks of "the Deity," "Almighty

God," and "Heaven" twice. A letter to a society of Quakers in 1789 uses "Divine Providence," "Almighty God," and "Maker." In subsequent letters to religious bodies, the largely Deistic language continues. Writing in 1790 to the "Roman Catholics in America," Washington speaks of "Divine Providence." His 1793 letter to a congregation of the Church of the New Jerusalem employs "an over-ruling Providence" once and "God" twice. To the "Convention of the Universal[ist] Church" in 1790, he uses "an intelligent and accountable Being." When he writes to six "Hebrew Congregation[s]" on the East Coast, he uses "Heaven," "the Deity," the "Wonder-working Deity," "father of all mercies," and "The Power and Goodness of the Almighty."

Finally, in a 1793 letter to "the Philadelphia Protestant Clergy," he refers to "the Divine Author of life and felicity."[11] An approximate count shows that at least half of these terms are clearly Deistic and that another five represent the kind of term that either a Deist or an orthodox Jew or Christian would employ. The remaining terms—mostly consisting of the word "God"—are those employed by orthodox believers. Even to Trinitarian congregations and clergy, Washington significantly makes no mention of Jesus Christ.

In Washington's official documents, the most common reference is to "Providence." This term—which Washington used for God as early as 1755—displays Washington's belief that the almost miraculous victory of the colonists as well as the successful creation of the new republic stemmed from the invisible workings of Providence. Though he sometimes appeared to have difficulty differentiating Providence from destiny, he seemed to view Providence as the actions of a benevolent, prescient, all-powerful God who created life and guided its development, but who remained at least partially distant and impersonal.[12]

Like Deists, Washington was more concerned with morality and ethics than with adhering to the doctrines of a particular church. He seemed to have no interest in theology. Unlike Jefferson and Adams, he did not seem particularly interested in why the world was so. Favoring freedom of conscience for all Christians, Jews, Deists, and freethinkers, he helped establish religious liberty and toleration as central principles in the new American government. He also believed

The Apotheosis of George Washington displays his near-deification by Americans upon his death.

that organized religion played a useful role in society by promoting morality, order, and stability. His replies to the concerns raised by various religious bodies during his presidency exhibit his considered reflections on these issues.

Thus Washington required Revolutionary military forces to have chaplains, insisted that his soldiers attend Sunday services, and ordered Thanksgiving services after victories. He talked about death with resignation and stoicism and referred to what lay beyond the grave as "the world of spirits." While on his deathbed—with Martha sitting close by, his personal servant standing near, his physician James Craik staring helplessly into the fire, his other physicians waiting downstairs, and a group of his house servants standing anxiously by the bedroom door—Washington never asked for an Episcopal clergyman. After uttering his last words of "'Tis well" and taking his own pulse, he died peacefully on the night of December 14, 1799. Four days later, he was buried after Episcopal and Masonic funeral services. All of this is in keeping with an interpretation of Washington as a Deistic Episcopalian.[13]

Yet some writers do not depict Washington as a Deist. Shortly after his death, the religion of the first president became the subject of controversy. Seeking to demonstrate the role that orthodox Christianity played in the founding of the United States, evangelical writers began to portray the Father of His Country as a devout Christian who devoted an impressive amount of time to prayer.

Books such as *The Life of George Washington* by Mason Locke Weems (a book that first appeared in 1800) and Edward C. McGuire's *The Religious Opinions and Character of Washington* (New York, 1836) informed readers of the supposed piety of George Washington. They contained stories of Washington holding Holy Communion services before battles; of a stranger who turned out to be Washington taking lodging in a humble home and spending most of the night in prayer; of Washington visiting small rural churches and inspiring the congregations with his religious fervor; of Washington escaping into the forests during encampments to pray in solitude.

Kept in continuous publication until the 1920s, the biography by "Parson Weems" became one of the best-selling books in American history. As late as the 1890s, in his biography of Washington, Woodrow Wilson passed on Weems's story of a little girl overhearing Washington cry out before a battle. Although the biblical battle cry of the Reubenites, the Gadites, and the Half-Tribe of Manasseh fails to come trippingly off the tongue, the child reportedly remembered Washington as saying: "The Lord God of gods, the Lord God of gods, He knoweth, and Israel he shall know; if it be in rebellion, or if in transgression against the Lord, save us not this day" (Joshua 22:22).[14] Recent decades have seen a number of works by evangelical writers reasserting the arguments that Washington (as well as many of the other founding fathers) was in reality an orthodox Christian.[15]

When these pious stories began to appear shortly after Washington's death, many of the general's contemporaries—including Jefferson, Madison, and Bishop White—disputed the depictions. "Sir, he was a Deist," one of Washington's pastors declared in a discussion of the question. Since then, disagreements over Washington's religious beliefs have periodically broken into public print. Early in the twentieth century, letters arguing for and against Washington's belief in the divinity of Christ occupied pages of a leading New York newspaper. Senator Henry Cabot Lodge was among those who argued for Washington's orthodoxy.[16] Unlike Washington's pastor or contemporaries, of course, none of the writers had known Washington or observed his religious practices.

In such disputes evangelical and patriotic authors tend to find orthodoxy and zeal in Washington's religion.[17] Professional historians, however, find the chain of evidence supporting the stories of Washington's exemplary piety weak. One author, for example, said that the "*Rev. D.D. Field* told *her* that a *Mrs. Watkins told him that when she was a girl,* Washington . . ." Such hearsay evidence (italicized in the quotation) is not valid historical proof.

Similarly, Parson Weems became famous for his story of young George Washington and the cherry tree, which he added to the fifth edition of his biography in 1806. Weems declared that he had heard the story from an old woman who was a cousin of Washington and who had grown up with him. In 1817, in the seventeenth edition of his biography, Weems added another story that has become a standard part of Washington lore. In it Washington is discovered kneeling and praying aloud in a snowy wood at Valley Forge by a pacifist Quaker and local inhabitant named Isaac Potts. Moved by what he sees, Potts converts to the Revolutionary cause. He goes home and tells his wife, Sarah, that Washington is a "man of God," who, with the aid of God, "will work out a great salvation for America."

The analysis of Frank E. Grizzard, Jr., the most recent writer on Washington's religion, calls this story into serious question. Although Isaac Potts owned the house in which Washington headquartered, he did not then live in Valley Forge. Instead, his home was rented to an ironmaster named William Dewees. Potts also did not marry Sarah until 1803—long after the supposed episode at Valley Forge. In addition, as Grizzard notes, "clergymen who knew Washington testified that he never knelt during service or at prayer." Grizzard also points out that the Reverend Nathaniel Randolph Snowden's *Diary and Remembrances,* written after Weems's version was published, not only names Isaac Potts's brother John as the witness to Washington's prayer, but also claims to have received the account directly from him. Grizzard speaks of "Weems's proclivity to make up stories out of wholecloth."[18] Weems billed himself as "Rector of Mount Vernon Parish"—a nonexistent parish—and had a low standing as a historian and truth-teller even among his fellow Episcopal clergy in Virginia.

"I should have thought it the greatest heresy to doubt his firm belief in Christianity," Nelly Custis wrote somewhat acerbically to a biographer who inquired about the religious views of her adoptive grandfather. "He communed with his God in secret. . . . He was a silent, thoughtful man."[19] No historian would be well advised to depict Washington as anything other than a Christian. But most historians today believe that the stories of Parson Weems and of other writers who depicted Washington as a model of Christian orthodoxy have no more basis in fact than the story of the cherry tree.[20] Nevertheless, these stories not only elevated Washington to near mythological status but also created legends about him that have refused to die. More accurate perhaps is the summation given by President James Madison to a biographer of Washington in 1830:

Mr. Madison does not suppose that Washington had ever attended to the arguments for Christianity, and for the different systems of religion, or in fact that he had formed definite opinions on the subject. But he took these things as he found them existing, and was constant in his observations of worship according to the received forms of the Episcopal Church, in which he was brought up.[21]

7

THE RELIGIOUS VIEWS OF
JOHN ADAMS

I f Washington's religious views remain a subject of disagreement today, those of John Adams arouse no such debate. Adams was the first president who was a Unitarian—a faith that, in Adams's case, could be described with some accuracy as "Christian Deism." Since the time of Adams, Unitarianism has broadened in America to include schools of thought that view themselves as neither theistic nor Christian. In the eighteenth and early nineteenth centuries, however, it was a form of supernaturalist Christianity that taught that God was one—a *unit*—and not three—a *tri-unit*. In doing so, Unitarians asserted that they had restored the original Christian belief that Jesus was in some way commissioned or sent by God but that he remained subordinate to him.

At one point in early Christianity, the majority of Christians did not believe in the doctrine of the Trinity. Citing such passages as Proverbs 8:22 ("The Lord created me at the beginning of his work, the first of his acts of long ago"), Colossians 1:15 ("[Jesus] is the image of the invisible God, the firstborn of all creation"), and John 14:28 (where Jesus says, "If you loved me, you would rejoice that I am going to the Father, because the Father is greater than I"), they believed that God was a unipersonality to whom Jesus was subordinate.

A leading example of Christian Deism and early Christian Unitarianism, John Adams believed in the biblical miracles, in a personal God, and in Jesus as the Redeemer of humanity.

Of the two kinds of anti-Trinitarians, one school held that Jesus was a demigod who had come down from Heaven as a messenger; their rallying cry was "Jesus was from above." The second school held that Jesus was a human being whom God had raised to a divine status because of his unique obedience and morality while on earth; their rallying cry was "Jesus was from below." Adams seems to have fallen into the second category.

The views of the principal leader of early Christian subordinationism—Arius of Alexandria—also fell into that second category. A Christian presbyter of the third and fourth centuries, Arius taught that Jesus was essentially a super-angelic being whom God had created out of nothing. "There was a time," Arius declared of Jesus of Nazareth, "when he was not." For Arius, Jesus was immensely superior to humans, but he was subordinate to God. For a time a majority of Christian clergy and laity believed similarly.

In the fourth century, however, Trinitarianism defeated subordinationism. Led by Athanasius, bishop of Alexandria, two church councils of the fourth century—Nicea (325) and Constantinople (381)—drew up the materials for what is called the Nicene Creed. The precise origins of this Trinitarian creed, still recited in Christian churches, are unclear.[1] But by the fifth century, it had become a hallmark of orthodoxy for Christianity. Somewhat erroneously, it came to be named for the council that had met earlier at Nicea. In the Book of Common Prayer used by Anglican founding fathers, this Nicene Creed in part reads:

I BELIEVE . . . in one Lord Jesus Christ, the only begotten Son of God, Begotten of his Father before all worlds, God of God, Light of Light, Very God of very God, Begotten, not made, Being of one substance with the Father, By whom all things were made: Who for us men, and for our salvation came down from heaven, And was incarnate by the Holy Ghost of the Virgin Mary, and was made man. . . .

The creed then continues with a definition of the divinity of the Holy Ghost (the Elizabethan word for "spirit"): "And I believe in the Holy Ghost, The Lord and giver of life, Who proceedeth from the Father and Son, Who with the Father and the Son together is worshipped and glorified, Who spake by the Prophets. . . ."[2] In the same period, another statement of orthodox faith—the Athanasian Creed—defined the Trinity as "the Father is God, the Son is God, and the Holy Spirit is God; and yet there are not three Gods, but one God."[3]

Since the late fourth century, the doctrine of the Trinity has been synonymous with orthodox Christianity. Although subordinationist churches continued for more than a century after the formal definition of the Trinity, the union of church and state in the Roman Empire meant that Trinitarianism became the only interpretation permitted.

For Christians, the doctrine was enormously important. It gave authority to the words of Jesus. It taught that the Son of God, and not simply a demigod, died on the cross for the sins of humanity. It placed the continual intercession for humanity at the right hand of God in the hands of the Son of God, and not in those of a chief angel (who, like Satan, could always defect).

Finally, Christians believed in the doctrine precisely because it had biblical support. Such New Testament passages as 2 Corinthians 13:13 ("The grace of the Lord Jesus Christ, the Love of God, and the communion of the Holy Spirit be with all of you"), Jude 20–21 ("pray in the Holy Spirit; keep yourselves in the love of God; look forward to the mercy of our Lord Jesus Christ that leads to eternal life"), 1 Corinthians 12:4–6 (in which the "varieties of gifts" are traced to a Spirit, Lord, and God), and Matthew 28:19 ("Go therefore and make disciples of all nations, baptizing them in the name of the Father and of the Son and of the Holy Spirit") can be interpreted as describing one God in three persons.

Driven from the empire, the anti-Trinitarians gradually disappeared. They revived in the Reformation period, though persecuted by Protestants and Roman Catholics alike. By the seventeenth century, the term "Unitarian" had begun to replace "anti-Trinitarian" as a description of the movement.

In eastern New England, Unitarianism emerged in the later eighteenth century in combination with Enlightenment thought. It also grew as a reaction against the revivalistic emotionalism of the Great Awakening. Objecting not only to the doctrine of the Trinity but also to such Calvinist teachings as total depravity (the corruption of humanity since the fall of Adam and Eve) and predestination (the election to heaven of some humans and the reprobation of others to hell, wholly without relationship to their faith and works), Unitarians became the left wing of the established Congregationalist churches. To orthodox Christians they were heretics, but in their own minds they were restorers of the primitive Christianity that had existed prior to the Trinitarian definitions of the fourth century.

For decades the orthodox Calvinists and the new "rational Christian" or "liberal Christian" Unitarians struggled in New England for control of both the denomination and Harvard College. By the second decade of the nineteenth century, it was clear that the rupture would be permanent. Finally, 125 Congregationalist churches—most located within forty miles of Boston—joined in 1825 to form the American Unitarian Association. Their number included First Parish Church in Quincy, the long-time church of the Adams family.

In 1815, Adams stated that in his experience Unitarianism in New England was not a new movement. Rather, he said, it had existed for at least sixty-five years. As it developed, Unitarianism was geographically restricted, making it difficult for New England adherents such as Adams to attend a Unitarian church when traveling. Unitarian churches were also tilted in membership toward the upper classes.

While increasingly holding Unitarian sentiments, Adams was technically a Congregationalist, though a liberal one, for most of his life. Raised in a churchgoing family in the established Congregationalist churches of Massachusetts and baptized in the parish church in Quincy, he planned at a young age to enter the ministry. While he was at Harvard, however, an acrimonious theological debate between

Lemuel Briant, his Enlightenment-influenced pastor at the Quincy church, and traditional Calvinists caused Adams to change his views. The controversy was prompted by a 1749 sermon of Briant's that seemed to deny the Calvinist doctrines of total depravity, unconditional election, and irresistible grace. To orthodox Calvinists, it also seemed to declare that humans possessed free will in accepting or rejecting divine grace.[4]

As was customary in Congregationalist circles, a council of clergy and laity from churches in the area convened to decide Briant's orthodoxy. The controversy raged for some years. Siding with the minister (as the majority of the parishioners and even his father did) and rejecting the dogmatism and intolerance that seemed to accompany religion, Adams became a schoolmaster and a lawyer rather than a minister. Retroactively, though the doctrine of the Trinity played no role in this doctrinal dispute, his parish church dated its adherence to Unitarianism to this controversy of the 1750s.

Religion and churchgoing remained important to Adams throughout his life. He married Abigail Smith, the daughter of a Congregationalist minister. Describing himself as "a church-going animal," he typically went to church twice on Sundays. He believed in a personal God, in a guiding Providence, in the resurrection of Jesus Christ, and in life after death. He rejected Paine's views of the Bible and Christianity, criticizing him for the antagonism he displayed. As president of the United States, he used such distinctly Christian phrases as "Redeemer of the World," "the Great Mediator and Advocate," and "the grace of His Holy Spirit" in his thanksgiving proclamations. These were phrases that Unitarians of the time (many of whom, like Adams, believed in the miracles recorded in the Bible) could use without contradicting their doctrine of the unipersonality of God.

Additionally, Adams continued a colonial tradition by twice calling for national fast days to renew the nation's sense of divine mission. Believing it imperative that the world follow the ethical teachings of Jesus, he viewed himself as a Christian. "The Christian religion, as I understand it," he declared to Benjamin Rush in 1810,

is the brightness of the glory and the express portrait of the eternal, self-existent independent, benevolent, all-powerful and all-merciful Creator,

Preserver and Father of the Universe. . . . Neither savage nor civilized man without a revelation could ever have discovered or invented it.[5]

Like other Deists, however, Adams substituted a simpler, less mysterious form of Christianity for the Christianity he had inherited. Reading and reflection caused him to discard such beliefs as the Trinity, the divinity of Christ, total depravity, and predestination. God, he declared, "has given us Reason, to find out the Truth, and the real Design and true End of our Existence." Thus he asserted that humans should study nature and use reason to learn about God and his creation.[6]

Above all, Adams opposed religious oppression and narrow-mindedness. "Twenty times, in the course of my late Reading," he wrote to Jefferson in 1817, "have I been upon the point of breaking out, 'This would be the best of all possible Worlds, if there were no Religion in it.'" Adams then qualified this self-described "fanatical" comment by declaring that "without Religion this World would be Something not fit to be mentioned in polite Company, I mean Hell."[7]

All of this displays the blend of Unitarian Christianity and rational thought that was the religion of John Adams. Like many of his contemporaries, he brought the religion in which he was raised into the court of his reason and common sense and judged it by what he found. His wife, Abigail—who shared her husband's Unitarian views—did the same. "Let the human mind loose," Adams once wrote in an outburst of Enlightenment passion. "It must be loosed; it will be loose. Superstition and despotism cannot confine it."[8] He followed these words with the assertion that Christianity would surely triumph if the human mind were loosed. This statement indicates that Adams belongs somewhere in the category of Unitarian Christian or Christian Deist.

8

THE RELIGIOUS VIEWS OF
THOMAS JEFFERSON

T homas Jefferson epitomized what it meant in America to be a man of the Enlightenment. At his estate of Monticello, he displayed busts of Bacon, Locke, and Newton. Incredibly broad in interests and abilities, Jefferson was sufficiently interested in religious matters that one scholar has described him as "the most self-consciously theological of all America's presidents." Religion, the writer declares, "mesmerized him, enraged him, tantalized him, alarmed him, and sometimes inspired him."[1]

Although no record of Jefferson's baptism exists, he was undoubtedly baptized as an infant by a priest of the Church of England. He could remember his mother teaching him prayers from the Book of Common Prayer. His father, Peter Jefferson, a planter and surveyor, served as a vestryman in the local Anglican parish. Educated in the academies of Anglican parsons, young Jefferson spent important years of study under the Reverend James Maury, an Anglican minister and graduate of William and Mary who owned an abundant scholarly library.

At age sixteen, Jefferson entered William and Mary. Of the seven clergy then on its faculty, six were Anglican clergy. But the seventh— a layman, William Small—proved by far the most influential. A product of the Scots Enlightenment, Small taught mathematics, ethics,

Thomas Jefferson's religion was monotheistic, restorationist, reason-centered, Jesus-centered, combative toward mystery, outwardly Episcopalian, but probably Unitarian.

rhetoric, and belles lettres. He introduced Jefferson to Enlightenment thinkers and sparked a lifelong passion in him for their teachings.

During and after his years at William and Mary, Jefferson copied an enormous amount of the writings of Deistic thinkers into his copybooks. By his thirtieth year, he had read and digested the writings of most of the principal thinkers of the Enlightenment. Since he could read French, Jefferson became one of the minority of American Deists who was strongly influenced not only by the Scots and English Enlightenment but also by its more radical French counterpart. Among America's founding fathers, he became the principal *philosophe*.

Despite his heterodoxy, Jefferson remained outwardly an Anglican and Episcopalian throughout life. In 1772, an Anglican clergyman presided at his marriage to Martha Skelton Wayles. He remained a lifelong friend of James Madison, the first Episcopal bishop of Virginia. Although the evangelical bishop of Virginia who succeeded Bishop Madison in 1814, Richard Channing Moore, seems to have maintained no relationship with him, Jefferson committed the religious care of his children to the Episcopal Church. He also contributed generously to the support of St. Anne's Parish (of which Monticello was a part) and continued to record the births, marriages, and deaths of family members in his father's prayer book.

In Jefferson's time, as today, the Anglican-Episcopal tradition permitted its members a broad channel of belief. To the left and right of that channel, the Book of Common Prayer and the creeds of early Christianity placed buoys to mark the boundaries of Anglican belief. "Here thou may go but no further," the buoys seemed to say. During his adult life, many of Jefferson's Deistic views went well beyond the markers on the left into heresy. But he never formally left his ancestral faith. When he died in 1826, an Episcopal minister presided at his funeral.

Knowing his political future and the controversial character of his religious views, Jefferson was reticent about his beliefs. When he sent his thoughts on religion (often in great detail) to friends, he generally requested that they show them to no one. Despite his caution, his opinions on religion had become well known in the country as early as 1800, when he ran successfully for the presidency. Jefferson himself was to blame for this exposure, for his one book, *Notes on the State of Virginia* (published in France in 1785 and in England in 1787), contained certain passages that seemed to display him as a Deist. "It does me no injury for my neighbour to say there are twenty gods, or no god," Jefferson wrote in his chapter on religion. "It neither picks my pocket nor breaks my leg." In addition to opposing established churches and religious coercion, he also wrote: "millions of innocent men, women, and children, since the introduction of Christianity, have been burnt, tortured, fined, imprisoned . . . ."[2]

Thus it was not surprising that Americans generally saw Jefferson's opponent, John Adams, as the believing Christian in the presidential election of 1800. Adams's Federalist ally, Alexander Hamilton, a long-time rival of Jefferson, smeared the Virginia candidate as "an atheist in religion and a fanatic in politics."[3] During the election, Congregationalist clergy—generally Federalists in political loyalty—went so far as to assert that Christians would be forced to hide their Bibles as well as to worship in secret if the "unchristian" Jefferson were elected.

In the years since 1800, many writers have analyzed Jefferson's religion. Essentially he seems—like many other Deists—to have been a "restorationist." The restorationist ideal exists in such areas as politics, constitutional theory, and world religion. In all fields, restorationists attempt to restore a lost set of truths. Christian restorationists believe in a golden era—generally the New Testament period—from which the church has fallen away (or "apostacized"). Protestantism is a form of Christian restorationism, though some of its forms—for example, the Churches of Christ or the Baptists—are more restorationist than others. Whatever their specific programs, the goal of all Christian restorationists is to restore the faith once delivered by Jesus to his followers to its supposed original purity and power.

Deism inevitably tended toward restorationism, in that many of the movement's adherents believed that some combination of external forces had added false doctrines to the original teachings of Jesus. For Ethan Allen, "Craft and Ignorance" had added "excrescences" to Christianity. For Thomas Paine, "Christian Mythologists, calling themselves the Christian Church," had "set up a system of religion very contradictory to the character of the person whose name it bears," a system of "pomp and revenue in pretended imitation" of Jesus's life of "humility and poverty."[4]

After initially fearing that he could no longer believe in the religion in which he was raised, Jefferson read Joseph Priestley's *History of the Corruptions of Christianity* at some point after the Revolution. In 1813, Jefferson wrote to Adams that he had read Priestley's book "over and over again."[5] A one-time Presbyterian minister, a noted scientist (the discoverer of oxygen), and the author of numerous unorthodox tracts on religion, Priestley moved left in his theological views and founded the Unitarian Society in London in 1791. Three years later, he fled England for America after publicly defending the ideals of the French Revolution, a stance with which Jefferson sympathized.

Through Priestley's book, Jefferson came to believe that the combined effect of power-hungry monarchs and corrupt "priests" had despoiled the original, pristine teachings of Jesus. Among the "band of dupes and impostors" he identified were "Platonizing Christians," Paul the Apostle (the "first corrupter of the doctrines of Jesus"), bishops such as Athanasius of Alexandria ("the fanatic") and Augustine of Hippo, a posse of medieval popes, the Protestant Reformer John Calvin (whose followers "introduced into the Christian religion more new obscenities than its leader had purged it of old ones"), and assorted other Christians throughout history.[6] But beneath these corruptions—which he labeled with such words as "nonsense," "dross," "rags," "distortions," and "abracadabra"—Jefferson, like Priestley, came to believe there lay a fulcrum of eternal truth. In 1803, he wrote to Benjamin Rush:

To the corruptions of Christianity I am, indeed, opposed, but not to the genuine precepts of Jesus himself. I am a Christian in the only sense in which I believe Jesus wished any one to be; sincerely attached to his doctrines, in preference to all others; ascribing to himself every human excellence, and believing he never claimed any other.[7]

Jefferson's view of Jesus displays his restorationism. He regularly read the Bible. He revered Jesus as a reformer and moral exemplar. But he did not see Jesus (as the Adamses, John Jay, and Elias Boudinot did) as a savior. Nor did he believe that the miracles attributed to Jesus were more than pious exaggerations. As a result, Jefferson used scissors and razor to excise from his New Testament the corruptions that he believed its writers had placed upon the original teachings of Jesus. Because Jefferson's God was a God of reason, not of irrationality, Jefferson removed from the gospels anything that appeared unreasonable.

Such an approach meant, of course, that the Sage of Monticello cut out the prophecies and miracle stories and focused instead on Jesus' ethical teachings and parables. His edited version of the New Testament ends with the death of Jesus. In scholarship, it has always been possible to declare that the Apostle Paul's profoundly influential letters took Christianity in the wrong direction. Choosing that option, Jefferson removed from the New Testament not only Paul's letters but also the book of Revelation and the letters attributed to Peter, John, James, and Jude. His Deistic version of the New Testament— titled *The Life and Morals of Jesus* (and other titles)—was not published until almost a century after Jefferson's death.

In 1820, Jefferson sent a copy of this edited version of the New Testament, which he then called the "Syllabus," to his one-time protégé and secretary, William Short. In his accompanying letter, he described Jesus of Nazareth as "no imposter himself, but a great Reformer of the Hebrew code of religion." Jefferson then declared that he disagreed with the Galilean on some matters: "It is not to be understood that I am with him in all his doctrines. I am a Materialist; he takes the side of Spiritualism; he preaches the efficacy of repentance towards forgiveness of sin, I require a counter-poise of good works to redeem it, etc, etc."

Having disagreed with Jesus, Jefferson then indicated what he admired about Jesus:

> It is the innocence of his character, the purity and sublimity of his moral precepts, the eloquence of his inculcation, the beauty of his apologues in which he conveys them, that I so much admire. . . . Among the sayings and discourses imputed to him by his biographers, I find many passages of fine imagination, correct morality, and of the most lovely benevolence.

Yet Jefferson also believed that the writers (the "biographers") of the New Testament had mixed in "so much ignorance, so much absurdity, so much untruth, charlatanism and imposture, as to pronounce it impossible that such contradictions should have proceeded from the same being."

All of "these palpable interpolations and falsifications of his doctrines," Jefferson declared to Short, led Jefferson to try to reestablish the true Jesus of history: "I found the work obvious and easy," Jefferson wrote, "and that his [Jesus'] part composed the most beautiful morsel of morality which has been given to us by man."[8] In good restorationist fashion, Jefferson believed he had removed the barnacles of corruption from the New Testament. He thought that the character of Jesus would now emerge as "the most innocent" and "the most eloquent . . . that has ever been exhibited to man."[9]

As indicated by his derogatory use of the word "priests" (a term he applied not only to medieval Roman Catholic clergy but also to contemporary Calvinist ministers), Jefferson's Deism made him anticlerical. "The Presbyterian clergy," he wrote in the same letter to Short, "are . . . the most intolerant of all sects, the most tyrannical and ambitious; ready at the word of the lawgiver, if such a word could now be obtained, to put the torch to the pile."[10] Thus it is no surprise that his favorite religious body (outside perhaps of Unitarianism) seems to have been the Quakers, a group that had neither clergy nor creeds. Yet where Christianity was concerned, Jefferson was not anti-institutional, for he firmly believed that morality was rooted in religion. Thus he contributed to the building funds of Episcopal, Baptist, and Presbyterian congregations.

Jefferson attended church with some regularity. He liked to listen not only to good speeches but also to good sermons. When he went to the "union services" conducted by ministers of various denominations at the Albemarle County Courthouse in Virginia, he even carried his own chair. "Mr. Jefferson used to bring his seat with him on horseback from Monticello," Bishop Meade noted, "it being some light machinery which, folded up, was carried under his arm, and unfolded served for a chair on the floor of the court-house."[11]

For a time in the 1780s Jefferson attended a church newly formed for the Reverend Charles Clay. He also helped to raise money to support Clay's ministry. An evangelical Anglican and patriot who left St. Anne's Parish (Jefferson's home Episcopal parish) after a disagreement with the vestry over salary, Clay was an excellent preacher. Jefferson not only liked him personally but also appreciated his sermons. He remained friends for life with the Reverend Mr. Clay, who left the active ministry after the 1780s but apparently remained an orthodox Episcopalian.[12]

That Jefferson attended and supported other churches does not make him a Baptist, Presbyterian, or evangelical Episcopalian, any more than his regular reading of the Bible makes him an orthodox Christian. Like many churchgoers, he was always able to tune out points of doctrine with which he disagreed. He remained a Deist in rejecting the rituals and sacraments of institutional religion as the proper forum for worship. For Jefferson, true worship consisted of love and tolerance for human beings according to the ethical teachings of Jesus. He viewed these precepts as "the most pure, benevolent, and sublime which have ever been preached to man."[13] Despite the frequent bickering of Christians about the fine points of dogma, he hoped that they and others could agree about the morals of Jesus.

Jefferson also opposed the strong influence that institutional Christianity had on the higher education of his time. When serving as a member of the board of visitors at William and Mary in the 1770s and 1780s, he helped to abolish its divinity school and its two divinity professorships. In their place he substituted professorships in the secular fields of science and law. When he saw that he could not remove the deeply embedded Anglican-Episcopal ethos from William and Mary, he established his own university, the University of Virginia.

For some decades, "Mr. Jefferson's university" was essentially a Deistic institution, with neither a religious curriculum nor a chaplain.

Its first board of visitors included three American presidents (Madison, Monroe, and Jefferson himself) of Deistic religion. Characterized by religious heterodoxy, its early faculty included the leading Unitarian George Ticknor. Several years after Jefferson's death, a sermon preached in Charlottesville by a highly regarded Episcopal cleric attributed a recent epidemic that had killed a significant percentage of students to the "irreligion and even infidelity" of the university's faculty and curriculum. "If such have not been the principles upon which this Institution was raised, or on which it is now conducted," the minister challenged his congregation,

> is it superstition or weakness to ask whether these visitations have not been sent to show the rulers thereof their entire dependency on God? See how easily the Almighty can blast all their high hopes and dash all their noble schemes to the earth. See how quickly he can send a plague or pestilence through these buildings. . . . Oh, it is a hazardous experiment to undertake to conduct such an institution . . . without constantly and earnestly imploring and seeking the aid of God.[14]

This sermon, which caused a furor, urged the Deistic university to dedicate itself "to Almighty God, and place it under his guardian care." It also urged not only that "the morality here taught be the morality of the Bible" but also that "the Bible . . . be the text-book of first esteem and most constant reference." The sermon was viewed as an assault by an influential, staunch Episcopalian not only on Deism but also on Jefferson. However it sounds to readers in the twenty-first century, it achieved changes in the university's practice.[15]

As his religious views developed, Jefferson's understanding of God went beyond that of many Deists. Like many of the founders, he believed in a governing and overriding Providence that guided the affairs of the United States. Like other Deists, he valued intellectual and spiritual freedom and abhorred organized Christianity's tendency toward dogmatism. He believed that no government had the authority to mandate religious conformity, and his Act for Establishing Religious Freedom (1786) helped guarantee the right to freedom of conscience.

Jefferson is often described as a Unitarian. Although he designed the first Episcopal church in Charlottesville, it is that city's Unitarian church that is named for him. This identification of Unitarianism with Jefferson seems accurate.

With the exceptions of Bishop Madison—whom he knew both from scientific investigation and from his work at William and Mary— and friends such as Charles Clay, Jefferson distrusted Trinitarian Christian clergy. He viewed most as enemies of the simple teachings of Jesus. As Jefferson saw it, rational empirical investigation determined what constituted reality. When viewed from this perspective, the Trinity was—in his words—"incomprehensible jargon," "metaphysical insanity," a "hocus-pocus phantasm of a god like another Cerberus, with one body and three heads," a "deliria of crazy imaginations, as foreign to Christianity as is that of Mahomet," and "abracadabra."[16] Like other Deists, Jefferson viewed mystery as a disguise for absurdity. "I should as soon undertake to bring the crazy skulls of Bedlam to sound understanding," he wrote to the Unitarian Benjamin Waterhouse, "as inculcate reason into that of an Athanasian."[17] In 1813, he wrote to John Adams: "It is too late in the day, for men of sincerity to pretend they believe in the Platonic mysticisms that three are one, and one is three; and yet that the one is not three and the three are not one."[18]

For this reason, Jefferson refused to serve as godfather for children of friends in Anglican baptisms, for godfathers had to profess a belief in what he viewed as the unreasonable doctrine of the Trinity. "The person who becomes sponsor for a child, according to the ritual of the Church in which I was educated," Jefferson politely wrote to a friend who asked him to serve as a godparent in 1788, "makes a solemn profession before God and the world, of faith in the articles, which I had never sense enough to comprehend, and it has always appeared to me that comprehension must precede assent."[19] Jefferson believed in a Supreme Being who created and sustained the universe, but this was not the triune God of the Anglican and Episcopal tradition.

Whether Jefferson would have formally left the church of his ancestors is unclear. He remains listed in many histories as an Episcopalian rather than a Unitarian for the probable reason that Piedmont Virginia contained no Unitarian church. Unitarian societies were established in Baltimore, Georgetown, and the District of Columbia in the early part of the nineteenth century, but these cities were much too far from Monticello. When Jefferson lived in Philadelphia, however, he attended Joseph Priestley's Unitarian church. In addition, in some famous correspondence with a Unitarian minister, he predicted that Unitarianism would soon sweep the nation:

> I rejoice that in this blessed country of free inquiry and belief, which has surrendered its creed and conscience to neither kings nor priests, the genuine doctrine of only one God is reviving, and I trust there is not a young man now living who will not die an Unitarian.[20]

Like Adams, Jefferson would have fallen into the category of Unitarians who believed that Jesus was "from below." But unlike some early Unitarians, he did not go beyond believing that Jesus became the moral example for humans while he was below. To him, Jesus was always a man. His view of Jesus contained no role for a virgin birth, incarnation, resurrection, miracles, or adoption into divine status.

In his last years, Jefferson clearly moved toward a more traditional interpretation of Christianity. He valued Jesus as a person even more highly. Unlike some Deists, he came to believe in prayer and in a life after death. But belief in an afterlife and in a God who hears prayer were standard Unitarian beliefs of the time. Holding them did not move him into the category of orthodoxy.

Jefferson's great-grandson classified him as a "conservative Unitarian."[21] While close to the truth, that classification may not be definitive. In Jefferson's era, the description better applies to figures such as John and Abigail Adams, who believed in Jesus as a savior and redeemer and who held a generally supernaturalist view of the Bible. Instead, the term that seems most accurate for Jefferson is "moderate Unitarian." In any event, that description may be as good as we can give of a man who classified himself religiously as "of a sect by myself, as far as I know."[22]

Thomas Jefferson's religion was monotheistic, restorationist, reason-centered, Jesus-centered, anti-medieval, anti-Calvinist, anti-clerical, and combative toward mystery. A reformer in religion as well as in politics, the founder of a major university he hoped would become a beacon of the Enlightenment, an American who believed he had separated the gold from the dross in government and religion, Jefferson wanted to tear down what he considered false to allow what he considered true to shine through.

9

THE RELIGIOUS VIEWS OF
JAMES MADISON

I n the 1850s, an Episcopal bishop who knew the Madison family and every clergyman who had ministered to it wrote down what he remembered and had been told about President Madison's religion:

> Mr. Madison was sent to Princeton College,—perhaps through fear of the skeptical principles then so prevalent at William and Mary. During his stay at Princeton a great revival took place, and it was believed that he partook of its spirit. On his return home he conducted family worship in his father's house. He soon after offered for the Legislature, and it was objected to him, by his opponents that he was better suited to the pulpit than to the legislative hall.
>
> His religious feeling, however, seems to have been short-lived. His political associations with those of infidel principles, of whom there were many in his day, if they did not actually change his creed, yet subjected him to the general suspicion of it. . . .
>
> Whatever may have been the private sentiments of Mr. Madison on the subject of religion, he was never known to declare any hostility to it. He always treated it with respect, attended public worship in his neighbourhood, invited ministers of religion to his house, [and] had family prayers on such occasions, though he did not kneel himself at prayers. Episcopal ministers often went there to see his aged and pious mother and administer the Holy Communion to her.

I was never at Mr. Madison's but once and then our conversation took such a turn—though not designed on my part—as to call forth some expressions and arguments which left the impression on my mind that his creed was not strictly regulated by the Bible.[1]

Born in 1751 in King George County, Virginia, while his mother was visiting her family at their estate of Port Conway, James Madison was baptized by an Anglican parson three weeks after he was born. He had three godmothers and two godfathers. His father, a small planter, was a justice of the peace and a vestryman of St. Thomas Parish of Orange County; his mother was known for her devoutness.

In his eleventh year his parents sent him to the school run by

An orthodox Christian into his twenties, James Madison was subsequently influenced by Deism.

Donald Robertson, a Scots schoolmaster in King and Queen County, three counties away. A graduate of the University of Edinburgh who was then in his mid-forties, Robertson had opened his academy shortly after arriving in Virginia. Besides teaching the standard curriculum of the time, Robertson especially exposed Madison to Latin and to Enlightenment thought. He was clearly a gifted teacher, for Madison later declared a lifelong indebtedness to him.[2]

After five years with Robertson, Madison returned to the family estate of Montpelier and continued his studies with the Reverend Thomas Martin, rector of St. Thomas Parish. That Martin was a product of the College of New Jersey and Robertson was undoubtedly raised Presbyterian in Scotland is significant. Their dual influence probably explains why the Madisons sent their son not to the Deistically inclined William and Mary but rather to the College of New Jersey. Known for its orthodoxy, the latter was then the principal training ground for American Presbyterian clergy.[3]

After graduating in 1771, Madison remained in Princeton for a year to study Hebrew and ethics under its president, the Reverend John Witherspoon. Witherspoon combined Presbyterian orthodoxy with an advocacy of the Scottish Common Sense philosophy, which gave a decided role to human reason. He later became the only clergyman to sign the Declaration of Independence.

Studying under Witherspoon at Princeton, Madison learned to read the Bible in both Hebrew and Greek, though he apparently did not continue to study it. When he left the College of New Jersey and returned to Virginia to read law, he conducted family worship, a mark (then as now) of orthodoxy. Almost immediately he witnessed the persecution and jailing of religious dissenters in adjacent Culpepper County by the Established Church—*his* church. At the age of twenty-two, he came down firmly on the side of religious freedom, arguing that only liberty of conscience could guarantee civil and political liberty.

Madison fought for religious liberty throughout his political career. When Virginia adopted a new constitution in 1776, he insisted that the document guarantee freedom of conscience rather than mere toleration. In 1785 he wrote the anonymous and influential *Memorial and Remonstrance against Religious Assessments*, which helped defeat a bill in the Virginia House of Delegates calling for state subsidies to religious bodies. He also devoted energy to ensuring the adoption of Thomas Jefferson's Act for Establishing Religious Freedom and worked to have its principle enumerated in the federal Bill of Rights. As the years went on, he increasingly became convinced that the separation of church and state was best not only for the state but also for the churches and synagogues.

Once he embarked on his legal and political career, Madison rarely wrote or spoke publicly about religious subjects. Yet religion remained one of his lifelong interests. When Jefferson asked him for a list of books on theology for the library of the new University of Virginia, he responded with a list that showed a wide familiarity with theological literature.

Madison maintained a similarly low religious profile during his presidency. He opposed, for example, executive proclamations that used religious language. When circumstances forced him to issue one (such as during the War of 1812), he kept the language as neutral

and nonsectarian as possible. His belief that citizens should voluntarily support religion led him to oppose the appointment of chaplains for Congress and for the army and navy.

As a result, American historians know relatively little about the
fourth president's private views on religion. Any investigator who
wishes to get beyond Madison's reticence must look not only at what
he did and did not do, but also at what he said and did not say, in the
area of religion.

During his presidency, Madison held the President's Pew at St.
John's Episcopal Church, adjacent to the White House. When he and
his wife went to church in Washington, they attended St. John's
Church. When they were at Montpelier and went to church, they
attended St. Thomas Church in Orange.

But the evidence is unclear about how frequently the Madisons
attended church. What is known is that Madison was never confirmed,
though his wife, Dolley, and his mother, Nelly Conway Madison, were.
Chapter 11 will discuss the confirmation of Dolley Madison. Interest-
ingly, two accounts remain of the confirmation of Madison's mother.
The first comes from Bishop Richard Channing Moore's report to
the annual convention of the Episcopal Church of Virginia in 1817.
"My labours commenced in the county of Orange," he wrote, "at
which place I preached to a large and attentive auditory, celebrated
the Lord's Supper, and administered the rite of Confirmation to a
goodly number."

Bishop William Meade, who had discussed the confirmation with
Moore and others, later expanded this report. "The visit of the good
Bishop," he later wrote:

> as well from its novelty as its effectiveness, was calculated to make, and did
> make, a great impression at the time. It was an event of unusual solemnity,
> and is still remembered with lively interest by some who were present. This
> was the first Episcopal visitation that had ever been made, and this was the
> first time the rite of Confirmation had ever been administered, in the parish.
> . . . Among the "goodly number" confirmed by Bishop Moore on this occa-
> sion was the aged mother of President Madison. She became a communi-
> cant at the age of twenty, and now at the age of fourscore and four she came
> forward to ratify her early baptismal vows. Until that day an opportunity
> had never presented itself for the reception of this solemn and sacred rite.[4]

Despite Madison's reticence, contemporaries gained some sense of his private religious views. At a White House dinner in 1815, he purposely seated the Boston gentleman-scholar George Ticknor between himself and Dolley. A co-founder of the Boston Public Library and a leading layman in the emerging Unitarian movement, Ticknor reported the contents of the conversation:

> He talked of religious sects and parties, and was curious to know how the cause of liberal Christianity stood with us, and if the Athanasian creed was well received by our Episcopalians. He pretty distinctly intimated to me his [high] regard for Unitarian principles. . . . Mr. M. gave amusing stories of early religious persecutions in Virginia, and Mrs. M. entered into a defence and panegyric of the Quakers, to whose sect, you know, she once belonged.[5]

"Liberal Christianity"—about which Madison inquired of his guest—was the name New England Unitarians such as John and Abigail Adams first used to describe their movement. Written in the fourth and fifth centuries, the Athanasian Creed was a creed that Madison, like other Anglicans, grew up reciting during church services:

> We worship one God in Trinity, and Trinity in Unity; Neither confounding the Persons: nor dividing the Substance. . . . as also there are not three incomprehensibles uncreated, nor three uncreated: but one uncreated, and one incomprehensible . . . . the Father is made of none: neither created, nor begotten. The Son is of the Father alone: not made, nor created, but begotten.
> The Holy Ghost is of the Father and of the Son: neither made, nor created, nor begotten, but proceeding. . . . He therefore that will be saved: must thus think of the Trinity . . . our . . . Lord Jesus Christ, the Son of God, is God and Man. . . . One altogether; not by confusion of Substance: but by unity of Person. . . . this is the Catholick Faith: which except a man believe faithfully, he can not be saved.

Containing what one critic has called "the incompressible jargon of the Trinitarian arithmetic," it was precisely the kind of statement of faith that caused Enlightenment figures to turn toward Deism or Unitarianism.[6] The Athanasian Creed was unpopular even among practicing Anglicans. When the newly independent Episcopal Church—then very small—was drawing up its version of the Book of Common Prayer in Philadelphia in 1786, the deputies voted decisively to remove it from their Prayer Book:

On the question, Shall the Creed commonly called the Athanasian Creed, be admitted in the Liturgy of the Protestant Episcopal Church in the United States of America? The Ayes and Nays being taken, were as follow:

NEW YORK.—Dr. Provoost, No; Mr. Duane, No; Mr. Rutherford, No.—Nay.

NEW JERSEY.—Rev. Mr. Ogden, No; Rev. Mr. Frazer, No.; Mr Cox, No; Mr. Wallace, Aye; Mr Waddell, Aye.—Divided.

PENNSYLVANIA.—Dr. White, No; Dr. Magaw, No; Rev. Mr. Blackwell, No; Mr. Hopkinson, No; Mr. Powel, No; Mr. Gilpin, No.—Nay.

DELAWARE.—Dr. Wharton, No; Rev. Mr. Thorne, Aye; Mr. Sykes, No; Mr. Grantham, No.—Divided.

SOUTH CAROLINA.—Rev. Mr. Smith, No; Mr. Rutledge, No.—Nay.

And so it was determined in the negative.[7]

Unless more material is discovered, only snippets of Madison's private religious views remain. In 1825, for example, he exchanged letters with the Reverend Frederick Beasley, an Episcopal clergyman who was provost of the University of Pennsylvania. Beasley sent Madison a tract he had published on proofs for "the being and attributes of God." Madison's impressive response, which uses the phrase "Nature's God," not only displays his sympathy with Beasley's theism but also declares that "The belief in a God All Powerful wise & good is so essential to the moral order of the World & to the happiness of man, that arguments which enforce it cannot be drawn from too many sources." He omits any references, however, to Jesus, to the Bible, to the Judeo-Christian tradition, or to the church. Thus Madison's letter seems more the response of a Deist than that of an orthodox Christian.[8]

In 1835, a cousin wrote to Dolley Madison and apologized for a disagreement she had had with Madison about keeping the Sabbath. "I hope my beloved Mr. Madison was not displeased at my reference to his opinions on the Sabbath," Sarah Coles Stevenson wrote. "They were to me new, & so adverse to my own, that I confess they startled me. . . . pray do not mention it to him again if it displeases him. I would not incur his censure for any consideration."[9]

Mrs. Stevenson, wife of an ambassador to Great Britain, was an active Episcopalian at a time when Virginia Episcopalians kept a strict Lord's Day, or Sabbath. In conversation, Madison had apparently shocked her with his more lenient views about what activities were permissible on Sunday.[10] Because this disagreement occurred only one year before Madison's death, it would appear to reaffirm his essentially Deistic form of Anglicanism. Yet two decades later the Episcopal bishop of Virginia concluded the review of Madison's religion that began this chapter with surprising words: "At his death . . . his minister, the Rev. Mr. [William] Jones, and some of his neighbours openly expressed their conviction, that, from his conversation and bearing during the latter years of his life, he must be considered as receiving the Christian system to be divine."[11]

Bishop William Meade held a tough-minded view of other people's religion. He possessed no sympathy whatsoever for Deism. If he was correct that James Madison returned to a more traditional view of Christianity, that development would be unsurprising. Old age is often the time when people return "home" by embracing the faith in which they were raised.

Yet Meade's testimony is the single indication historians have that Madison returned to the orthodoxy of his childhood and college years. In "the entire Retirement corpus of Madison's writings . . . ," the senior associate editor of the James Madison Papers reports, "what there was did not indicate in any way that Madison at the end of his life returned to the orthodox piety of his youth."[12] Except for the account of Meade (who also argued for the religious orthodoxy of George Washington in the same book), the pattern of Madison's religious associations and the comments of contemporaries clearly categorize the fourth president of the United States as a moderate Deist.

In his comments on Beasley's tract in 1825, Madison analyzed how the minds of many people tend to assent "to the self-existence of an invisible cause possessing infinite power, wisdom and goodness." They choose that option, Madison declared, rather than the more negative concept of "the self-existence of the universe, visibly destitute of those attributes." He concluded by declaring that "all philosophical reasoning on the subject of existence and attributes of God will end up in one of those two opposing camps."[13]

Like so many other founding fathers, James Madison seems to have ended up in the camp affirming the existence of a Deistic God. By the time he died in 1836, Christianity in the United States had moved into a more traditional and orthodox model. Some of his contemporaries may have doubted Madison's religious orthodoxy. But as one wrote, "as to the purity of his moral character, the amiableness of his disposition toward all, his tender affection to his mother and wife, kindness to neighbours, good treatment of his servants, there was never any question."[14]

10

THE RELIGIOUS VIEWS OF JAMES MONROE

J
ames Monroe was born on April 28, 1758, in a home four miles
from the birthplace of George Washington. He was the eldest
son of Spence Monroe, a small planter in Westmoreland County.
Born into an Anglican family, Monroe was baptized in Washington Parish. He studied at Campbelltown Academy, a noted academy run by the Reverend Archibald Campbell, the rector of Washington Parish; future Supreme Court Justice John Marshall was a
classmate. In 1774 he went to an Anglican college, William and Mary,
where the president and most of the faculty were clergy of the Established Church. There Monroe was required to attend not only daily
morning and evening prayer in the College chapel but also Sunday
worship at nearby Bruton Parish Church.

As political tension with Great Britain mounted, Monroe became
active in the revolutionary cause and later served as an officer in the
Continental Army. In 1780 he left the army as a colonel to study law
at William and Mary and later in Richmond under Thomas Jefferson,
who became his lifelong friend and political mentor. In the next decades, Monroe practiced law in Fredericksburg and served in the
Virginia House of Delegates and on the Council of the State of Virginia. He gained additional political experience in the Congress, as a
minister to France, Great Britain, and Spain, and as secretary of state

Possibly a skeptic in his private beliefs, James Monroe set a pattern of religious "commitment" that later became normative for many politicians in American history.

and secretary of war during the War of 1812. In 1816, Monroe was elected fifth president of the United States. His two terms as president are noted for the Era of Good Feelings, the Missouri Compromise, the establishment of the Indian Territory, the purchase of Florida, and especially the Monroe Doctrine.

In 1786, at age twenty-eight, Monroe met and married seventeen-year-old Elizabeth Kortright. Daughter of a New York City merchant, she was noted for her beauty. Their marriage occurred at her home parish church, Trinity Church in lower Manhattan. The couple raised their two daughters, Eliza and Maria Hester, as Episcopalians. Thirteen years later, Monroe built and moved to the plantation of Highland, adjacent to Jefferson's estate of Monticello in Albemarle County, Virginia. After serving two terms and leaving the presidency at the age of sixty-seven, Monroe gave up his dream of retiring to Highland. Selling it to satisfy creditors, he settled on his plantation of Oak Hill in Loudoun County, Virginia, which was closer to the nation's capital.

Elizabeth Monroe, whose increasingly fragile health had provided another reason for moving closer to the District of Columbia, died on September 23, 1830. Ten months later, on July 4, 1831, Monroe died in New York City at the home of his younger daughter, Maria Hester Gouverneur. He was the third American president—Jefferson and John Adams were the other two—to die on July 4.

Monroe's funeral occurred at Trinity Church, where the church's rector and the Episcopal bishop of New York conducted the service from the Book of Common Prayer. In the same month, the Episcopal bishop of Virginia conducted a memorial service for Monroe in his native state. In 1858 his coffin was disinterred from its burial vault in a private cemetery in Manhattan and moved to the Episcopal Church of the Annunciation on West 14th Street in Manhattan, where the public could view it. The coffin was then moved by steamer to Richmond and reinterred with pageantry in Hollywood Cemetery. A Presbyterian minister delivered the prayer of commitment.

During his lifetime, Monroe lived in six Virginia parishes—Washington (where he was born), Bruton (where he went to college), Henrico (where he studied law and served as governor), St. George's (where he practiced law), St. Anne's (when he lived at Highland), and Shelburne (when he retired to Oak Hill). He also served on the board of visitors of William and Mary, where Episcopal membership was almost a prerequisite for service. While president, he occupied the President's Pew in St. John's Episcopal Church opposite the White House; its rector officiated when Maria Hester was married at the White House in 1820. Yet Monroe's biographers have rarely mentioned his religious views. Even those who have written books on the religion of the American presidents have found little to say when they have reached the religion of the fifth president of the United States.

The family papers of James Monroe are missing, as are the papers of his daughters. Tench Ringgold, a friend of Monroe during his later years, reported that Monroe burned his correspondence with his wife after her death. These family letters are the most likely places where Monroe would have discussed religious matters. While a substantial number of private letters of Monroe have survived, as have his public papers and writings, they contain remarkably little about religion.

One letter written during the American Revolution to Peter S. Duponceau does contain clear religious sentiments. A native of France, Duponceau served as military secretary to Frederick Wilhelm Augustus von Steuben, the Prussian-born inspector general of the Continental Army. During the winter of 1778, he and Monroe (who were close in age) became good friends. Receiving word that Duponceau had become seriously ill, Monroe wrote to him from Valley Forge in April 1778:

> From what the Baron has informed us, much heightened by your melancholy letter, I am induced to believe that declining nature scarce supports human existence. Your turn of mind I observe . . . is well adapted to the

gradual decay of life. . . . tis the summit of christian fortitude and heroism to prevail over the views of this transitory life, and turn the mind on the more lasting happiness of that to come. The blessed influence of heaven is, I hope, on you: beware of heresy: danger, ruin, and perpetual misery await it. But while life remains, it is necessary you should have some thing more than mere repentence [*sic*] to amuse your thoughts on.

Monroe then declared that he was sending Duponceau (who had been raised a Roman Catholic) some books by two Anglican authors. "The moral of the one," he concluded, "[was] so correspondence [correspondent?] with the scripture of the other that you will esteem it a well calculated discourse on virtue and religion."[1]

The letter was the work of a nineteen-year-old who had been through three battles and had narrowly escaped death at the Battle of Trenton. It may have displayed a certain amount of rote piety, for Monroe had a strong background of religious instruction and knew the language of orthodox Christian belief. Nevertheless, the letter spoke of "christian fortitude and heroism," mentioned heaven, warned against "heresy," and indicated that its writer was sending several books "on virtue and religion" written by Anglican clergy.

To draw too many conclusions from a single letter written by a young man in the midst of war would be unwise. But the letter does permit speculation that Monroe's view of Christianity may have changed at some point between the Revolution and his emergence into public service. He had not yet, for example, spent many months in daily contact with Thomas Paine. For in later years Monroe's public statements and speeches were remarkably silent about religious matters. Neither his public utterances nor his writings—including his autobiography—cite the Bible, nor do they make references to Jesus Christ.

In his first inaugural address, Monroe praised the concept of religious freedom, boasting that Americans may worship "the Divine Author" in any manner they choose. This same address declared that "the favor of a gracious Providence" had guided the United States. It concluded with Monroe declaring that he entered the presidential office with "fervent prayers to the Almighty that He will be graciously pleased to continue to us that protection which he has already so conspicuously displayed in our favor."

Monroe's second inaugural address spoke of his "firm reliance on the protection of Almighty God." When his speeches referred to the Deity, he used only the stock Deistic phrases. No more than half of the numerous short speeches he made while on his tour of the nation in 1817 contained religious references. Instead, Monroe talked about the virtues of citizenship.

Though many of Monroe's published letters deal with political issues, they did make passing references to personal matters. All discussion of religion, however, was absent. Even the surviving personal correspondence of Monroe avoided religious issues. In his era, gentlemen customarily wrote letters of advice to children, including godchildren and children of friends. When they wrote to sons in college, for example, fathers might urge them to attend religious services. In one such letter, Jefferson began by advising his nephew Peter Carr on books to read but then changed to advising him about scriptural interpretation and theological claims.[2]

Nothing of the sort appears in Monroe's extant letters of advice. When he wrote detailed letters advising his nieces and nephews how they could live happy and productive lives, he included no comments about spiritual matters. When James Monroe, Jr.—the son of Monroe's brother, Joseph Jones Monroe—became unruly while a cadet at West Point, Monroe sent him a detailed letter full of advice. But the letter mentions neither God nor religion. Even though Monroe had many connections in New York, he did not counsel his nephew, as was customary in such letters, to see any noted ministers or to attend certain churches.

When his only son, James Spence Monroe, died in 1800 before his second birthday, Monroe was clearly overwhelmed. The funeral service and burial were at St. John's Episcopal Church, Richmond, where the family worshiped while Monroe was governor. But the letters Monroe wrote to others about the death include no references to the consolation of religion. When Elizabeth died in 1830, Monroe wrote to a number of their friends saying how devastating her death was, but he failed to mention any religious beliefs that might have proved comforting. In contrast, when John Adams and Jefferson exchanged letters upon the death of Abigail Adams, both spoke of the consolations of a future state where they would meet loved ones again.[3]

James and Elizabeth Monroe did own a substantial collection of art that included religious subjects. As documented by inventories, their collection included a Madonna and Child, a depiction of John the Baptist, a painting of the Virgin Mary, and a painting of Mary Magdalene. But the inclusion of religious art was typical in a collection of that time and says little about religious belief. Monroe's selection of art parallels that of Jefferson and of other Virginia and English contemporaries. A typical Protestant gentleman's home might have paintings of religious subjects by continental Roman Catholic artists, mixed with landscapes, old masters, contemporary art, engravings and prints, and classical sculpture. In addition, the evidence indicates that Elizabeth Kortright Monroe, who was especially interested in art and architecture, was instrumental in the collecting.

Monroe's known library included three copies of the Bible. Fewer than a dozen books in the library (some of which are plainly presentation copies) were theological or biblical. He knew Bishop James Madison—second cousin of President Madison—from their years together at William and Mary. But when Madison became the first Episcopal bishop of Virginia in 1790 and Episcopalians could participate in the rite of confirmation for the first time, Monroe did not seek to be confirmed. He does not seem to have been anti-clerical, as Jefferson was. But he appears to have corresponded with Bishop Madison only on William and Mary affairs and he does not appear to have initiated correspondence with other clergy.

During his decades at his Albemarle estate of Highland, Monroe may have attended Forge Church, a deteriorating colonial structure within easy riding distance of his estate. The Episcopal bishops never allude to him in their reports of visitations to the church, however, nor does Bishop Meade include the Monroes in his list of families that supported the Episcopal Church in Albemarle County.[4] Jefferson never reported being accompanied by his neighbor Monroe when he attended services at the Albemarle County courthouse in Charlottesville.

On his three-month national goodwill tour in 1817, Monroe visited ten states, going as far west as Ohio. Throughout New England as well as in Pittsburgh, his visits to towns and cities included clergy in receptions and in ceremonial processions. On some Sundays Monroe went to church—usually to Episcopal services, but sometimes to those of other denominations.

The record is unclear as to how many Sundays Monroe attended church on the tour, but one service stands out because of his reaction. On June 22, 1817, accompanied by Horace Holley (a leading Unitarian minister in Boston), Monroe attended the Congregational meeting house in New Haven pastored by the Reverend Nathaniel Taylor. A stern defender of Calvinism, Taylor and his "New Haven Theology" married conservative Calvinism with the evangelical currents of the Second Great Awakening. Taylor's sermon on that Sunday may have included not only the hard marrow of traditional Calvinism but also the critiques of Unitarianism and the Episcopal Church for which he was also known. In any event, an observer declared that "Mr. Monroe was taken by surprise by a sermon from Rev. Dr. Taylor, an extreme Calvinist, much to the chagrin of the Rev. Horace Holl[e]y, a high Unitarian."[5]

Religion was not a primary concern of Monroe. When he died, he left no deathbed statement. Instead, historians have only the assertion of a friend that he died resigned to his fate. The eulogies by his contemporaries at his funeral commemorations in New York, Richmond, and Boston speak of Monroe in terms of patriotism and statesmanship; none even mentions his religious faith. Following Monroe's death, writers did not circulate pious literature about his religious beliefs, as they did about Washington.

Also significant are the reminiscences of Bishop Meade, who knew the Virginia founding fathers and their families well. When Meade discusses their religion in his two-volume *Old Ministers, Churches and Families of Virginia*, he devotes considerable space to Washington. Additionally, he gives detailed information on the religious beliefs of Madison and dismisses Jefferson's views as "disbelief." But in five mentions of Monroe—who had served with the bishop's father in the Revolution—he says nothing about religion. Similarly, Monroe's biographers rarely introduce the subject. "When it comes to Monroe's . . . thoughts on religion," one such writer declares, "less is known than that of any other President."[6]

But one known item about Monroe may shed additional light on his religious beliefs: he was a Freemason. The ties between Deism and Freemasonry were close. Freemasonry claims ancient origins, but probably originated in England in the twelfth century as a religious society that guarded the secrets of the craft of masons. Over the centuries it developed into a secret international fraternity concerned with the moral and religious improvement of its members. From England it spread to France, Germany, Italy, and other countries.

The movement took on a new character in the eighteenth century. In Roman Catholic countries, the Masonic lodges tended to form an underground movement antagonistic not only toward Roman Catholicism but also toward organized religion in general. Hence from the eighteenth century until recent years, Popes prohibited Roman Catholics from joining the Masons. In Protestant countries, Freemasonry tended to require a belief in a monotheistic God from its members and to advocate an undogmatic religion that claimed to represent the essence of all religions.

Wherever Masonry went, its rituals used drama and allegory to emphasize its message but gave a preeminent place neither to the Bible nor to Jesus. A Muslim, Jew, or Christian—or anyone who could accept its statements about a divine being—could belong. When the founding fathers use such terms as "the Grand Architect" to speak of God, they are using language that comes directly from Freemasonry and not from the Bible.

A fraternal organization that provided a club for men at a time when clubbing represented a principal form of entertainment, Masonic lodges appeared in the American colonies early in the eighteenth century. Like Deistic belief, these lodges grew in popularity in the decades following the Revolution, and Deistic views were widespread in them. Masonic membership was common among leading figures in the Revolution. Franklin and Lafayette were both Masons. Washington not only took his oath of office on a Masonic Bible but also laid the cornerstone of the U.S. Capitol using a Masonic trowel. Monroe became a Mason in 1775 while a student at William and Mary, joined the lodge in Fredericksburg while practicing law, and remained at least somewhat involved in the Masons throughout his life. During his second term as president, he was made an honorary member of the Washington Naval Lodge No. 4.[7]

As his Episcopal marriage, wedding, and funeral indicate, James Monroe maintained a lifelong affiliation with the church in which he was raised. The Episcopal Church ministered to the Monroe family and claimed them as its own. The Monroes had their children baptized. And Elizabeth and the daughters appear to have been relatively active Episcopalians.

Yet the surviving evidence implies that Monroe was not a Christian in the traditional sense. Neither his private nor his public writings indicate that he ever experienced a sense of the mystery or awe that is at the heart of orthodox Christianity. No evidence exists to show that he was an active or emotionally engaged Christian. How the Anglican interpretation of Christianity influenced his character and personality, and what depths of religious feelings he may have experienced while attending worship, scholars may never know.

Like Washington, Monroe was neither a philosophical nor a highly intellectual man. He was most effective when he solved problems and worked on practical matters. Unlike Franklin, Adams, Jefferson, and Madison, he did not seem to spend extensive time considering why the universe was so. These personality traits may explain the lack of information about his spiritual side.[8]

In sum, Monroe seems to have been an Episcopalian of Deistic tendencies who valued civic virtues above religious doctrine. No one cared more for the identity of the new nation. In his adult years, his passion always seems to have been directed toward the cause of the United States. From his eighteenth to his seventy-third year, he was almost continually in public service. "He had found [the nation] built of brick," John Quincy Adams declared in his eulogy of Monroe, "and left her constructed of marble."[9] Reflective, tactful, practical, simple in his tastes, democratic in his convictions, Deistic in his religion, James Monroe may have been the most skeptical of the early American presidents.

11

THE WIVES AND DAUGHTERS OF THE FOUNDING FATHERS

The Appeal of Christian Orthodoxy to Women[1]

Ll of the first five presidents of the United States were influenced to a great extent by Deism. Of the ten wives and female children (natural or adopted) of these presidents, however, seven appear to have been orthodox Christians. These seven include Elizabeth Kortright Monroe and her two daughters, Eliza Hay and Maria Hester Gouverneur, whom family tradition describes as orthodox Episcopalians.

Of the three presidential wives or daughters who held unorthodox Christian views, one seems to have become orthodox in her last years. Yet even the remaining two were Unitarian Christians who believed in the divine mission, miracles, resurrection, and second coming of Jesus. Although significant exceptions existed here and there, the women associated with the Revolutionary and post-Revolutionary generations were significantly more orthodox in religious belief than the men.

Why American women in this era turned to the rationalistic religion of Deism in far smaller numbers than men has never been satisfactorily explained. Virtually all historical narratives have focused on the spread of Deism among men rather than on its simultaneous

A more active Episcopalian than her husband, Elizabeth Kortright Monroe initiated the tradition of White House weddings with the marriage in 1820 of her daughter, Maria Hester.

failure to spread among women.[2] To fill that void lies beyond the scope of this book. But future scholars who attempt to complete this missing piece in the historical puzzle will probably consider at least the following six points.

First, Deism spread in colonial America concurrently with Freemasonry. After the introduction of Freemasonry into the colonies in Philadelphia in 1731, the Masons had several dozen lodges in the colonies by the time of the Revolution. Operating like "a network of churches of the same denomination," the lodges—in essence, metaphysical secret societies—"offered fellowship to members of other lodges who might be traveling in the area."[3]

Like the Deists, the Masons taught a natural religion where the "Grand Architect" or "Architect of the Universe" was a God of nature identified with natural laws. The symbols used in Masonic rituals—the compass, the square, the trowel, the maul, the level, the plumb line, the working apron of the stonemason—came from the building trades. And like those in the building trades, the Masons were all male; they prohibited women from membership.

The exact number of the leaders of the new republic who were Masons varies from book to book and website to website, but a significant percentage clearly belonged to lodges. Yet none of their wives or daughters was a Mason. Thus one reason that Deism spread largely among men may be that women lacked the constant reinforcement of Deistic ideas that Masonic lodges might have given them.

Second, women were barred from another institution that propagated Deism: college. Young men would enter such institutions as Harvard or William and Mary, read and discuss such authors as Paine, Voltaire, Rousseau, Allen, and Palmer, and often change their views of Christianity. To be sure, some women received good private educations. Women read, and often widely. But they never had the opportunity to experience the college environment that for some decades nurtured Deism.

Third, any religion a woman embraced had to address suffering. In early America women constantly faced the specter of suffering, both physical and emotional. They underwent childbirth without epidurals, endured sickness without modern medicine, and lost child after child to diseases now preventable. Nelly Custis was in labor for a week with her first child and lost four children before they reached the age of three. Martha Jefferson, who lost four of six children, had a son die after three weeks and a daughter after eighteen months. Elizabeth Monroe's only son—a little boy named for his father and grandfather—contracted whooping cough, failed to respond to treatment, and died in his seventeenth month.

Although fathers suffered immensely because of such deaths, they almost always returned to their work. Women were left to remain in the house of mourning. To grieving mothers or widows, Deism could offer only the consolation of a "Grand Architect" who did not interfere with his creation and an assertion that life continued after death. For women, prayer was a resource in their times of trial and tribulation, but no one prayed to the First Cause.

On the other hand, Christianity proclaimed a Lord who raised the dead, cured the sick, cast out demons, and enabled the blind to see. Its scripture contained a book entitled Job that meditated on suffering. Its central figure was a suffering servant who endured an ignoble death on a cross and who promised comfort to those who mourn. To such a God, a person could pray, ask for guidance and assistance, and give thanks.

Fourth, Deism may not have accounted for the abundant mystery of life satisfactorily enough to persuade women. In Deistic religion, there was no mystery, no need for any revelation beyond that given by nature and by what Deists considered God's supreme gift to humanity, human reason. In fact, a fountainhead book of Deism—written, like other Deistic books, by a man—was entitled *Christianity Not Mysterious*.[4] But women may have sensed more clearly that existence itself was a mystery. After all, it was women, not men, who conceived children, carried them for nine months, gave birth, and then experienced a child's first breath. For them, Deism may have seemed an oversimplified explanation of a mysterious universe.

Fifth, the role of women in raising and teaching children may have reduced the chance that they would endorse Deism. Wives spent a larger amount of time with children than husbands. Traditionally, they had the responsibility of overseeing the secular and religious education of the children. They taught manners, behavior, morals, and religion. They tended to arrange the baptisms. Many women may simply have thought that the Judeo-Christian tradition and Sundays devoted to churchgoing gave a better preparation for life than the rationality of Deism.

Finally, there was a social dimension to the decision for religious orthodoxy. Church was a place where women could socialize with each other and with the larger world. Men encountered more of such opportunities during the week. In addition, appearing in church had something to do with social standing, for other parishioners would notice a family's presence or absence. Women wanted their children to conform to the highest expectations of the community. More specifically, in the case of sons and daughters, they wanted their children to be socially acceptable. Thus remaining with a stable organization such as the church may in part have been a pragmatic decision.

Whatever the causes, most Deists in late colonial and post-Revolutionary America were male. In American religion from at least the late seventeenth century on, women—and not their Deistically inclined male counterparts—kept the churches going. In home after home, orthodoxy had a female face. Religious commitment was not universal, as the following survey will demonstrate. But the wives and daughters studied will more frequently display religious orthodoxy than rationalism.

Martha Custis Washington

Born in 1731 in the Tidewater county of New Kent and widowed prior to her marriage to George Washington, Martha Custis Washington seems clearly to have been an orthodox Anglican and Episcopalian. If researchers seek the basis for asserting her orthodoxy, however, they will find it more in her actions than in her letters.

Martha's surviving correspondence generally deals with house-hold matters, and the mentions of religion are few. The first 171 pages of her collected correspondence, for example, contain no references to religion, though they cover the years from 1757 to 1774. In a letter written in 1778, she twice refers to "providence": "indeed I think providence was very bountifull in her goodness to your state. . . . Would bountiful providence aim a like stroke at Genl. Howe, the measure of my happyness would be compleat." A Christmas letter in 1789 includes the phrase, "I wish the best of Heaven's blessings." In 1791, she speaks about an illness: "I am thank god recovering."[5] In the longest expression of religious sentiment that seems to survive in a letter, she writes to Tobias Lear, Washington's secretary:

> It is the nature of humanity to mourn for the loss of our friends; and the more we loved them, the more poignant is our grief.—It is part of the precepts of religion and Philosophy, to consider the Dispensations of Providence as wise, immutable, uncontroulable; of course, that it is our duty to submit with as little repining, as the sensibility of our nature is capable of, to all its decrees.—But nature will notwithstanding, endulge, for a while, its sorrows.[6]

If the language of these letters provided the only evidence, Martha would qualify, like her husband, as a moderate Deist. Moreover, if the letters written in her name to mourners after Washington's death in 1799 were considered, the case would be strong, for those letters similarly use Deistic terms for God.

But these responses were written by Lear, a Deist himself. When letters of condolence poured in to Mount Vernon addressed to the grieving widow, Lear took over the daunting task of answering them. During his fourteen years

Like many wives of American political leaders influenced by Deism, Martha Washington remained an orthodox, practicing Christian.

with Washington, he had learned to reproduce not only Washington's handwriting but also his written and spoken style. When answering the letters of condolence to Washington's widow, Lear may simply have used the Deistic language that expressed his and Washington's beliefs.

Martha's spiritual practices, however, shed an entirely different light on her religiosity. From the time of her first marriage, she put aside a period during each weekday for devotions. "She never omitted her private devotions," her granddaughter Eleanor Parke Custis Lewis wrote.[7] She read the Bible daily, a mark of orthodoxy. She included first her children and then her grandchildren in these devotions.

In addition, she worshiped in church regularly. When married to Daniel Parke Custis and living in New Kent County, she attended St. Peter's Church. From Mount Vernon, she rode in the carriage to Pohick Church in Fairfax County or to Christ Church in Alexandria. When the national capital was in New York, she attended St. Paul's Chapel of Trinity Parish twice a day. She worshiped with her family in the morning but with the children alone for the service of Evening Prayer. When the government moved to Philadelphia, she attended Christ Church.

The first president's wife typically stayed in the church when the quarterly service of Holy Communion followed the regular service—another sign of orthodoxy. In a Deistic period, the clergy of Philadelphia plainly considered her the kind of devout parishioner they were grateful to have in their parishes. Mrs. Washington "habitually occupied" the presidential pew at Christ Church, the first Episcopal bishop of Pennsylvania declared, and "was regularly a communicant"—that is, someone who received Holy Communion.[8] "On communion Sundays, he left the church after the blessing, and returned home," Nelly Custis Lewis wrote about attending Christ Church in Alexandria with General Washington, "and we sent the carriage back for my grandmother."[9]

The manner of Martha's death in 1802 further displays her devoutness. Whereas her husband had died more in the manner of a Roman stoic than a Christian believer, Martha called her children to her deathbed. She then talked to them at length about the Christian faith and its responsibilities. Raised an orthodox Anglican, she seems to have not departed from that orthodoxy throughout her lifetime. Nelly Custis Lewis—in words that would not have been used to describe a Deist—remembered her as "eminently pious."[10]

Eleanor Parke Custis Lewis

Martha seems to have passed on her orthodoxy to her granddaughter, Eleanor Parke Custis Lewis, known as "Nelly." "I had the most perfect model of female excellence ever with me as my monitress," Nelly later wrote.[11] Born to Martha's son and daughter-in-law in 1779, Nelly was two years old when her father was killed at the battle of Yorktown. When her mother later remarried and had additional children, the Washingtons reached an agreement—relatively common at the time—that they would adopt the two children born during her marriage to Martha's son.

The Custis grandchildren lived as if they were Washington children. When the capital was in New York and Philadelphia, Nelly not only reveled in being a member of the first family but also looked back on the years in Philadelphia as the happiest in her life.[12] She formed a lifelong friendship with William White, the first Episcopal bishop of Pennsylvania and Washington's principal pastor in Philadelphia.

Martha Washington trained her granddaughter rigorously in domestic as well as in religious matters. As a young girl, she participated in Martha's daily religious devotions. She attended church with the Washingtons in Fairfax County, Alexandria, New York City, and Philadelphia. In 1799 she married Lawrence Lewis of the Fairfax County estate of "Woodlawn."

The surviving letters of Mrs. Lewis indicate that her churchgoing habits did not change after her marriage. She remained a practicing Episcopalian until her death. In 1821, returning from a stay in the District of Columbia, she made sure to attend church on her way home. In 1824, when the family was visiting in the Hudson River Valley during August, she wrote to a friend: "We go to a pretty Little Church on Sundays & hear very good sermons."[13] Like many antebellum Virginia Episcopalians, she strictly observed the Lord's Day, or Sabbath. In 1834, when she and her husband were visiting a married daughter in Louisiana, she lamented:

There are no schools, no churches here for many miles. Sunday among the French & Creoles & indeed among the Americans too is like any other day. Pedlars go about, cake sellers, & they really appear to have no idea beyond this world & its enjoyments. We do not visit or receive visits on Sunday, but it is a gala day here generally.[14]

In 1844, after an Episcopal church had been established near her daughter's home, Mrs. Lewis rejoiced that "after so many years without religious services, they have church now and the communion service." By 1848, she was complaining that she had become so deaf that she sometimes could not hear the services of worship.[15] When she had a stroke two years later, having outlived six of her eight children, Episcopal clergy visited Woodlawn and wrote to her.

Mrs. Lewis's letters are consistently orthodox in sentiment. They refer to her prayers for the concerns or illnesses of others[16] and employ such terms for God as "the Almighty," "maker and redeemer," "giver of all good," and "Him who giveth and taketh away."[17] She speaks of the "goodness of the Almighty" in preserving her children during an epidemic.[18] When one daughter dies and is buried in Bishop White's family vault, Mrs. Lewis writes of a vision: "I dreamed last night that I was in a new Catholic Chapel, & saw there a monument to my child, on the altar, which was of marble as white as snow—& that I heard a most eloquent and affecting prayer from a Priest in white robes."[19] Upon the death of a son in 1847, she writes: "It is the *belief* of his eternal happiness, his reunion with my other Angels in Heaven that reconciles me to his loss."[20] She comments after her stroke: "I bowed in submission to the will of God."[21]

If colleges had then been open to women, Eleanor Parke Custis Lewis could have been a student during the period when Deism was dominant. But far from being a Deist, as many of her male contemporaries were, she disparaged the movement. In 1821 she wrote about Charles Carter Lee and Henry Lee of Stratford Hall: "I am sorry to hear that Carter is travelling about with his vile Brother, they are both *Deists*." She ended, "May the Almighty change Carters [*sic*] heart for the sake of his amiable Mother & Sister."[22] In 1821 she sent her son to Yale College (which had largely returned to orthodox Congregationalism) rather than to William and Mary, which still had a

Deistic reputation. Her pastors represented a succession of Episcopal evangelical clergy who revived the Anglican tradition in antebellum Virginia. They included William Holland Wilmer, who became president of William and Mary in 1826 when its Board of Visitors attempted to bring the college back to orthodoxy.

Nelly Custis Lewis lived into the period when Deism had almost disappeared, but she represented a generation that was exposed to it during their formative years. From childhood until death, however, she remained an orthodox Christian. "Brought up by her grandmother as a devout Episcopalian," Patricia Brady writes, "she was genuinely and unself-consciously religious all her life."[23]

Abigail Smith Adams

"Remember the Ladies," Abigail Smith Adams wrote her husband in well-known words during the Second Continental Congress. Wife of a founding father, second of the First Ladies, mother of a president, pioneer advocate for women's rights, Abigail Adams occupies a special place in American history. She also differs from many of her contemporaries in another important way. Influenced by Deism, she left orthodox Christianity and became a Unitarian.

The daughter of William Smith (Sr.), a Congregationalist minister, and his wife, Elizabeth Quincy Smith, Abigail was born in 1744 in Weymouth, Massachusetts. Although a frailty diagnosed as rheumatic fever caused her to be educated at home and to receive no formal education, she not only possessed a keen mind but was also an avid reader. As such, she would have been attentive to the theological discussions around

Daughter of a liberal Congregationalist minister, Abigail Adams shared her husband's Unitarian faith.

her. Significantly, during her formative years, Congregationalism—the state church of all of New England except Rhode Island—was in the process of developing a liberal wing.

Abigail did not come from a conservative Calvinist family. Easy-going, empathetic, and popular with his congregation, her father seems to have been concerned more with the moral dimensions of Christianity than with traditional Calvinist theology. Parson Smith neither worried about eternal damnation nor went through a conversion experience. He opposed the Great Awakening. He doubted the doctrine of original sin. In his view, the sovereignty of God—so stressed by his Calvinist forebears—did not exclude the existence of free will in humans; hence it did not lead inexorably to predestination. When it came to the relationship of Jesus of Nazareth to God, he seems to have been a subordinationist.[24] Parson Smith's liberalism provided his daughter the first step in a theological journey that ultimately led to Deism and Unitarianism.

When Abigail—"a feisty female," in the words of one biographer—married John Adams in their "marriage of equals," she formed a life-long partnership with a liberal Congregationalist who shared her theological concerns.[25] "Abigail's record," a scholar writes, "is her letters."[26] Those letters—often written to her husband, but also to friends and to other members of the family—display her religious views. Above all, three letters stand out.

Two that date from the 1780s display an intermingling of Christianity and Deism. Writing to her son, John Quincy Adams, Abigail declares:

> The only sure and permanent foundation of virtue is religion. . . . The foundation of religion is the belief of the one only God, and a just sense of his attributes, as a being infinitely wise, just, and good . . . who superintends and governs all nature, even to clothing the lilies of the field . . . but more particularly regards man, whom he created in his own image, and breathed life into him an immortal spirit, capable of a happiness beyond the grave; for the attainment of which he is bound to the performance of certain duties, which all tend to the happiness and welfare of society, and are comprised in one short sentence, expressive of universal benevolence, "Thou shalt love thy neighbour as thyself."[27]

Like the five points of Deism, this letter, written in her thirty-sixth year, equated religion with morality. It spoke of "the one only God" without mentioning Jesus Christ. It declared that the "performance of certain duties" assured "happiness beyond the grave." A Deist could have made all of these assertions.

But the letter also mixed Christian with Deistic beliefs. It described, for example, a God of "all nature" who is "infinitely wise, just, and good." In addition, it asserted Abigail's belief in a life after death. To be sure, all of these beliefs were standard convictions not only of Christianity but also of Deism. Yet Abigail's biblical orientation provided the letter's foundation. Her statements about God creating man "in his own image" and breathing life in him as well as her phrases "the lilies of the field" and "love thy neighbour as yourself" come directly from the Bible.

A second letter, sent in 1786 to her sister, displayed a similar mixture. Beginning with a strikingly Deistic statement, it supported that assertion with a New Testament parable. It then went on to cite the Deistic argument that "priestcraft" had corrupted the world's religions. It ended with a reference to the New Testament:

> The Universal Parent has dispensed his blessing throughout all creation. . . .
> [including] Christian, Jew, or Turk. What a lesson did the great author of our
> religion give to mankind by the parable of the Jew and the Samaritan; but
> how little has it been regarded! To the glory of the present age they are
> shaking off that narrow contracted spirit of priestcraft and usurpation which
> has for so many ages tyrannized over the minds of mankind, and deluged
> the world in blood. . . . Religion [should be] . . . a wise and benevolent
> system, calculated . . . to harmonize mankind to the temper of its great Au-
> thor, who came to make peace, and not to destroy.[28]

By 1816, the date of the third letter, Abigail was openly Unitarian. The formation of the American Unitarian Association did not occur until 1825. But by the time of this letter, the liberal wing of Congregationalism in New England had essentially broken away from the Trinitarian Congregationalist churches. "There is not any reasoning which can convince me, contrary to my Senses," Abigail wrote to John Quincy in 1816, "that Three, is one, and one three. . . . The first commandment forbids the worship of but one God." Discussing her views of Jesus, she cited passages from the New Testament that she believed exhibited his subordinate relationship to God:

> From these and many other passages of Scripture, I was led to believe in the unity of the Supreme Being and that Jesus Christ was divinely inspired and specially delegated to communicate the will of God to man, and that after having fullfil'd his Mission upon Earth, he ascended into heaven, from whence we are assured he shall come to Judge the World in Righteousness, all power being given him *by the Father*.[29]

In its early decades of existence in the United States, Unitarianism was distinctly Christian, though subordinationist in its understanding of Jesus. Many Unitarians of the time would have affirmed the writer's belief in the divine inspiration and commission of Jesus, in the ascension, in the second coming, and in God's granting of all power to Jesus. "My own loss is not to be estimated by words," Abigail wrote after the death from breast cancer of her daughter, Abigail (or "Nabby"), "and can only be alleviated by the consoling belief that my Dear Child is partaking in the Life and immortality brought to Light by him who endured the cross and is gone before to prepare a place by those who Love him and express his commandments."[30] As the decades went on, American Unitarianism moved away from its Christian moorings. Abigail Adams—like her husband—was representative of the generation of New Englanders who broke with orthodox Congregationalism but who retained much of their parent church's scriptural orientation and supernaturalism.

During their marriage, the Adamses attended the First Parish Church in Quincy, which had essentially accepted Unitarian teachings since the 1750s. During the years they lived in Boston, they attended the affluent Brattle Street Church. Just as John Adams described himself as a "church-going animal," so Abigail was a regular church attender throughout life. When she became a grandmother, she advised her daughter to accustom her young children "to a constant attendance upon public worship, and enforce it by your own example and precept. . . . It is a duty, for which we are accountable to the Supreme Being."[31] She visited Anglican and Roman Catholic churches in Europe, but liked none of them as well as the simple meetinghouses of New England.

In her letters, Abigail referred constantly to her reliance on religion to get her through births, deaths, and the extended absences of her husband. "Abigail's religious beliefs . . . fundamentally affected her life," Edith Gelles writes: "Religion provided her a perspective for understanding the world and her place in it. Religion explained the vagaries of existence and gave her hope." Dying in 1818 from typhus, Abigail was buried in the cemetery of First Parish Church, where her husband was also interred eight years later.

Martha Wayles Skelton Jefferson

Thomas Jefferson's wife, Martha Wayles Jefferson, was born in 1748 at "the Forest," the large Charles City County estate of her father, John Wayles. Because the Church of England was the established church in Virginia during the colonial period, she would have been baptized—probably at home—and reared an Anglican.

At the age of eighteen, Martha married Bathurst Skelton, a graduate of William and Mary. A mother at nineteen, she was widowed within two years. After she returned to Charles City to live in her father's home, she lost her son, John, who died before his fourth birthday. Jefferson, then a member of the House of Burgesses that met in Williamsburg, began courting Martha in December 1770. When the period of mourning for John was over, the couple was married at "the Forest" on New Year's Day, 1772, in a ceremony with two clergy present. Two weeks after the wedding, the Jeffersons rode through snow drifts to move into Jefferson's partially completed estate of Monticello.

Most of Martha's correspondence has disappeared, for the grieving and private Jefferson apparently destroyed her papers after her death. Virtually no records exist of her religious views

Martha "Patsy" Jefferson Randolph, raised by her Deistic father in the Anglican tradition.

or practices, but no indication exists that she was other than an ortho-dox Christian. Monticello was in St. Anne's Parish, on whose vestry Jefferson served. On Sundays the Jeffersons would have attended the nearest church of the parish; Forge Church was a short drive on the mountain road.

During the ten years of her marriage to Jefferson, Martha gave birth to six children. A son and two daughters died as infants. Lucy Eliza-beth Jefferson, the last child—born in Richmond, where the govern-ment had moved in 1780—died in her second year from whooping cough. Only two daughters, Martha Jefferson and Maria Wayles Jefferson, lived beyond childhood. Unless the children died too soon, Martha would have had them baptized at Monticello, probably by the rector of St. Anne's Parish, Jefferson's friend Charles Clay. Jefferson entered these baptisms in his father's Book of Common Prayer.

A letter from Jefferson to the Marquis de Chastellux declared that Martha never recovered from the complications associated with the birth of her last child in May 1782. Lingering through the summer, she died in September. "A single event wiped away all my plans," Jefferson declared in the letter, "and left me a blank which I had not the spirits to fill up."[32] With an Anglican priest presiding, Martha was buried in the graveyard at Monticello. Translated, the epitaph from the *Iliad* that Jefferson placed on his wife's tomb reads: "Nay if even in the house of Hades the dead forget their dead, yet will I even there be mindful of my dear comrade."

Jefferson's Daughters:
Martha Jefferson Randolph
and Maria Jefferson Eppes

The Jeffersons' daughter, Martha Jefferson Randolph, was born late in September 1772. With Martha still mourning the death of her son, the Jeffersons fortunately had a child quickly. To distinguish her from her mother, she was known at Monticello as "Patsy." She was ten years old when her mother died. Her sister Maria was born in 1778.

In 1784 Jefferson went to Paris to serve as commissioner and then as Franklin's successor as minister to France. Taking along Martha, he enrolled her in the Abbaye Royale de Panthemont, a convent school. Abigail Adams, who assisted Jefferson in getting established in Paris, opposed the enrollment until she learned that the Marquis de Lafayette was Martha's sponsor. Although Jefferson was no more an admirer of French Roman Catholicism than Abigail, he had developed reservations about the morals of Parisian society. A convent school seemed to him the best way to insulate a growing daughter from such influences. When Maria, who had been staying with Jefferson's brother and wife in Virginia, joined her father and sister in Paris in 1786, he also sent her to the convent school.

Martha and Maria had been educated well at Monticello by their mother and, after her death, by their father. Jefferson played an active role in their education, drawing up outlines of their daily schedules of studies. In Paris he strictly instructed his daughters about what they could and could not do at the convent. He assured Protestant correspondents that the "Panthemont" offered a high level of instruction in music, art, dancing, Italian, and the social graces. "It is a house of education altogether the best in France, and at which the best masters attend," Jefferson wrote friends. "There are as many Protestants as Catholics, and not a word is ever spoken to them on the subject of religion."[33]

Jefferson later tempered his endorsement of the school. The description of his great-granddaughter, Sarah Randolph, remains vivid more than one hundred years after its publication:

> The gentle and loving kindness lavished on [Martha] by the inmates of the convent won for them her warmest affection, while the sweet amiability of her disposition, the charming simplicity of her manner, and the unusual powers of her mind endeared her to them. Thus her school-days flowed peacefully and gently by.
>
> But while their father had so carefully secured for his daughters a good mental and moral training by the situation in which he had placed them, he overlooked the danger of their becoming too fond of it. He was startled, therefore, by receiving a note from Martha requesting permission to enter the convent and spend the rest of her days in the discharge of the duties of a religious life.[34]

Jefferson was concerned with the possibility of losing a sixteen-year-old daughter to the cloistered life of a nun. He was also troubled by Martha's recent revelation to him that she was losing the ability to speak or to think in English. After receiving Martha's note, he waited a day or two. Then he went to the convent, met with the Abbess, and removed both of his daughters from the school. Randolph concluded:

Martha was soon introduced into society at the brilliant court of Louis the Sixteenth, and soon forgot her girlish desire to enter a convent. No word in allusion to the subject ever passed between the father and daughter, and it was not referred to by either of them until years afterwards, when she spoke of it to her children.[35]

The story comes from Jefferson family tradition. Its details are unverifiable, but it is true that Jefferson was on his way back to the United States by the fall of 1789, the year that Martha would have written her note.[36] In the next year, she married a cousin, Thomas Mann Randolph, at Monticello. During the ceremony, the Episcopal minister held the family Bible of Martha's mother. Seven years later, Martha's younger sister, Maria, married John Wayles Eppes at Monticello.

Both of Jefferson's sons-in-law became active in politics. Thomas Randolph served in the Virginia General Assembly, as governor of Virginia, and as a congressman, though his later years were troubled. After Jefferson retired from politics in 1809, he and Martha and her husband moved to Monticello. John Eppes, Maria's husband, had studied law under Jefferson. He eventually served in both the House of Representatives and in the U.S. Senate.

The surviving correspondence of Jefferson's daughters contains few references to religious matters. In a collection of hundreds of Jefferson family letters, religion is mentioned so infrequently that the editor speaks of a letter by Jefferson to Martha in 1803 as "one of the very few allusions to his religion which he ever made to any of his family."[37]

The reasons are probably not far to seek. Throughout life, Jefferson considered religion a private matter — and no more so than in the years before he ran for president. For him to have written about his religious views to his young daughters was unlikely. According to family tradition, both of the Jefferson daughters, like their mother, were orthodox Episcopalians. Thus they were unlikely to correspond in later years about religious matters with a father whose religious views were so entrenched.

Yet one detailed letter written by Jefferson to Martha on a religious topic has survived. In her eleventh year he writes about predictions regarding the imminent end of the world that have apparently troubled her:

> I hope you will have good sense enough to disregard those foolish predictions that the world is to be at an end soon. The Almighty has never made known to any body at what time he created it; nor will he tell any body when he will put an end to it, if he ever means to do it. As to preparations for that event, the best way is . . . . never to say or do a bad thing. If ever you are about to say . . . or to do any thing wrong, consider beforehand you will feel something within you which will tell you it is wrong. . . .Our Maker has given us all this faithful internal monitor, and if you always obey it you will always be prepared for the end of the world, or for a much more certain event, which is death.[38]

Although Martha died fifty-three years after receiving this letter, Maria was buried only twenty-one years after Jefferson wrote it. When she failed to recover from the effects of childbirth, Jefferson had her carried in a litter to Monticello for her last weeks. When Martha went to Jefferson on the day Maria died, she found him with a Bible in his hands.

Both of the Jefferson daughters died at Monticello. When Jefferson invited Thomas Paine to stay at their mountain home, Martha and Maria—as orthodox Christians—reportedly protested that they would rather not associate with him, given his religious views. Jefferson is said to have replied that Paine was "too well entitled to the hospitality of every American, not to cheerfully receive mine."[39]

Dolley Payne Madison

The major religious question surrounding the life of Dolley Payne Madison is not whether she left orthodox Quakerism—she did—but whether she became a Deist or an orthodox Episcopalian. Until at least her last years, the answer seems to be that she believed something in between.

Raised a Quaker, Dolley Madison went through a lifelong spiritual journey and finally was confirmed as an Episcopalian late in life.

Dolley's mother, Mary (Molly) Coles, was a birthright Quaker from Virginia. Her father, John Payne, had converted to the Religious Society of Friends from the established Anglican Church of Virginia. One of eight children, Dolley was born in 1768 in a pioneer Quaker community near what is today Guilford College (a Quaker institution) in Greensboro, North Carolina. On both sides the Paynes came from Virginia families of substance, with Patrick Henry numbered among Molly Payne's relatives.

After several years of farming in North Carolina, the Paynes returned to Hanover County, Virginia, where they rose to positions of influence in the local Quaker meeting. Increasingly prosperous, Payne farmed and purchased additional land. By 1775, he had relocated his growing family to Patrick Henry's former plantation of "Scotchtown." As Quakers, the Paynes remained pacifists during the American Revolution. Like many Quakers, they also came to the conclusion that they should not own slaves. Thus in 1783, just as the Revolutionary War was concluding with the Treaty of Paris, Payne sold his Virginia land and moved the family to Philadelphia, a center of Quakerism.

Due to lack of demand, the business Payne started—the manufacturing of laundry starch—was unsuccessful. By 1789, he was not only bankrupt but also disowned by his Quaker meeting for failing to pay his debts. Disgraced, he went into seclusion and died three years later. To support her family, Molly Payne opened their house to boarders, one of whom was a rising attorney and politician named Aaron Burr.

Because the egalitarian Society of Friends educated its female members, Dolley was probably better educated than most American women at the time. Besides instruction at home, she may also have attended a Friends school in Hanover County. She once declared that she was "educated in Philadelphia," a city that had noted Friends schools.[40] A biographer notes:

> The subjects offered probably included reading, mathematics, history, geography, religion, fancy sewing, French, and sometimes the classics. Dolly's earliest surviving letters were penned in an elegant Italian script, and her spelling was far superior to that of many leading Americans of the century. She also knew French.[41]
>
> Attractive both in appearance and in personality, Dolley was pursued by many suitors.

Even in Philadelphia she displayed the personality that later made her such an outstanding hostess in the White House. "She came among our comparatively cold hearts in Philadelphia," the family friend Anthony Morris wrote, "at the age of sixteen . . . with all the delightful influences of the summer sun."[42] This was the background out of which the Dolley Madison known to history emerged.

As a young woman, marriage was clearly on her mind; a letter she wrote to a friend during this period discusses three marriages and two elopements of members of their circle.[43] In 1790 Dolley and a young Quaker lawyer, John Todd, Jr., "passed meeting" and married. In the first two years of their marriage, the couple had two sons, John Payne and William Temple.

In 1793, however, disaster struck when yellow fever ravaged Philadelphia. Approximately five thousand of the city's 55,000 citizens died. Among the victims were Dolley's husband, both of his parents, and their second child, William Temple Todd. At the age of twenty-five, Dolley Payne Todd was a widow.

After her husband's death, the new widow drew up a will. Although most of the beneficiaries were her Quaker relatives, she entrusted "Aaron Burr to be the sole Guardian" of her surviving son, John Payne Todd. That a Quaker widow would leave the guardianship of her son to a non-Quaker undoubtedly says something about her state of mind toward the Society of Friends. Her younger sister, Lucy, had already eloped with President George Washington's nephew and been disowned for it.

In May of 1794, James Madison, then a congressman from Virginia, asked Aaron Burr for an introduction to Dolley Payne Todd. Madison was seventeen years older and a lifelong bachelor. Initially hesitant when Madison proposed, Dolley soon agreed to marry "the man who of all other's I most admire," as she wrote to a friend.[44] Both the Payne family and their Pine Street Meeting strongly disapproved of the marriage to a non-Quaker. In September Alexander Balmaine, an Episcopal clergyman from Winchester and Madison's cousin by marriage, performed the wedding at "Harewood," the plantation of Dolley's brother-in-law, George Steptoe Washington. Three months later, the meeting disowned Dolley Todd Madison for "having disregarded the wholesome order of our discipline, in the accomplishment of her marriage with a person not in membership with us, before a hireling priest."[45]

As writers have frequently noted, the Madison marriage turned out to be one of the most celebrated of the presidential marriages. Much of the style of White House life stems from the influence of Mrs. Madison and of her successor as First Lady, Elizabeth Monroe. For the remainder of her life, Dolley Madison moved back and forth between Washington, D.C., and the family estate of "Montpelier" in Orange County, Virginia.

Though the Madisons had no children, they experienced lifelong embarrassment and expense because of Dolley's son, Payne Todd. A spendthrift alcoholic and gambler who was imprisoned several times, the restless Todd spent his life involved in drunken escapades. Though often hard pressed to do so, James Madison continually redeemed his stepson's substantial debts. "The tendency towards dissipation . . . seems to be irresistible," John Quincy Adams wrote in his diary about Payne Todd; "there is a moral incapacity for industry and application."[46]

Mrs. Madison's religious views elude easy classification. Despite being disowned, she continued to display some Quaker characteristics. In the first years following marriage she wore plain, Quaker-like dresses during the day and changed to more fashionable dress only in the evening. She seems also to have kept her "pretty little Quaker cap(s)" for some years.[47] Quakers did not dance, and at her husband's first inauguration, she refused to dance. As late as 1813, she referred to herself as "a Quaker" in a letter.[48] Accustomed to hearing women speak freely in Quaker meetings, she expressed a desire to hear an itinerant female preacher in 1827.[49]

As the years went on, however, Dolley plainly left her Quaker heritage further and further behind. She came to love gowns, wigs, jewelry, and the very French practice of wearing rouge—all the paraphernalia of parties. She loved to shop, not only for herself but also for others. She displayed a social savior-faire and sense of style that were definitely non-Quaker. Writing in 1805 to a sister who had also left the Religious Society of Friends, she reflected negatively on their religious heritage:

> I had a visit last night from Nancy Miflin & Sally Lane, who remonstrated with me—on seeing so much company—they said that it was reported that half the City of Phil[a] had made me visits—this lecture made me recollect the times when our *Society* used to controle me entirely & debar me from so many advantages & pleasures—& tho so entirely from their clutches, I really felt my ancient terror of them revive to disiagreable [*sic*] degree.[50]

When discussing Dolley Madison's religion, most writers list her as an Episcopalian. After 1845, at least, that statement is accurate. On July 15, 1845, she and her niece Anna Cutts (her companion in her last years) were confirmed at St. John's Episcopal Church, Lafayette Square, by Bishop William Whittingham of Maryland. It was a special occasion. Not only was Whittingham—who had responsibility for all the Episcopal churches in the District of Columbia—present but also the eloquent bishop of New Jersey, George Washington Doane, who preached.

Apparently nervous, Mrs. Madison sent a note to the rector of St. John's, the Reverend Smith Pyne, asking for any advice he could give about confirmation. Pyne replied, "I have no counsel to give, but to go on as you have begun. God bless you and keep you in His Holy Favor. Gladly I will enroll you in my list of candidates."[51] Mrs. Madison described her and Anna's confirmation in a letter written to a nephew the next day: "I will tell you on what, our thoughts have dwelt a great deal—it was to become worthy of membership in the Church which I have attended for the last forty years. . . . Yesterday this wish was consummated as far as confirmation extended."[52]

Mrs. Madison had attended St. John's since it was built during her husband's administration. She and her husband not only occupied the President's Pew at the church's dedicatory service but also, like a number of their successors, viewed it as their parish church. After retirement, the Madisons spent long periods at Montpelier, though Dolly occasionally returned to Washington for the "seasons."

When at Montpelier, the Madisons attended St. Thomas Church in Orange, Virginia. To what extent she shared her husband's Deism during these years is unknown. Also unknown is how frequently the couple attended either church, but in James Madison's last years they may have attended St. Thomas with some regularity.[53] Although no record seems to exist of Mrs. Madison's baptism, confirmation in the Episcopal Church represented a renewal of baptismal vows. Thus she could not have been confirmed if she were unbaptized.

Mrs. Madison's available letters contain such sentiments as "relegion [*sic*] and time, can alone reconcile us to bereavments." They speak of "Heaven," as in "trust Heaven will preserve you" or "may the blessings of Heaven rest on you."[54] Her letters do not seem to discuss church events, however, even in passing. Clergy also rarely appear either as correspondents or as names mentioned in passing. One letter written to her by the Reverend Mason Locke Weems has survived. His letter, however, is a treacly solicitation seeking to persuade her to endorse a book he is publishing.[55]

What Mrs. Madison's religious views may have been when she was confirmed in the Episcopal Church is unknown. But two letters written in the 1830s seem to show her religious views as of that decade. The first is a letter of condolence written in 1832 to a friend whose son had died:

> My heart akes for you and your precious daughter! Who can find words to sooth you under such a loss? None. I feel that even the tears of a friend must be an intrusion on your sacred sorrow! "God tempers the wind" and I pray that he may extend his goodness to you both! To you my beloved, who have been tryed as in a furnace, & come forth as pure gold.[56]

Written the next year from Montpelier, the second letter replies to a niece who had reported visiting a fortune teller:

May your fortune, dearest Mary, be even better than the Sybil's predictions. There is a secret she did not tell you, however, it is, that we have all, a great hand in the formation of our own destiny. We must press on, that intricate path, leading to perfection and happiness, by doing all that is good and handsome before we can be taken under the silver wing of our rewarding angel.[57]

Well written, showing genuine concern, the two letters display a poetic turn of phrase—but no specifically Christian content. Their theology seems to rest somewhere between Deism and Christianity. "Dolley Madison served as an American icon for decades," a contemporary author has declared.[58] After spending her final years beset by financial difficulties, Mrs. Madison died in Washington on July 12, 1849, at the age of 81. Her funeral was conducted four days later in St. John's Church by her friend and rector, Smith Pyne. Dolley's body was later buried next to that of James Madison at the family graveyard at Montpelier. "Although few would deny that Dolley Madison considered herself a religious woman," one writer declares, "even in matters of faith she seems to have exercised a remarkable talent for flexible adaptation to her times and surroundings."[59] A student of First Ladies put it even more succinctly: she described Dolley Madison as "an odd bird for a Quaker nest."[60]

12

A LAYPERSON'S GUIDE TO DISTINGUISHING A DEIST FROM AN ORTHODOX CHRISTIAN

The Christian Right is trying to rewrite the history of the United States as part of its campaign to force its religion on others," declares the website of *Free Inquiry*—one of many sources that rejects the assertion that the United States was founded as a Christian nation.

They try to depict the founding fathers as pious Christians who wanted the United States to be a Christian nation, with laws that favored Christians and Christianity. This is patently untrue. The early presidents and patriots were generally Deists or Unitarians, believing in some form of impersonal Providence but rejecting the divinity of Jesus. . . .[1]

Similar views are found in a work by a professional historian who won the Pulitzer Prize:

Most of the founding fathers had not put much emotional stock in religion . . . . Most of the revolutionary gentry only passively believed in organized Christianity, and, at worst, privately scorned and ridiculed it. Jefferson hated orthodox clergymen. . . . Even puritanical John Adams thought that the argument for Christ's divinity was an "awful blasphemy". . . .When Hamilton was asked why the members of the Philadelphia Convention had not recognized God in the Constitution, he allegedly replied, speaking for many of his liberal colleagues, "We forgot."[2]

Standing in direct contrast are the views expressed by another book on the founders. Written by a conservative evangelical who belongs to what *Free Inquiry* calls the "Christian Right," it maintains that "left-wing scholars tend to lionize and exalt the statements of those who agree with them and ignore those who hold a religious or conservative viewpoint."[3] The author asserts that "even secular humanists, if they were honest, would have to admit to the religious (particularly the Christian) origins of this nation."[4] The perspective of the book is expressed by its chapter titles: "Help! We've Been Robbed!" "Who Secularized America?" "Who Fathered America?" "The Christian Consensus of America in 1787," and "A Constitution for the Ages—If We Can Keep It."[5] A final quotation captures its author's objectives:

> Fortunately, a groundswell of concerned citizens is getting involved. They are becoming so informed that they will wrest control of this nation from the hands of the secularizers and place it back into the hands of those who founded this nation, citizens who had a personal and abiding faith in the God of the Bible.[6]

This marked, often contentious division of opinion over the religious views of the founding fathers stems from methodology followed in research, from the educational training of the scholars, from the religious belief or lack of belief on the part of authors, and from the intentions of writers. Most of the founding fathers of the United States were members of Christian churches. Yet widespread disagreement exists about their beliefs.

The religious beliefs of the founders seem to have fallen into three categories: Non-Christian Deism, Christian Deism, and orthodox Christianity. To reduce misrepresentations, historians and readers require a common definition. How can students of early American history distinguish a Deist from an orthodox Christian? Readers seeking the answer should consider at least the following four points.

First, they should look—to a point—at the *actions* of America's founding fathers in the area of religion. If a founder belonged to a church, attended a church, or served on a governing body such as a vestry, those involvements did not guarantee his orthodoxy. A colonial church served not only religious but also social and business functions. Thus no reader of American history should classify all churchgoers as orthodox believers. Nevertheless, readers should regard regular church attendance by a founder as more clearly indicative of orthodoxy than sporadic attendance. Devout Christians among the founders would be more likely to go to church.

Second, investigators should look at the participation of the founders in what some colonial churches called "ordinances" and others called "sacraments." That a founder was baptized says little about his adult beliefs. During the colonial period, most churches baptized children shortly after birth. The children therefore had no choice about whether to be incorporated into the Christian faith or not; as all viewers of the film *The Godfather, Part I* understand, godparents even articulated their assents for them during the baptismal rite. As a result, the most thoroughgoing Deists could be and probably were baptized. A far better indicator of the religious stance of founders is whether or not they had their own children baptized. Yet even there, the orthodoxy of their wives usually caused the children to be baptized.

But if most of the founders had no choice about their own baptism, they did have a choice about confirmation. Consisting of the laying on of hands by bishops, this rite represented a reaffirmation of baptismal vows by an adult or young adult. It conferred full church membership. Hence founders raised in churches that practiced confirmation—Roman Catholic and Anglican—made adult choices about confirmation. And following the Revolution, these two denominations—which had lacked bishops throughout the colonial period—secured their own bishops.

From the 1780s on, Episcopalians had bishops in New York, Pennsylvania, and later Virginia and Maryland. From 1790 on, Roman Catholics had a bishop in Maryland. After that point, Episcopalians and Roman Catholics who lived in dioceses headed by bishops had to decide whether to be confirmed.

Technically or ritualistically speaking, Episcopal and Roman Catholic laity really had little choice. If they wished to receive Holy Communion in their churches, they had to be confirmed. The American Book of Common Prayer, for example, contained a rubric (or

After becoming bishop of Charleston in 1820, the gifted John England organized the scattered Roman Catholics of the southeast into permanent dioceses.

ceremonial rule) that declared: "And there shall none be admitted to the Holy Communion, until such time as he be confirmed, or be ready and desirous to be confirmed."

But the American bishops of both churches tended to view such rubrics liberally for some decades, for they realized the problems that could occur if a bishop suddenly asserted his authority over churches. Nevertheless, once these churches had bishops, the avoidance of confirmation by a church member represented a conscious omission.

George Washington, for example, lived in New York, Pennsylvania, and Virginia during the period when these states had Episcopal bishops, but he was never confirmed. James Madison of Montpelier never arranged for confirmation, though his cousin and namesake James Madison of William and Mary held the office of bishop of Virginia during twenty-two years of President Madison's life. If confirmation had been available when Madison returned to Montpelier from Princeton in 1772, he might have sought it, for he was then a believing Christian. But by the 1790s, when the future president's cousin was available to confirm Virginians, Madison had been aligned with the Deists for twenty years. It was too late for him to express beliefs that he did not hold.

Thus if a founder was an Anglican or a Roman Catholic and decided not to be confirmed, Deism had probably influenced him to some extent. Episcopalians and Roman Catholics who sought confirmation after their American bishops took office were more likely to be orthodox believers than those who avoided the rite. Because confirmation was not held in the highest regard in either church during the eighteenth and early nineteenth centuries, this litmus test is helpful but not entirely indicative of a founder's religious belief. A second rite readers should heed is the Lord's Supper or Holy Communion.[7] Participation or abstention from this sacrament or ordinance represents another way of distinguishing between Deists and orthodox Christians. Few founders who were Deists would have received the bread and the wine distributed at the communion. If they attended church, even sporadically, they would have been least likely to attend on Sundays when the Holy Communion was being administered. In the Anglican or Episcopal churches, where the Lord's Supper came after the preaching service, members influenced by Deism might attend only the first part of the service and then leave without communicating, as Washington did.

If a reader asks why Deists were reluctant to receive the Holy Communion, the answer seems to stem from at least two causes. First, the Lord's Supper represented the most supernatural level of church activity. Churches such as the Roman Catholic, Anglican, and Lutheran—and, if their heritages were examined, some other denominations as well—taught that God was in some way present (and, in some interpretations, encapsulated) in the bread and wine. A Deist would therefore have seen the Holy Communion as the part of Christian worship that was least connected with reason. That earthly bread and wine could in some way become the body and blood of Christ vexed founders such as Jefferson and Adams. Their correspondence often employed the derogatory term "hocus-pocus"—a term that probably comes from the words said by a Roman Catholic priest—"*hoc est enim corpus meum*" (or "this is my body")—in the Mass.

Deists, in fact, would have encountered problems believing in the purpose of the Holy Communion service even in churches that did not teach a "real presence" in the bread and wine. Every Christian tradition taught that a worshiper vicariously participated in the Last Supper through the Lord's Supper. The Holy Communion services of virtually all churches included the defining words, "This is my body broken for you." Thus the Lord's Supper physically linked participants with the Christian doctrine of the atonement (the belief that Jesus of Nazareth had paid the penalty for the sins of humanity by dying on the cross). All orthodox Christians believed not only that

Jesus had died for *them*, but also that his body had been given and his blood had been shed for *them*. Thus even more than the regular preaching service, the service of Holy Communion represented a principal way by which Christians could affirm their belief that "while we were still sinners, Christ died for us."[8]

But Deists believed neither in the doctrine of the atonement nor in the presence of Christ in the elements. They did not believe that Jesus was a savior who had died for them. Hence they found much to oppose in this central ordinance or sacrament of Christianity. Because Deists denied what the Lord's Supper signified, they had no reason to participate in the rite.

Third, readers attempting to classify the religious views of the founding fathers should also consider the dimension of *inactivity* versus *activity*. Few thoroughgoing Deists would have taken an *active* part in the rituals of the Christianity that surrounded them. And most Deistic Christians would have participated in these rituals *less actively* than orthodox churchgoers.

Confirmation was an *active* affirmation of Christian belief, for example. To be confirmed, worshipers had to walk forward and stand in full view of a congregation. If Episcopalians, like Washington or Madison or Monroe, they had to answer the following question from a bishop:

> Do ye here, in the presence of God, and of this congregation, renew the solemn promise and vow that was made in your name at your Baptism; ratifying and confirming the same in your own persons, and acknowledging yourselves bound to believe, and to do, all those things, which your Godfathers and Godmothers then undertook for you?

Upon receiving an audible "I do," a bishop would lay hands upon a candidate's head. Most Deists would have resisted such active involvement in worship. They would also have been unable to answer the bishop affirmatively. And none would have believed for a moment that a bishop could transmit divine grace through the laying on of his hands.

If participating in confirmation was an *active* affirmation of Christianity, so was "receiving" or "taking" the bread and wine in a service of Holy Communion. The New Testament words of Jesus concerning the Lord's Supper—"do this in remembrance of me"—direct future generations to actively reenact the Last Supper in his memory. Thus in the Roman Catholic and in some Protestant churches in eighteenth-century America, worshipers walked forward to the altar, or holy table, to "receive" the sacrament. Other Protestant churches passed loaves or plates of bread and cups of wine among the pews, and worshipers "took" them. Regardless of whether Christians "received" or "took," the Holy Communion represented highly active participation in organized Christianity.

Thus it comes as no surprise that Jefferson omitted the story of the Last Supper from his version of the New Testament. His cut-and-paste account moves from Jesus washing his followers' feet, to his prophecy of betrayal, to his giving a new commandment—"that ye love one another"—and finally to his arrest and crucifixion. In the Jefferson Bible, the followers of Jesus do not share a last meal with him. Jefferson's excision undoubtedly stemmed from his belief—universal among Deists—that Christianity had corrupted and exaggerated the meaning of the Lord's Supper over the centuries. But he could hardly have failed to note that the command "do this in remembrance of me" was so *active.*

Thus Deism had a converse effect on participation in Christian ritual. The greater the influence of Deism, the less a person participated. Non-Christian Deists rejected all sacraments and rarely attended church. Deistic Christians attended church regularly or sporadically, but seldom participated in the Lord's Supper and confirmation. Orthodox Christians attended regularly and participated in both sacraments. Hence one way a reader can identify the orthodox Christians of the Revolutionary and early national era is that they were *not passive.* Through regular attendance, confirmation, and Holy Communion, they played an *active* role in their faith.

Finally, in determining where a founder stood religiously, readers should look carefully at his *religious language.* Non-Christian Deists such as Paine described God with such terms as "Providence," "the Creator," and "Nature's God," but they refused to use specific Christian terminology.

Similarly, Deistic Christians often used Deistic terms for God. Occasionally or frequently, however (depending upon the degree of Deistic influence on their religion), they added a Christian dimension to the terms—such as "Merciful Providence" or "Divine Goodness." In addition, they used the name of Jesus and employed terms—"Supreme Being" or "Supreme Ruler of the world," for example—that rode the boundary between Deism and Judeo-Christian orthodoxy. But they did not go further and employ terms that would indelibly commit them to orthodoxy. As for the orthodox Christians among the founders and populace, they affirmed the Trinity and used language ("Savior," "Redeemer," or "the Resurrected Christ," for example) that clearly conveyed their orthodox views.

An examination of history cannot capture the inner faith of any man. But in the case of the founders of the United States, readers can use these four indicators—church attendance, approach to sacraments or ordinances, level of activity, and religious language—to locate the founders on the religious spectrum with some confidence. When readers use these guidelines, four prominent members of the revolutionary generation, for example, seem to fit easily into religious categories of Non-Christian Deist, Christian Deist, and orthodox Christian.

A hero of the Revolutionary War, largely self-educated but immersed in the theological and philosophical issues of his day, *Ethan Allen* began his theological writing as an opponent of the established Calvinist faith of New England. Soon he became an advocate of an infinite, perfect, and moral God of Nature and developed an overall anti-Christian position.

No record exists of Allen attending church after a certain point or of his participating in the ordinances of a Christian church. Instead, he found biblical revelation contradictory and erroneous. He came to believe that organized religion had been carried away by "a torrent of superstition." When discussing religion, he used such words as "Providence" and "God" but gave no salvific role to Jesus. He criticized such Judeo-Christian practices as prayer. In *Reason, the Only Oracle of Man*, he quoted the New Testament to prove that Jesus himself had said he was not divine. Allen is almost a textbook case of a non-Christian Deist.

A vestryman in both Anglican and Episcopal parishes, *George Washington* attended church with some regularity, held organized religion in high regard, and was known to pray privately. But he was never confirmed, and apparently avoided Holy Communion for most or all of his adult life. Although Washington's most common term for God was "Providence," he also used such terms as "Heaven," "the Grand Architect," "the Deity," and "the Great Ruler of Events." Both his official and his private correspondence, however, omitted such words as "Lord," "Savior," and "Redeemer," and he rarely referred to Jesus Christ. On the spectrum of early American religion, he would clearly be classified as a Deistic Christian.

A minister's daughter, *Abigail Adams* retained a lifelong interest in religious matters. She regularly attended a Congregationalist church in Massachusetts so influenced by the Enlightenment that it later joined the American Unitarian Association. Her correspondence used such words as the "one only God," the "Supreme Being," the "Universal Parent," and the "Great Author." Although Adams did not believe in the doctrine of the Trinity, she did believe that God had sent Jesus to earth as a special messenger. In addition, like most Unitarians of her time, she believed in his resurrection, his ascension, and in life after death. She would be classified as a Deistic Christian.

The son of an Anglican vestryman and the nephew of an Anglican rector, *Patrick Henry* was strongly influenced by an evangelical leader of the Great Awakening. An active Episcopalian, he read the Bible daily, paid for the printing and distribution of two attacks on Deism by British authors, and distributed religious tracts while riding circuit as a lawyer. His letters and addresses typically spoke of "Almighty God," "the gospel of Jesus," and "the merits of Jesus." In his last words he expressed gratitude to God. His will declared that "the religion of Christ" would give his family the inheritance "which will make them rich indeed." Henry would clearly be classified as an orthodox Christian.

While the founding fathers held diverse religious views, little reason exists for a continued distortion of them. A careful examination should place most of the founders in one of these three major classifications. Because Christian Deism was somewhat diverse, some reason exists for confusion about such figures as Washington, Monroe, or Dolley Madison. Although readers should keep in mind that one person can never quite know the inner faith of another person, historians can do a better job of deciphering the religious views of the founders than they have in the past.

13

THREE
ORTHODOX CHRISTIANS

Samuel Adams

A radical in the politics of his time but a traditionalist in religion, Samuel Adams has been titled the "father of the American Revolution." Because he consistently urged New England to return to its earlier and simpler life, writers have also called him "the Cato of the American Revolution." But Adams is best known as "the Last of the Puritans," a title that accurately portrays his orthodoxy in a time of religious change.

On the day of his birth in 1722, Adams was baptized in Boston's "New" South Congregational Church on Summer Street, one of the established, tax-supported Puritan or Congregationalist churches of Massachusetts. The Adams family Bible lists a succession of Samuel Adamses, none with a middle name.[1] Of the twelve children born to his parents, Samuel and Mary Fifield Adams, only three—a daughter and two sons—survived.

The owner of a brewery and other businesses, the elder Samuel Adams was a man of influence in Boston, though he later went through financial reversals. He was a justice of the peace, a selectman (or city councilman), and a representative to the Massachusetts Assembly. Answering to the title "Deacon Adams" because of a long association

In a Deistic era, Samuel Adams said grace before meals, led daily devotions in his household, kept a strict Sunday, and remained loyal to the Calvinist orthodoxy of his ancestors.

with the Old South Congregational Church, he was also a founder of the New South Church. A highly religious woman, Adams's mother rocked her children to sleep with hymns, used the Bible to teach them the alphabet, and assured they had memorized the Lord's Prayer at an early age. "To the scrupulous attention of his parents to devotional subjects," an early biographer noted, "must have been due the religious turn of mind which was a prevailing trait throughout the life of the son."[2]

After attending the Grammar School of Boston and Boston Latin School, young Adams entered Harvard at age fourteen. If his father's interests lay in religion and business, the son's lay in religion and politics. At Harvard, he copied such Lockean statements into his notebooks as "It is the right of the people to withdraw their support from that government which fails to fulfill its trust. . . . it is the right of the people to overthrow it."[3] The few records that exist of Adams's years at Harvard indicate a studious undergraduate life.

In 1743, Adams received an M.A. from Harvard, answering affirmatively in his thesis the following question: "Whether it be lawful to resist the supreme magistrate if the commonwealth cannot be otherwise preserved." Six years later he married Elizabeth Checkley, daughter of the pastor of New South Church. When she died following childbirth in 1757, leaving two young children, Adams married Elizabeth Wells, by whom he had no children. Following college Adams studied law, worked in a counting house (or bank), lost his funds in an unsuccessful business venture, and finally was given employment in the family brewery. "Until he reached the age of forty-two," in the words of a biographer, "he was a miserable failure . . .

the laughingstock of Massachusetts Bay. . . . then he sniffed the most precious of perfumes, the scent of freedom, and everything was changed."[4]

From approximately 1763 on, when the British announced their plan to "tax the colonies, for the purpose of raising a revenue," Adams became a principal opponent of British intervention in the affairs of Massachusetts. He organized groups that favored independence, founded the Committees for Correspondence, served on other committees, and led the Boston Sons of Liberty. Elected to the Massachusetts legislature, he participated in the writing of report after report and published widely read essays in the Boston *Gazette* denouncing England's tyranny, "Popery," and plans to send bishops to the colonies.

Adams may also have instigated not only the protest that precipitated the Boston Massacre but also the Boston Tea Party. During this period, his cousin John Adams described him as possessing "the most thourough [sic] Understanding of Liberty . . . as well as the most habitual, radical Love of it" of all the leaders of the revolutionary cause in Boston.[5] By the time he became a delegate to the First Continental Congress in 1774, he was known even to the King of England.

Adams served in the Continental Congress from 1774 to 1781. Working closely and tirelessly with such figures as Washington, Franklin, and Jefferson, he was instrumental in securing the passage of significant bills and resolutions, including the Declaration of Independence and the Articles of Confederation. A leader of the congress from the start, he was probably its most adroit politician.

Religiously, he remained orthodox although surrounded by Deists. While at Harvard, Adams had been influenced by the Great Awakening, as had his family. His mother was a follower of Jonathan Edwards. His sister maintained a journal listing the clergy she had heard preach and the content of their sermons. Adams, however, may have needed the inspiration of the Awakening less than many of his classmates. He entered Harvard an orthodox Congregationalist, and he remained one throughout his life.

Whether as an adult he believed in the traditional five points of Calvinism is unknown.[6] Neither the traditional terms of orthodox Calvinism nor the new evangelical language used by converts of the

Awakening stand out in his correspondence and writings. Also un-known is which of the two major strands of the Calvinism of the time—the New Divinity (which tried to reconcile the evangelicalism of the Awakening with classical Calvinism) or the "Old Calvinism" (which resisted the Awakening)—he favored.

But his orthodoxy is indisputable. He opposed Freemasonry, led his family in grace before meals, read to them from the Bible, led morning and evening devotions in the household, and strictly ob-served the Lord's Day. Until old age prevented it, Samuel Adams walked to church on Sunday with his family, a sight that neighbors were accustomed to seeing. As early as 1765, John Adams wrote that his cousin possessed "real as well as professed piety."[7]

His religious language is also strikingly orthodox. Like other or-thodox Christians of the time, he was able to describe God in terms shared with Deism. But most of his religious phrasing, even in state documents, is unabashedly Christian. He uses such terms as "the common Master," "our Divine Redeemer," "Him . . . who has given us his Son to purchase for us the reward of eternal life," and "all those who love the Lord Jesus Christ in sincerity." Even at the height of Deism, when governor of Massachusetts, Adams issued a Thanks-giving proclamation anticipating "that holy and happy period when the kingdom of our Lord and Saviour Jesus Christ may be every-where established, and all . . . willingly bow to the sceptre of Him who is the Prince of Peace."[8]

Adams's will declared that he recommended "my soul to that Al-mighty Being who gave it, and my body I commit to the dust, relying on the merits of Jesus Christ for a pardon of all my sins." Similarly, the will of Elizabeth Wells Adams declared that she "commend[ed] my soul into the hands of my blessed Lord and Saviour Jesus Christ." It also stated that she depended "absolutely, entirely, and exclusively on his atonement and finished work of righteousness for the pardon of my sins and acceptance with God to eternal life."[9]

Because the religious views of Adams display a restorationist strain, it was not surprising that he attempted to revive the Puritan covenant theology in post-Revolutionary Massachusetts. "Almost all varieties of Puritans . . . held that God enters into covenants with nations," Mark Noll writes, especially those that are granted special insight into the truths of the Bible. Guidelines from the Bible indicate to nations what they must do to enjoy divine blessing, while scriptural examples concerning ancient Israel provide harrowing warnings about what will happen to nations that violate their covenant with God.[10]

In the first covenant, or solemn contract, God said to Adam: "Obey my commandments and you will live; disobey them and you will die."[11] In this teaching, the sovereign God offered grace and salvation to humanity—on his terms.

The early leaders of Puritanism visualized all of New England as a new Israel that lived according to God's commandments. In a sermon preached en route to Massachusetts, Governor John Winthrop spelled out the covenantal relationship the Puritans believed they had with God:

> We are entered into Covenant with Him for this worke. Wee have taken out a commission. . . . Now if the Lord shall please to heare us, and bring us in peace to the place we desire, then hath hee ratified this covenant and sealed our Commission, and will expect a strict performance of the articles contained in it; but if wee shall neglect the observation of these articles . . . the Lord will surely breake out in wrathe against us; be revenged . . . and make us knowe the price of the breache of such a covenant.

If the Puritans will keep to the conditions of their covenant with God in New England, Winthrop concluded: "Wee shall finde that the God of Israell is among us. . . . hee shall make us a praise and glory that men shall say. . . 'the Lord make it like that of *New England*.' For wee must consider that wee shall be as a city upon a hill."[12]

As an heir to this tradition, Adams believed that God rewarded or chastised a society according to the morality it exhibited. Moreover, he believed that the king of England had broken his contract with the American colonies. Thus from at least 1776 on, he linked the covenant tradition with the American quest for liberty: "Public Liberty will not long survive the total extinction of morals," he declared in 1776. "Righteous Heaven will surely smile on a Cause so righteous as ours is," he similarly wrote, "and our Country, if it does its Duty will see an End to its Oppressions."[13] When the British left Boston,

Adams hoped that their departure would allow the old Puritan commonwealth to reestablish "ancient Principles and purity of manners." Adams believed he saw a decline in morals all around him in Massachusetts. Late in 1776, he lamented to his wife that he wished "we were a more religious people."[14] In 1780, he complained about the extravagance in clothes, furnishings, and entertainments that had become routine for supposed "men of religion" in Boston. In a parallel to what he saw occurring in Massachusetts, he also argued that the anti-Puritan advisors to King Charles II of England had diverted the concern of English citizens for their liberties by "making them extravagant, luxurious, and effeminate." He added: "I love the people of Boston. I once thought the city would be the *Christian Sparta*. But alas! Will men never be free? They will be free no longer than while they remain virtuous."[15] His proclamation for "A Day of Public Fasting, Humiliation, and Prayer" spoke of the need for the citizens of Massachusetts to "express sorrow and repentance for the manifold transgressions of His Holy Laws."[16]

By the post-Revolutionary period, however, the religious zeal that had made Puritan New England so distinctive among the American colonies had almost died out. Although the Federalist aristocracy of Boston had long viewed the Republican Adams as "a dictator . . . who controlled a trained mob," the Boston masses idolized Adams.[17] Few in any social class, however, became enthusiastic about his desire to return Massachusetts to the old paths of Puritanism. Thus Adams did not accomplish the reformation of morals he desired, though he continued to believe that a genuinely religious people produced a moral society.

The role Adams played in drafting the provisions about religion—known as "Article 3"—in the Massachusetts Constitution of 1780 is unclear. But the constitution's assertions that the citizens of Massachusetts had a "duty" to worship "the Supreme Being," that religion preserved morality and hence was essential to society, and that the legislature could continue Congregationalism as the established, tax-supported church were consonant with Adams's religious beliefs. Article 3 represented a distinct counterpoint to the Deistic approach to the same subject.

The last writing of Adams that has survived was addressed to Thomas Paine. Hearing that Paine (whom he had known since 1775) intended to publish a work similar to *The Age of Reason*, Adams, then eighty years old and in ill health, wrote a sharply critical letter:

> When I heard you had turned your mind to a defence of Infidelity, I felt myself much astonished, and more grieved, that you had attempted a measure so injurious to the feelings, and so repugnant to the true interest of so great a part of the citizens of the United States. . . . Do you think that *your pen*, or the pen of any other man, can unchristianize the mass of our citizens, or have you hopes of converting a few of them to assist you in so bad a cause? . . . Neither Religion nor Liberty can long subsist in the tumult of altercation.[18]

Paine's reply, written with candor but in a tone of great respect, is classic Tom Paine. "If I do not believe as you believe," he tells Adams at one point, "it proves that you do not believe as I believe, and this is all that it proves." He ends with the expression of "hearty good-will" to a "dear friend."[19]

"Samuel Adams was one of the most perfect models of disinterested patriotism and of republican genius and character, in all its severity and simplicity, that any age or country has ever produced," a British historian wrote. "[He was] a sincere and devout Puritan in religion."[20] Overshadowed in later years by so many extraordinary contemporaries, Adams has become one of the least known of the founding fathers. A man who saw a need for American independence earlier than most of his contemporaries, he was so much a supporter of American liberty that many colonists believed he wrote Paine's *Common Sense*.

Thomas Jefferson profoundly respected him. When Jefferson received reports that Federalists were insulting and denigrating the elderly Adams in Boston, he declared that a biblical passage had immediately come to his mind: "Father, forgive them, for they know not what they do."[21] The Deistic Jefferson and the orthodox Adams differed on the subject of religion and on the question of tax support for churches, but they thought alike in politics.

Increasingly feeble and plagued with palsy, Adams died in 1803. Though he was known as "the Last of the Puritans," he was not a

Puritan in the sense that such Massachusetts predecessors as John Winthrop, John Cotton, and Cotton Mather were Puritans. Rather, in a Deistic age, he was a New England Congregationalist who remained staunchly loyal to the Calvinist orthodoxy in which he had been raised.

Elias Boudinot

Elias Boudinot, president of the Continental Congress and brother-in-law of a leader of the Great Awakening, compiled a resume that sounds like a roll call of orthodoxy. In a lifetime of eighty-one years, he was president of the General Assembly (or chief legislative body) of the Presbyterian Church in the United States of America, president of the New Jersey Bible Society, founding figure and first president of the American Bible Society, and a leading figure in the establishment of Princeton Theological Seminary.

In addition, Boudinot wrote books on such topics as the refutation of Deism, the imminent Second Coming of Jesus, and the life of a leader of the Great Awakening. So much did he view the world through a biblical prism that he wrote a fourth book arguing that the Native Americans were descendants of the Israelites. Thus Elias Boudinot stands as a principal representative of Christian orthodoxy among the founding fathers.

A Huguenot (or French Calvinist) descendant, Boudinot was the fourth in direct succession to carry that name. He was born in 1740 in Philadelphia, where Benjamin Franklin was a neighbor. George Whitefield, the principal evangelist of the Great Awakening, baptized him. Whitefield performed the baptism because Boudinot's father, Elias, a silversmith, was an original member of Philadelphia's Second Presbyterian Church. A congregation of "New Lights" founded during the Great Awakening, Second Presbyterian had as its pastor the leading evangelical William Tennent.

The elder Boudinot subsequently moved his family from Philadelphia to Princeton, where he became postmaster. Although Boudinot was interested in entering the Presbyterian ministry, thc family was financially unable to send him to the College of New Jersey. As a result, he studied law under Richard Stockton of "Morven," a signer of the Declaration of Independence. Each of the men subsequently wed the sister of the other.[22] Marriage into the affluent and well-connected Stockton family elevated Boudinot socially and professionally. During this period, Alexander Hamilton became a protégé. Increasingly influential and affluent, Boudinot was in his mid-thirties when the Revolutionary War broke out. He served not only as the president of the Continental Congress but also as a member of the committees of correspondence in New Jersey and as commissary general of prisoners—a thankless but important position. As the principal civil officer of the new United States, Boudinot signed the Treaty of Paris ending the Revolutionary War. He served as a U.S. Representative from New Jersey and, from 1795 through 1805, as the director of the national Mint. Retiring from politics in 1805, he moved to a large home in Burlington, New Jersey, where he recouped the losses caused by public service and increased his wealth through land speculation, rentals, and stocks.[23] Because the town had no Presbyterian church, he regularly attended St. Mary's Episcopal Church and became thoroughly involved in its affairs.[24]

Boudinot spent his last decades immersed in philanthropic and religious work. In Burlington he often led daily prayers for his family and domestic servants—a sign of Christian orthodoxy. The language of his letters, addresses, and writings also displayed his orthodoxy. Like the Deists, Boudinot occasionally used the word "Providence" alone, but more often used such phrases as "gracious God," "Providence of God," "all gracious Providence," the "Almighty," and "Almighty Being." He spoke of "the Gospel," a "gospel ministry," and "our divine religion." When critically ill in 1817, he wrote to a friend, "Our Immanuel overcame Death Hell and the Grave." When his wife died, he concluded the record of her death in the family Bible with the traditional words, "The Lord Gave and the Lord hath taken away, blessed be the name of the Lord."[25]

Boudinot wrote all of his books in the final decades of his life. In 1801, when the Deistic Jefferson was president, Boudinot published *The Age of Revelation,* a book intended as a point-by-point refutation of Paine's *The Age of Reason.* The book's subtitle was *The Age of Reason Shewn to be an Age of Infidelity.* "One of those vicious and absurd publications, filled with ignorant declamation and ridiculous representation of simple facts," Boudinot declared. "I confess, that I was much mortified to find, the whole force of this vain man's genius and art, pointed at the youth of America, and her unlearned citizens."[26]

Boudinot's treatment of Deistic assumptions that humans should rely on reason alone and discount mystery illustrates his approach. "These objectors find it difficult to submit to the faith of the gospel," he wrote,

> because many things are above their reason; while they continually exercise the same principal in temporal things . . . they will mount the horse recommended by its owner or enter a public carriage provided for passengers, without doubting of their safety. . . . Does any person refuse to swallow his victuals, before he fully understands the method of digestion . . . ? In short, innumerable important facts, the causes of which, with their modes of operation, we cannot comprehend . . . are yet firmly believed; and, in the course of life, acted upon by us.[27]

Seeing Paine's work as "sapping the foundation of our holy religion" from Americans, Boudinot's refutation defended the authority of the Bible, the Mosaic law, the divinity of Christ, the doctrine of the Trinity, and "the miraculous facts of revelation." Because it was only one of a number of attempted refutations of Paine, *The Age of Revelation* received less attention than Boudinot had hoped.[28]

Five years later, Boudinot wrote a lengthy letter for a religious magazine about his brother-in-law, the Reverend William Tennent. In 1813 a publisher turned the letter into a small biography. The book aroused interest because it narrated the life-after-life experience of Tennent.[29] Becoming a "living skeleton" when he was preparing for his ordination exam, Tennent apparently died one morning when speaking with his brother, Gilbert, about life beyond the grave. His body—cold and stiff—was laid out for a funeral on the next day.

But a friend who was a physician believed Tennent was not dead. Over firm objections he insisted that the mourners postpone the funeral. After several days of holding off burial, the physician was finally able to show signs of life. Tennent reported experiencing "an ineffable glory" and hearing "things unutterable; I heard their songs . . . of thanksgiving and praise, with unspeakable rapture." He reported that his "conductor" had then said, "you must return to the earth." Tennent next remembered seeing his brother and the physician standing by his side, arguing about his burial. "The three days during which I appeared lifeless," he concluded, "seemed to me not more than twenty minutes."[30] Two years later, Boudinot published his most substantial work, *The Second Advent*. The result of twenty-five years of reflection about biblical prophecies, it was one of a number of books written on the Second Coming during the nineteenth century. In any era, authors who write about an imminent Second Coming inevitably see "the signs of the times" in current events. Many also believe that the prophesied Antichrist has appeared in their time. For Boudinot, the French Revolution and other events in Europe had displayed some of those signs, with Napoleon Bonaparte as the Antichrist. Though he gave no precise date, Boudinot thought that Christ might return before the century ended.[31]

Boudinot's final book, *A Star in the West*, seems initially to represent an entirely new subject matter. But the subtitle—*A Humble Attempt to Discover the Long Lost Ten Tribes of Israel, Preparatory to their Return to Their Beloved City, Jerusalem*—shows that it is tied in with his *The Second Advent*. *A Star in the West* also displays affinities with Boudinot's earlier attack on Deism.

Like many writers on the Second Coming then and now, Boudinot believed that the nation of Israel had to reunite before Christ could come again. The crucial question, of course, involved the locations of the scattered members of Israel. In *The Second Advent*, Boudinot suggested that the Native Americans are the "lost tribes of Israel." *A Star in the East* not only developed that theory but also displayed what for Boudinot constituted the evidence for it.

Because it presupposed that the discovery of the Native Americans as the lost tribes of Israel would demonstrate that the Bible and its prophecies were accurate, the book represented a continuation of Boudinot's defense of scripture in *The Age of Revelation*. A worldwide conversion to Christianity would follow the discovery. Just as the nineteenth century produced many books that predicted an imminent second coming of Christ, so Boudinot's work represented only one in a series of books declaring that Native Americans stemmed

from Hebrew origin. Boudinot, Ethan Smith, and—some would say—
the Mormon prophet Joseph Smith are three of the principal American writers in that tradition.

Elias Boudinot died in 1821. His will included substantial bene-
factions to Bible societies, to the Presbyterian denomination, to
Princeton Theological Seminary, to Christian missions to Native
Americans, to hospitals and prisons, to the College of New Jersey, to
societies to aid the poor, and to similar organizations. He even be-
queathed money to buy spectacles for people who could not read the
Bible without them.

A man of deep convictions—eloquent, poised, well informed—
Boudinot was viewed by his peers as a person of character. As a
founding father, he has been overshadowed by others, though Supreme Court Justice William Rehnquist found Boudinot relevant
enough to cite in a recent opinion on church and state.[32] Boudinot's
religious faith mixed traditional Calvinism with the new spirit of
evangelism spreading through early America. Although Franklin was
his neighbor and Washington held him in high regard, Elias Boudinot
moved in very different religious circles.

John Jay

In a letter to Thomas Jefferson, John Adams once satirically commented that John Jay had retired "to study prophecies to the end of
his life."[33] Although a self-described "church-going animal," Adams
found Jay almost too religious. An evangelical Episcopalian who
believed "the Bible contains . . . a connected series of divine revela-
tions and dispensations,"[34] John Jay differed from most of the founders
in both orthodoxy and religiosity. Only Elias Boudinot became as
active in moral and religious matters.

John Jay held more high-level appointments than all but a few of
the founders: president of the Continental Congress, minister to Spain
during the war, negotiator (with Franklin and John Adams) of the
Treaty of Paris, secretary for foreign affairs, first chief justice of the
Supreme Court, and second governor of New York. Along with
Alexander Hamilton, he conceived the Federalist Papers but wrote
only five because of illness. Although he did not attend the constitu-

tional convention, he was instrumental in securing its ratification in New York. At Washington's request he went to London in 1794 to negotiate the highly controversial "Jay Treaty." All of these honors came to Jay despite his initial hesitancy to support a revolution. An instinctively conservative man, he initially desired reconciliation with England and even left Philadelphia before the signing the Declaration of Independence.

Born in New York City in 1745, the seventh child of Peter and Mary Van Cortlandt Jay, Jay came from a socially elite family. His father, a wealthy merchant, was of French descent. His mother was a descendant of one of New Netherland's great patroon, or large landowning, families. In the year of Jay's birth, a smallpox epidemic ravaged New York. Jay's father moved his family to a four hundred-acre farm adjacent to Long Island Sound in Rye, New York.

Although Jay's mother was of Dutch descent, historians generally classify him—as they do Elias Boudinot, Francis Marion, Henry Laurens, and other American revolutionary leaders—as a Huguenot. Too scattered to form a lasting French Reformed Church in the colonies, the Huguenots tended to become Presbyterians or Anglicans. The Jay family gradually affiliated with the Church of England, for it was the established church in the lower counties of New York. Like his grandfather, Jay's father served on the vestry of Trinity Church, though

he had his children baptized in their mother's ancestral Dutch Reformed Church. Calvinist in background and pious on both sides, the Jay family carried their inherited Calvinism with them into the Church of England—a more common practice than some historians presume, for Anglicanism

An evangelical Episcopalian active in moral and religious societies, John Jay differed from most of the founders both in orthodoxy and in piety.

had supported a Calvinist wing since the Reformation. As believers in the sovereignty of God, the Jays saw God's hand everywhere—a trait John Jay demonstrated throughout life.

Jay attended an academy run by an Anglican priest of French descent in the Huguenot settlement of New Rochelle, New York. After further tutoring at home, he matriculated at the age of fourteen at King's College, the colony's small (when Jay entered, it had three faculty) Anglican college. Two Anglican clergy—the noted philosopher Samuel Johnson (who as president kept Deistic works out of the curriculum) and Myles Cooper, his successor—were especially influential during Jay's college years. Jay was studious and focused in college, so much so that he later joked about his lack of exposure to women during those years.

After graduating in 1764, he read law with a noted attorney and entered the legal profession four years later. For a time he had a joint practice with Robert R. Livingston, a lifelong friend who later became a member of the Continental Congress and a negotiator of the Louisiana Purchase. Jay's steadiness of purpose and unflagging work ethic caused him to rise quickly in New York's legal ranks.

In 1774, Jay married the vivacious Sarah Van Burgh Livingston of Elizabethtown, New Jersey. The marriage associated the rising young barrister with one of the most influential families in New York and New Jersey. Already well known for his writing, William Livingston, Sarah's father, would shortly become a member of the Continental Congress and the first governor of New Jersey. The wedding at the Livingston home also marked the beginning of a devoted marriage. So much did Jay rely on his wife that she even journeyed abroad with him on his ministerial duties, a highly unusual action at the time. John and Sarah Jay had five children. Three of the sons—William, Peter, and John, Jr.—later became active both in the Episcopal Church and in the effort to emancipate slaves.

Jay inevitably had detractors, especially among some subordinates and among the Spanish with whom he negotiated during the American Revolution. Elsewhere in Europe and in the colonies, however, he was generally praised not only for his competence but also for his ideals and character. He displayed these characteristics, for example, during his two terms as governor of New York. To a remarkable extent, he avoided partisanship while governor and remained as free from control as practicable from his Federalist party. When political adversaries had performed well, he tended to keep them in office. As governor he improved New York's prison system, outlawed the flogging of prisoners, reduced the number of executions, and secured the passage of a bill that gradually outlawed slavery in New York. He was highly popular.

In 1801, after finishing his second term as governor, Jay declined the request of John Adams to resume the office of chief justice of the U.S. Supreme Court. Sarah Livingston Jay died the next year. Jay "retired to an estate, which he has in his native County of Westchester," the Reverend Timothy Dwight (president of Yale) wrote. "Here he employs his time partly in the cultivation of his lands, and partly in a sequestered and profound attention to those immense objects, which ought ever supremely to engage the thoughts, wishes, and labors of an immortal being."[35]

Jay's "immense objects" included the American Bible Society, the Episcopal Church, various interdenominational Bible and Sunday School societies, and societies working toward the manumission of slaves. Because ill health and inclination kept him in Bedford most of the time, in many cases he simply endorsed a society and allowed it to use his influential name.

The principal of Jay's organizations, the American Bible Society, had the purpose of distributing free Bibles to Americans, especially in their native languages. It also coordinated the work of the regional Bible societies that already existed. Jay became its vice president upon its founding in 1816 and (following the death of Elias Boudinot) its president in 1822. Although he rarely attended its meetings, even while president, he wrote addresses for the Society's spring meeting each year.

Jay's first four annual addresses show that he believed in a literal fall of humanity, in a literal Noah, in the worldwide flood, in the tower of Babel, and in a future millennium. A concern for Christian cooperation in distributing the Bible "everywhere," however, rather than an emphasis on literalism characterized the addresses.

For Jay to accept the presidency of the Society was appropriate, for he was what twenty-first century Americans would call "a Bible believer." In his addresses, proclamations, and general correspondence, he employed *church* language—language that a reader will not find in the writings of most of the founders. He did use Deistic designations for God, such as "Providence," "Creator," and "Divine Providence." But most of his language was that commonly used in the orthodox Protestant circles of his time: "Saviour," "King of Heaven," "Author and Giver of the Gospel," "Lord of the Sabbath," "Almighty God," "Lord of Hosts," "Almighty and benevolent Being," "Master," and "Captain of our Salvation."

In addition, Jay used Christian terms that would rarely turn up in the writings of a founding father: "gospel," "gospel ministry," "mercy," "grace," "Divine ordinances," and "apostolic succession." He frequently displayed a close knowledge even of minor biblical episodes. One of his letters written in 1818 about Christianity and warfare, for example, mentioned Moses, Paul, Solomon, David and Absalom, the Last Supper, Peter, and John the Baptist in quick succession. Jay's willingness to use religious language in his public addresses was especially evident in the passionate address he wrote to New York constituents in 1776. It was also prominent in such documents as his Thanksgiving proclamation to the citizens of New York in 1795.[36]

When Jay moved to Bedford, he found no Episcopal church there. After attending the Presbyterian church for several years, he was instrumental in financing the construction of an Episcopal church. His ties with the denomination in which he was raised were strong throughout his life. In 1783, Robert R. Livingston spoke of Jay's "love to [for] the established Church."[37]

Educated largely in Anglican institutions, Jay served (like his grandfather and father) on the vestry of Trinity Parish in New York City. Along with Mayor James Duane of New York and Robert Livingston, he served as a lay delegate to the second annual convention of the national Protestant Episcopal Church in 1786. He helped the convention draft an important letter to the bishops of the Church of England. At a time when Episcopalians had high church (or more medievally oriented) and low church (or Reformation-oriented) wings, he was a strong low churchman. "If it be asked, whether the ministers of the Calvinistic and of such other churches are of apostolic succession," he wrote to the corporation of Trinity Church,

> it is answered by all our bishops and clergy that they are not. It follows, therefore . . . that our bishops and clergy, and their congregation, when they offer up their prayer to Almighty God, must offer it with the meaning and understanding that the gracious promise mentioned in it is confined to Episcopalian ministers, and therefore excludes the ministers of all other denominations of Christians. Who is there among us that can be prepared to declare, in solemn prayer, and in such positive and unqualified terms, that none but Episcopalian ministers have any part or lot in this important promise?[38]

Jay's sons later became active in Episcopal Evangelical organizations that opposed the high-church Oxford Movement and sought to keep the Episcopal Church resolutely Protestant.

As these associations indicate, Jay was far from a Deist. He had many friends, such as Franklin, who were Deists—but the indications are that he avoided discussing religion with them. In religious matters he consistently championed the authority of the Bible over the use of human reason. Certain writers, he wrote in 1825,

> have attempted to penetrate into the recesses of profound mystery, and to dispel their obscurity by the light of reason. It seems they did not recollect that *no man can explain what no man can understand.* Those mysteries were revealed to our faith, to be believed on the credit of Divine testimony; and were not addressed to our mental abilities for explication.[39]

During the 1820s Jay steadily declined in health. In 1825, he suffered a stroke. Unable to attend the Episcopal church in Bedford, he asked its clergy to administer the Lord's Supper to him in his bedroom. Dying with his children gathered around him, he was buried in the Jay family cemetery in Rye after the simple Episcopal service he had requested. Among his last words were "the Lord is good" and "the Lord is better than we deserve."[40]

Jay firmly believed in life after death. In 1780, when a daughter died, he wrote Livingston that he fully expected to see her again in heaven. When his long-suffering sister finally died, he expressed the belief that "she will have reason to rejoice in the change." When his wife died unexpectedly in her forties, Jay led the children who surrounded her bed to an adjoining room. He then read to them the apostle Paul's discussion of the resurrection of Jesus in chapter 15 of his first letter to the Corinthians. The contrasts between the manner of Jay's death and the stoic deaths of such founders as Washington and Monroe are significant. Although all were Episcopalian, their religious faiths differed markedly. Washington and Monroe were influenced significantly by Deism; Jay was not. "While my children lament my departure," Jay wrote in his will, "let them recollect that in doing them good I was only the agent of their Heavenly Father, and that he never withdraws his care and consolations from those who diligently seek him." On his tombstone a son placed the simple epitaph, "He was in his life and death an example of the virtues, the faith and the hopes of a Christian." At the time of his death, Jay was the last surviving member of the first Continental Congress.[41] He proved to be a paragon not only of political excellence but also of Christian orthodoxy.

14

THE PAST IS A
FOREIGN COUNTRY

What, then, is definitely known about the religion of the founding fathers of the American republic? Three months after the death of James Monroe, Bird Wilson, a professor at the General Theological Seminary in New York City—the oldest theological seminary in the Episcopal Church—preached a sermon purporting to answer that question.[1] His credentials for providing the answer were excellent. Wilson's father, James, was himself a founding father. One of George Washington's original appointments to the U.S. Supreme Court, James Wilson had been a member of the Continental Congress and a signer of the Declaration of Independence. In the Constitutional Convention of 1787, his influence had probably ranked second only to that of James Madison.

A conservative in politics, James Wilson had been a communicant of Christ Church in Philadelphia. He was an intimate friend of Bishop White, who had been Washington's pastor. White was, in fact, the godfather of Bird Wilson, who subsequently became his theological protégé. When White retired, he wanted Bird Wilson to succeed him as Bishop of Pennsylvania—a position Wilson subsequently missed securing by only one vote. Wilson later became White's first biographer.

Born in 1777, Bird Wilson was raised in Philadelphia, the city most associated with the American Revolution and with the founding of the new republic. More than most residents of the city, he grew up in close contact with the leading personalities of the new republic. Wilson was twenty-three years old when the national capital moved from Philadelphia to the District of Columbia. Prior to his death in 1798, his father had been one of the leading figures in Philadelphia. One can easily imagine the visitors to their home and the conversations the young Wilson must have overheard or participated in while growing up.

Additionally, Wilson had a distinguished career as a lawyer and jurist in Philadelphia before being ordained to the Episcopal ministry by his godfather. His access to the circles of political power as well as his theological training made him especially qualified to assess the founders' religious beliefs. He had known those men personally. Moreover, he possessed a theologically informed understanding of religious orthodoxy. If anyone in 1831 knew the difference between appearance and reality in the religious beliefs of the founding fathers, it would have been Bird Wilson.

In his sermon delivered in Albany, New York, in October of that year, Wilson attacked the current stories that were circulating about the admirable religious piety of such founders as George Washington. Washington, he said in the sermon, had not been an orthodox Christian; in reality he had really been an eighteenth-century Deist. Wilson cited support on this point from clergy who had known Washington and whom he himself knew. Then—in significant words—he went on to state that "among all our presidents downward, not one was a professor of religion, at least not of more than Unitarianism."[2]

Fourteen months later, an Episcopal cleric wrote to Bishop White to inquire about the religious beliefs of George Washington. A new generation of biographers had begun to depict Washington as an orthodox Christian, thus fueling a debate about the first president's beliefs. Wilson's sermon articulates his disgust with these books. The Episcopal cleric wrote to the most reliable source of information he knew—the man who had been chaplain of the Continental Congress and Washington's pastor when the national capital was in Philadelphia. On December 1, 1832, White replied in words as significant as those of Wilson: "I do not believe that any degree of recollection will bring to my mind any fact which would prove General Washington to have been a believer in the Christian revelation."[3]

In the almost 175 years since Bird Wilson's sermon and Bishop White's letter, writers have continued to examine the religious faith of the revolutionary generation. They have tended to place the founders' religion into one of three categories—non-Christian Deism, Christian Deism, and orthodox Christianity. Those best remembered by history—Franklin, Washington, and Jefferson, for example—were Deists of varying degrees. In recent decades evangelical writers, decrying a secular bias among academic historians, have argued that all but a few of the founders genuinely adhered to Christian belief.

Yet the men and women surveyed in this study appear to have been a diverse group theologically. Deists and orthodox Christians alike composed the revolutionary generation. Whatever their private beliefs, most maintained formal affiliations with Christian denominations. In the spirit of the times, some questioned doctrines that they believed could not be reconciled with human reason. As a result, they rejected such Christian teachings as the Trinity, the virgin birth, the resurrection, and the divinity of Jesus. Yet orthodox Christians participated at every stage of building the nation, and many of the founders' wives and daughters displayed an orthodox Christian commitment.

Despite this diversity of belief, the founding generation held certain convictions in common. Most believed in a guiding Providence and in a life after death. These affirmations separated them from the radical Deists of their time. They respected the ethical teachings of Jesus. Many believed that simple virtue and morality were of greater importance than adherence to a particular set of religious doctrines. Above all, they valued freedom of conscience and despised religious tyranny. By enacting laws to protect religious freedom, the founders ensured that Americans would maintain the right to worship in any manner they chose. In the circle of the founding fathers, both men and women embraced these religious ideals.

That many founding fathers adopted certain Deistic patterns of thought is unsurprising. It would have been far more surprising if they had become evangelical Protestants, Roman Catholics, Russian Orthodox, Scandinavian Lutherans, or Orthodox Jews. In the formative years of their lives, Deism was a prevailing religious sentiment not only in parts of the United States but also in France and in other European countries. In Virginia it was the dominant interpretation of religion among educated males. To a greater or lesser extent, many founding fathers accepted and "expressed the characteristic ideas and prepossessions of [their] century—its aversion to 'superstition' and 'enthusiasm' and mystery:

> its dislike of dim perspectives; its . . . clarifying scepticism; its passion for freedom and its humane sympathies; its preoccupation with the world that is evident to the senses; [and] its profound faith in common sense, in the efficacy of reason for the solution of human problems and the advancement of human welfare."[4]

The founding fathers of the United States were remarkable, even noble men. Like most people, they understood their religion in the terms of their background and of their day. Those trained in parsons' academies had studied the Bible more thoroughly than all but a small percentage of Christians today. In the spirit of their times, they appeared less devout than they were—which seems a reversal from modern politics.

Today many Americans are concerned that their presidents be sincere men and women of faith. These founding men and women were often sincere believers. But their faith differed—often markedly—from that which many Americans have held in later centuries. Writers need not revise history to align the founders' beliefs with their own. Americans can tell their story unhesitantly, warts and all. To do otherwise is to be untrue not only to history but also to the founders themselves. "The past is a foreign country," a twentieth-century writer accurately observed in words that apply to the religion of the eighteenth century. "They do things differently there."[5]

EPILOGUE

Only a few of the founding fathers who lived into the early decades of the nineteenth century would have known of the evangelical interpretation of Christianity that has nurtured the recent presidents of the United States. Although the evangelist Billy Graham had served as an unofficial chaplain to most presidents from Dwight David Eisenhower on, the brief presidency of *Gerald Rudolph Ford* seems to introduce the first glimmers of the partisan evangelical influence in the White House to which Americans have become accustomed.

Raised as an Episcopalian in Grand Rapids, Michigan, Ford lived in Alexandria, Virginia, during most of his congressional career. There he and his family belonged to the Episcopal parish of Immanuel Church-on-the-Hill. Although immersed in the work of Congress, Ford regularly volunteered for some of Immanuel's many outreach programs. When Ford was nominated to replace the disgraced Spiro Agnew as vice president, a Democratic fellow-parishioner was impressed that "after seven hours before the Senate Committee testifying for his fitness for the Vice Presidency, he still came to the All Saints Service at the church."[1]

Early on the morning of Sunday, September 8, 1974, one month after he had assumed the presidency following the resignation of President

Richard Nixon, Ford left the White House to receive Holy Communion at adjacent St. John's Episcopal Church. When he returned to the Oval Office, he completed arrangements for the pardon of Nixon. Although Ford later declared that he had prayed about the pardon, his press secretary, a long-time associate, resigned in protest. Ford himself tended to view the pardon not only in a political but also in a religious light. Polls subsequently showed that the pardon was one of the principal reasons he lost the 1976 election to Jimmy Carter.

That Gerald Ford was an active, believing Episcopalian was well known during his presidency. Less well known was his apparently close relationship with evangelist Billy Zeoli, president of Gospel Films Inc. (now Gospel Communications International). Based in Grand Rapids, the organization distributed evangelical films, videos, and software. A creationist in his views on the origin of life, Zeoli often led chapel services for professional football teams. He was closely associated with the conservative evangelical entrepreneurs who formed the Amway Corporation.

Beginning in the 1960s, Zeoli played a significant role in Ford's spiritual life. From 1973 on, he sent him weekly devotionals. At the invitation of Ford, then the Republican minority leader, the evangelist also delivered the opening prayer in the House of Representatives on the day after Spiro Agnew resigned. Both as vice president and president, Ford also prayed privately with Zeoli on occasion.

When the evangelical Jimmy Carter's candidacy for president gained support from many Americans who belonged to born-again churches, Ford had to scramble to display his own right to their allegiance. In the words of an astute observer of the religious dimensions of the 1976 election, Ford

> began scraping together his minor claims to be an evangelical. An Episcopalian, he appeared before the Southern Baptist Convention to remind them that his ministerial son had attended one of their colleges; and he assured a convention of national religious broadcasters that he was indeed of the evangelical persuasion.
>
> He reminded newsmen that he prayed and read his Bible daily. He described in some detail a recent experience in which he had met God personally, and his son later identified it as a rebirth. He made a point of having

Billy Graham stop by for White House chats and of stopping off at Graham's alma mater, Wheaton College. . . . He attended the First Baptist Church of Dallas to collect the endorsement of Southern Baptist power W. A. Criswell.[2]

By 1976, many Americans realized that not only Jimmy Carter the Southern Baptist but also Gerald Ford the Episcopalian could be considered an evangelical. Since 1976, every presidential election except that of 1988 has had at least one self-avowed evangelical Christian running as a major party nominee. The closing year of Gerald Ford's presidency marked the beginning of the evangelical surge in White House politics.

When *James Earl ("Jimmy") Carter* was elected president, a largely secular press corps spent substantial time pondering what an "evangelical" and a "Southern Baptist" were. At one of his early press conferences, Carter said that if reporters wanted to know what a Baptist believed, they needed only to read the New Testament. Being a Southern Baptist was a major part of who America's thirty-eighth president was—so much so that the Secret Service referred to him as "the Deacon" in their communications. But Jimmy Carter was a different kind of Christian and a different kind of Southern Baptist. The combination made him a somewhat different kind of president and a very different kind of ex-president.

Unlike most of his predecessors, Carter was not an undifferentiated, middle-of-the-road Protestant. Rather, he was an evangelical—the kind of Christian who saw the Bible as the supreme authority for faith and conduct, who emphasized a conversion experience as the entrance to Christianity, and who believed that a personal relationship with Jesus Christ was not only possible but also essential to salvation. For him, religion was a public matter. Newspapers and television reported his regular church attendance. That he also taught Sunday school was well known and generally viewed as remarkable. Carter spoke forthrightly, frequently, and with little urging about his personal faith.

The Plains in which Jimmy Carter grew up was a traditional southwest Georgia town, where religion was very much a way of life. In an era when church and state were loosely separated in much of the South, public school began in Plains each day with "chapel" (a daily assembly that included prayer) and sponsored annual Christmas pageants. Following a conversion experience, Jimmy was baptized in his family's Baptist church of Plains in his eleventh year. After leaving the United States Navy and returning to Plains, he became first a Sunday school teacher, then a leader of the junior division of the Sunday school, and finally a deacon (the highest lay office in a Baptist congregation). Prior to running for president, he maintained a nearly impeccable record of church attendance.

The Carter family was not just Baptist but Southern Baptist—one of "the last great repositories of the Puritan tradition in America."[3] All Baptists believe the New Testament teaches that only believing adults (or young adults) should be baptized—and then only by immersion. The Baptist tradition also teaches that a Christian must go through an experience of "conversion" or "rebirth" prior to immersion and formal admission to the church.

But the Southern Baptists, unlike their Puritan cousins in the north, have also been markedly influenced by revivalism, or the organized effort to reawaken Christian faith through emotional conversions. Separating in the 1840s from their northern (or American Baptist) brethren over slavery, they have grown to become the largest Protestant denomination in the United States. Over the years, they have felt no compulsion to align themselves with other denominations. As a result, they have remained not only independent but also to a large extent insular. In a decision typical for a Southern Baptist, Carter passed up the required chapel services (which, for Protestant cadets, were Episcopalian) when enrolled at the U.S. Naval Academy and secured permission to attend instead a Baptist church in Annapolis, where he also taught Sunday school.

Yet in his adult years Jimmy Carter did not accept all the tenets of the Southern Baptist tradition. Though traditionalist in many of his interpretations, he did not believe that the Bible was without error. A Darwinist rather than a creationist, he supported the kind of scholarly examination of the Bible pursued in theological seminaries. He also rejected any interpretation of the Bible that subordinated women to men in church and society.

Moreover, although many Southern Baptists supported segregation, Carter was at first a quiet and later an outspoken integrationist.

During the 1950s, he was the only white businessman in Plains who did not join the White Citizens Council. He and his mother were among the only members of their Plains church to vote to integrate the congregation. Carter later joined Maranatha Baptist Church of Plains, an integrated and theologically more moderate congregation than Plains Baptist Church. In 2000, he announced that he was reluctantly leaving the now highly conservative Southern Baptist Convention in order to support the more moderate Cooperative Baptist Fellowship.

Carter's intense study of the New Testament, his mother's influence, and his reading of theology caused him to adopt many of the positions he later advocated as governor and president. Prior to the 1980s, most Southern Baptists believed that the church should not sully itself by becoming involved in political activity. Carter sided with the small wing of Southern Baptists who believed that Christian churches had a fundamental obligation to work on behalf of social justice.

After a stormy campaign in 1962, he was elected to the Georgia senate and reelected two years later. In the state legislature he exhibited the same combination of strengths and weaknesses that would later characterize his one-term presidency: keen intelligence, egotism, vindictiveness, hard work, self-righteousness, Christian idealism, and micro-management.

Defeated in his campaign for governor in 1966, he "lost faith in my own ability, the political system, and God's will for my life." On the advice of his sister Ruth, an evangelist, he immersed himself in missionary work and experienced what he considered a second rebirth.[4] In 1970, after what opponents viewed as a deceptively conservative campaign, he was elected governor of Georgia. His inaugural address brought him national attention when he told his constituents:

I say to you quite frankly that the period for racial discrimination is over. No poor, rural, or weak black person should ever have to bear the additional burden of being deprived of the opportunity of an education, a job, or simple justice.

As governor, Carter concerned himself with integration, with improving educational opportunities for the poor, with the environment, and with reforming Georgia's prison system. By 1974, a portrait of the Reverend Martin Luther King, Jr., an Atlanta native, hung in the state capitol.

Starting out as a dark horse—an obscure "peanut farmer" from Georgia—Carter secured the Democratic nomination for president and defeated Gerald Ford in 1976. Unpretentious, homespun, rural, and yet experienced as a businessman, he seemed to recall an older and better America to voters disenchanted by Watergate and Vietnam. As president, he read several chapters of the Bible with his wife, Rosalynn, every night, witnessed about his Christian faith to foreign leaders, and taught Sunday school both in Plains and in Washington's First Baptist Church. As a low-church Protestant, Carter did not believe that the Most High God liked elaborate ritual, so he eliminated some of the quasi-royal trappings of the presidency. Southerners, of course, were accustomed to political leaders who embodied Southern Baptist piety, but the United States as a whole was not.

Carter clearly saw the presidency as a religious vocation. His securing a peace treaty between Israel and Egypt, his returning the Canal Zone to Panama, his support for human rights legislation, his national address about a festering spiritual crisis and a need for repentance and sacrifice—these and similar actions stemmed, in the opinion of Carter's aides, from his religious beliefs. Above all, what many critics viewed as his apparent paralysis in dealing with the Iranian hostage crisis of the late 1970s can be seen as reflecting a Christian concern that human life must be preserved. If a rescue effort into the heart of Tehran fell short of perfection, Carter knew that the American hostages could be killed.

During Carter's presidency, an activist and increasingly disciplined "Religious Right" began to coalesce as a force in American politics. The movement combined religious conservatism, Republican politics, patriotism and national pride, and traditional views of family life and sexuality. Focused on preserving the Christian heritage in the United States, it supported what it saw as biblical values and advocated pro-life and creationist views. Well funded, it endorsed and financially supported candidates who agreed with its positions. The Religious Right steadily grew during an administration increasingly perceived as weak and ineffectual. Many evangelicals who had voted for Carter in 1976 felt betrayed by his policies. By 1980, they were openly campaigning against him. Since that year, most evangelicals have supported Republican candidates in state and national elections. Decisively defeated by Ronald Reagan, Carter left office to a certain extent politically discredited. His stature steadily grew, however, in the years after 1980. His work for world peace, his founding of the Carter Center in Atlanta as a mediation center for national and international conflicts, his establishment of a major project to assist Atlanta's poor, and his support of similar initiatives have given him international respect. In 2002, he was awarded the Nobel Peace Prize.

But the most striking image of Carter's ex-presidency may be his manual labor in building homes for the poor with the Georgia-based charity Habitat for Humanity. The nation is accustomed to seeing former presidents playing in golf tournaments or turning out books in an attempt to give their side of history. For many Americans, the idea of a president, accompanied by his spouse, taking long bus rides and working on houses for a week in places such as the South Bronx is novel and arresting.

Carter's presidency never reached its goals. Yet twenty-five years after Carter assumed the presidency, a reader can still find the same idealism in his acceptance speech at the Nobel Prize ceremony. His words differ strikingly from those most presidents of the United States would have chosen:

> I worship Jesus Christ whom we Christians consider to be the Prince of Peace. As a Jew, he taught us to cross religious boundaries, in service and in love. He repeatedly reached out and embraced Roman conquerors, other Gentiles, and even the more despised Samaritans. . . .
>
> In the industrialized world there is a terrible absence of understanding or concern about those who are enduring lives of despair and hopelessness. We have not yet made the commitment to share with others an appreciable part of our excessive wealth. This is a necessary and potentially rewarding burden that we should all be willing to assume. . . .
>
> War may sometimes be a necessary evil. But no matter how necessary, it is always an evil. Never a good. We will not learn how to live together in peace by killing each other's children. . . .
>
> God gives us the capacity for choice. We can choose to alleviate suffering. We can choose to work together for peace. We can make changes—and we must.

"I was raised in the Christian Church which as you know believes in baptism when the individual has made his own decision to accept Jesus," *Ronald Wilson Reagan* once wrote to an inquirer. "My decision was made in my early teens."[5]

Although most historians of Christianity would not classify the Christian Church (Disciples of Christ) as "evangelical," Reagan's words describe the kind of decision for Jesus Christ that lies at the heart of evangelical religion. He often used similar words to describe his faith. Evangelicals believe that the crucial distinction between their interpretation of Christianity and other interpretations involves whether the believer "*knows* Christ" or merely "knows *about* Christ." Asked precisely that question in 1980 by the president of the Southern Baptist Convention, Reagan answered, "*I know him.*"[6]

Reagan's father—John (or "Jack") Reagan—was an Irish-American Roman Catholic. He took his religion lightly enough, however, that he married a Protestant, attended Mass sporadically, and allowed his two boys to be raised in his wife's church. Of Scots-Irish and nominal Methodist background, Reagan's mother, Nelle, became a devout and active member of the Christian Church (Disciples of Christ) in Dixon, Illinois. Insisting on raising her two sons in her church, she had Neil and Ronald baptized by immersion in 1922. Neil—"as much his father's son as Ronald was his mother's"[7]—later converted to Roman Catholicism, but Ron remained active in his mother's denomination.[8] He regularly accompanied her to services of worship and prayer meetings, cleaned the Dixon church, taught Sunday school, and at age fifteen led an Easter Sunrise service. "Nelle's great sense of religious faith rubbed off on me," he once declared.[9]

By high school, two new influences—Ben Cleaver, his pastor, and Cleaver's attractive and intelligent daughter, Margaret—had entered Reagan's religious life. Reagan spent large amounts of time at the Cleaver parsonage and often engaged in serious conversations with the minister. Because Margaret had enrolled at Eureka College, the denomination's nearby liberal-arts college, he decided to matriculate there as well. He entered Eureka "as close to being a 'minister's kid' as one can be without actually moving into the rectory."[10] Although he became engaged to Margaret in college, she later broke off the engagement. By the time Reagan became a radio announcer in Iowa following graduation, a co-worker could describe him as "a deeply religious man [though] not the kind who went to church every Sunday. A man with a strong inner faith. Whatever he accomplished was God's will—God gave it to him and God could take it away."[11]

The description seems to characterize Reagan's religious practices for the rest of his life. In California, both as an actor and governor, he attended church irregularly. For a time his attendance improved when his parents moved to the coast and his mother became active in the Hollywood-Beverly Christian Church. Reagan's first wife, Jane Wyman, not only attended that church with him but also taught in its Sunday school when their children, Maureen and Michael, were enrolled.[12] But after marrying Nancy Davis, Reagan switched his affiliation to Bel Air Presbyterian Church, which belonged to the evangelical wing of mainstream Presbyterianism. The couple attended on and off from 1964 on, but did not formally join the church until 1989, when they were about to return to California from Washington.

This pattern continued during his two terms as president. After initially affiliating with the National Presbyterian Church, Reagan— in the words of its pastor—"attended several services" in the two and a half months between the Sunday before his inauguration and the attempt on his life.[13] Following the failed assassination, the Reagans essentially stopped attending church in Washington. Both attributed their absence to heightened security precautions, which they said they found oppressive and disruptive not only to themselves but also to other worshipers.

Yet some observers saw these as the excuses of a couple already disinclined to attend church. "It must be noted," a politically conservative author wrote, "that such concerns did not stop either . . . George Bush or Bill Clinton . . . from attending church services outside the White House."[14] The criticisms had some merit. St. John's Church was specially outfitted to meet the rigorous security requirements of the Secret Service. Richard Nixon had regularly held services in the White House. Moreover, the Reagans spent many weekends at Camp David, but seem not to have arranged for services there. The real explanation seems to be that the Reagans did not view regular church attendance as important. "His faith was deep, secure, and part of his daily life," one biographer notes, "rather than a Sunday ritual."[15]

From childhood on, Ronald Reagan prayed often—something Nelle taught him to do. While president he not only spent time in private prayer but also prayed with visitors. Throughout life Reagan steadily tithed, giving a tenth of his income to the churches to which he belonged. He rarely took the Lord's name in vain. He firmly believed that God had a special plan for the United States and for all people. In addition, he believed that God had intervened in the major events of his life—leading him not only into his marriage to Nancy, but also into the presidency. He attributed his survival of the assassin's bullet to the will of God. Diagnosed with Alzheimer's disease, he never asked why God had allowed him to become a victim.

Unlike Jimmy Carter, Reagan read little theology. He was clearly less reflective about his religion than Carter. In his appeals for prayer in the public schools and for America to "return God to the classroom," he frequently supported his arguments by quoting Deistic founding fathers. Above all, he quoted the Deistic Franklin, the Unitarian Jefferson, and—remarkably—the Deist icon Thomas Paine. "I did not think he was astute in theology," Louis Evans, the pastor of National Presbyterian Church, declared of Reagan, "but he was a believer."[16]

If nonevangelicals such as Evans appreciated Reagan as a human being and a Christian, they did not necessarily agree that his strong political views were rooted in Judeo-Christian values. Heirs either of the Protestant Social Gospel or of the social teachings of Roman Catholicism and Judaism, many of Reagan's critics believed that government should play a significant role in protecting "the last, the least, and the lost." A long-time aide commented: "He cares about people as individuals. I'm not sure that he ever looks upon the masses and says, 'I must go do something, there are my people.'" A Washington observer described what he termed "the clash" between Reagan's decent instincts and his conservative, anti-government ideology. "If you were down on your luck," he wrote,

and you got past the Secret Service into his office [and said] "Mr. President, I'm down in my luck," he'd give you the shirt off his back. And then, in his undershirt, he'd sit down at his desk and he'd sign legislation . . . throwing kids off the school lunch program, other people off welfare, all in the name of fiscal responsibility, as he sat there shivering because he'd given you his shirt. He had a good heart . . . but when it came to his ideology, his philosophy . . . [was] "off with their heads."[17]

Reagan's mother raised him in a particularly earnest form of Protestantism. Despite the influence of the worldly movie industry and of his second wife, Nancy—who put great faith in horoscopes and astrology—Reagan retained the outlook and many of the values of his childhood religion. If anything, over the years he moved to the right of his denominational heritage. When he ran for office, he blended conservative Christian theology with attacks on big government. If these religious and political views were unpalatable to many Americans, to tens of millions of others they represented unchanging American values and beliefs that went back to the founding fathers. They swept Reagan into two landslide victories in presidential elections. Just as opponents and journalists continually underestimated Reagan's appeal to American voters, so they seem also to have underestimated the genuineness and depth of his religious convictions.

A throwback to the era of the founding fathers, *George Herbert Walker Bush* was an aristocratic Episcopalian in the tradition of George Washington. Appropriately, he was sworn into office on the same Bible used at Washington's inauguration.

Bush's Episcopalian family was highly religious as well as extremely wealthy. The compilers of the Book of Common Prayer, the principal liturgical book of the Episcopal Church, intended that heads of families use it to lead daily worship in their homes. George's father, Senator Prescott Bush, often did precisely that. Each morning he and his wife, Dorothy, also read a Bible lesson to the family. On Sundays, a day the family observed as a strict Sabbath, the Bush parents and children regularly attended Christ Church in Greenwich, Connecticut. When staying at their eight-bedroom seaside home in Kennebunkport, Maine, the family attended St. Ann's by the Sea Episcopal Church (a summer chapel) during the summer and the First Congregationalist Church during the spring and fall.

Following decorated service in World War II as a Navy pilot, Bush married Barbara Pierce, the Presbyterian daughter of the president of the McCall Corporation. Ultimately, Barbara and George Bush had four sons and two daughters. Moving after his graduation from Yale to west Texas to work in the oil industry, Bush eventually settled his family in Midland, Texas. In the spring of 1953, his daughter, three-year-old Pauline Robinson ("Robin") Bush, was diagnosed with advanced leukemia. Despite the best treatment then available, Robin died seven months later.

On weekdays the First Presbyterian Church of Midland opened its doors at 6:15 A.M. for Bible study classes. During Robin's illness, Bush began to stop in the sanctuary to pray at 6:30 every morning before going to work. "I really learned to pray," Bush later remembered. "I would ask God why? Why this little innocent girl?" For both parents, the death was a trauma.[18]

When the Bushes moved to Houston in 1959, they affiliated with St. Martin's Episcopal Church, one of Houston's wealthiest congregations. In Midland, the Bushes had taught Sunday school, and he had been elected one of the church's elders. At St. Martin's, they continued to teach Sunday school, and Bush was elected to the church's vestry, or governing body.

When Bush served as American liaison to the People's Republic of China in the mid-1970s, the family worshiped on Sunday on the second floor of a "beat up old house" that served as a Protestant Bible school and church. At that time, Christianity was severely regulated in Communist China, and the first service Bush attended in Beijing had a congregation of just fourteen, all but four of them foreigners like the Bushes.

Because of what Barbara described as "deaths, politics, long distances, and floods," the Bushes had deferred the baptism of their last child, Dorothy ("Doro"), four times. On what Bush noted in his diary as a "pleasant, wonderful . . . very special day," Doro was baptized in the little Chinese church in 1975 by smiling Chinese ministers. Suspicious representatives of the government photographed and taped the ceremony. As far as the Bushes were aware, their daughter was the first American to be baptized in China since the Communist government assumed power in 1949.[19]

Like most of the postwar presidents before him, Bush had a close relationship with Billy Graham and with his wife, Ruth. The evangelist gave Bush the Bible on which he was sworn in as vice president, corresponded with Bush, exchanged telephone calls with him, stayed at the White House, and inevitably played golf with him.

Graham also acted as spiritual advisor to Bush during the Gulf War—a war presided over by a president, White House chief of staff, secretary of defense, and chairman of the Joint Chiefs of Staff, all of whom were Episcopalian. As he approached the decision to invade Iraq in January 1981, Bush discussed his options with three clergy. The presiding bishop of the Episcopal Church urged him not to go to war. The advice given by the chaplain of the U.S. Senate is unknown. Billy Graham, however, quoted James Russell Lowell's words, "Once to every man and nation comes the moment to decide." In his diary Bush noted that Graham "offers his help . . . talks about Saddam Hussein being the anti-Christ [*sic*] himself . . . [and] wants to speak out in any way he can."[20]

On the day of the deadline he had given to Iraq, Bush received not only a cable from Pope John Paul II but also a telephone call from the Roman Catholic archbishop of Boston. In a last-minute appeal, his presiding bishop telephoned again. All three opposed the invasion.[21] Graham, whom Bush had invited to the White House, was the last person with whom the president conversed as that day closed. When the bombing of Iraq began at 7:00 P.M. on the next day, George Bush, Barbara Bush, and Billy Graham watched it together on CNN.

Bush was a "low church" (or Protestant-inclined) Episcopalian. He attended churches of other denominations, never insisted that his wife leave her Presbyterian faith, had a Southern Baptist as spiritual advisor, and was willing to allow Doro's baptism to be delayed until she was sixteen years old. During his presidency, he heeded certain evangelical social teachings—he changed his position on abortion, for example. But in contrast to the strict Episcopal orthodoxy of his father and the religious pilgrimages of two of his sons (George became an evangelical following conversion and Jeb a Roman Catholic after marriage), Bush remained a religious moderate.

On his mother's side, *William Jefferson Clinton* was descended from struggling farmers named for such founding fathers as George Washington and James Monroe. Clinton's mother, father, stepfather, and grandparents rarely attended church. But in Arkansas, "a state composed mostly of white Southern Baptists and blacks," young boys had no lack of religious influence outside the home.[22] Thus Clinton was brought up a Southern Baptist and remained one.

In 1943 Clinton's mother, Virginia, met William Jefferson Blythe III, a high school dropout who (unknown to Virginia) was in his fourth marriage. Shortly before he left for military service overseas, they were married. Seven months later Blythe was secretly divorced from his fourth wife. Discharged from the Army at the end of 1945, he was killed in a freak automobile accident three months before Bill Clinton's birth in August 1946.

Four years later, Virginia married the divorced Roger Clinton in a Baptist parsonage in Hot Springs, Arkansas. A gambler, an alcoholic, and a notorious womanizer, Clinton was also an abusive husband prone to jealous rages. Although Roger Clinton never officially adopted his stepson prior to his death in 1967, in his teens Bill Clinton changed his name legally to William Jefferson Clinton.

Young Clinton's initial experience with church came at the First Baptist Church in Hope, when his grandmother enrolled him in the Sunbeams program, which introduced preschoolers to Jesus. Virginia took him to Sunday school and summer vacation Bible school, but worshiped in the church herself only on Christmas and Easter. In 1952, Roger Clinton moved the family to his hometown of Hot Springs.

A cosmopolitan resort town, Hot Springs then had a population of approximately 35,000 but attracted as many as 100,000 visitors a year to its baths, hotels, gambling, and multiple other legal and illegal activities. In Clinton's words, it was an "amazingly diverse" city for Arkansas.[23] Besides the Baptist and other Protestant churches, the city had two synagogues, two Roman Catholic churches, and a Greek Orthodox church. In their new city, Virginia and Roger Clinton continued to attend church only twice a year, but Virginia encouraged young Billy to go regularly. On most Sundays he walked three blocks to Park Place Baptist Church, usually attending both Sunday school and then church. To the pastor, it seemed that Billy was at the church "every time the door opened."[24]

Near the end of each service of worship, a Southern Baptist church has an invitation or "altar call." Worshipers who wish to commit their lives to Jesus Christ and be baptized, as well as baptized persons who wish to rededicate their lives, are invited to come forward. Counselors and prayer leaders then take them aside for counseling. "In 1955," Clinton later remembered, "I had absorbed enough of my church's teachings to know that I was a sinner and to want Jesus to save me. So I came down the aisle at the end of the Sunday service, professed my faith in Christ, and asked to be baptized."

Clinton later described this decision to be baptized as his "first serious religious experience."[25] In 1976, when he was running for attorney general of Arkansas, members of Jerry Falwell's Moral Majority often asked Clinton whether he was a "born-again Christian." He always answered as most Southern Baptists would: he said *yes*.[26]

In his early teens, Clinton went through a "major spiritual crisis." The crisis developed, he later reflected, "because I couldn't understand why a God whose existence I couldn't prove would create a world in which so many bad things happened."[27] In the same period, he heard Billy Graham speak at a crusade in segregated Little Rock. When the evangelist "gave the invitation for people to come down onto the football field to become Christians or to rededicate their lives to Christ," Clinton remembered, "hundreds of blacks and whites came down the stadium aisles together, stood together, and prayed together."[28] Moved, he secretly contributed part of his small allowance to Graham's ministry for months after the crusade.

Clinton enrolled at Jesuit-run Georgetown University in the fall of 1964 to study at its prestigious School of Foreign Service. Ninety-six percent Roman Catholic in enrollment, the College of Arts and Sciences had a faculty composed largely of Jesuits and lay Roman Catholics. The more diverse School of Foreign Service had several hundred Protestant and approximately forty Jewish students, but it was also overwhelmingly Roman Catholic in enrollment.[29]

At Georgetown, Clinton did so well in introductory philosophy that the young Jesuit scholastic who taught the course invited him to dinner and suggested that Clinton consider becoming a Jesuit. When Clinton replied that he was Southern Baptist, the instructor was stunned. "I saw all the Jesuit traits in him—serious, political, empathetic," he later said. "I just assumed he was Catholic."[30]

Following his loss of the Arkansas governorship to a conservative evangelical, Clinton's church attendance reemerged in 1980. In what his opponents saw as a calculated attempt at political rehabilitation, he began attending Immanuel Baptist Church in Little Rock and singing in its choir. Clinton's wife, Hillary Rodham Clinton, suggested that her husband again take churchgoing seriously.

Raised in an upper-middle-class Chicago suburb, Hillary belonged to Park Ridge's First United Methodist Church, a church noted for its Sunday school program. The effect its youth minister, the Reverend Don Jones, had on her social consciousness during her teens cannot be overestimated. Hillary later recalled:

> He was filled with the teachings of Dietrich Bonhoeffer and Reinhold Niebuhr. Bonhoeffer stressed that the role of a Christian was a moral one of total engagement in the world with the promotion of human development. Niebuhr struck a persuasive balance between a clear-eyed realism about human nature and an unrelenting passion for justice and social reform. . . . Jones stressed that a Christian life was "faith in action." I had never met anyone like him.[31]

Jones established what he called "the University of Life" for his high-school youth group. Introducing them to the literature, theology, and art they had not yet discovered, he led challenging, wide-ranging discussions. Jones also arranged joint meetings and discussions with the youth groups of black and Hispanic churches in inner-city Chicago. Once, he took his charges to hear Martin Luther King, Jr., speak. Through Jones, Hillary first learned that life consisted of more than the comfortable existence and manicured lawns of Park Ridge. The University of Life caused her to come home from church on Sunday nights "bursting with excitement."[32]

When Hillary left suburban Chicago to study at Wellesley College, she was still a Republican. By the end of her sophomore year, she was not. She retained her religious convictions during college but attended church less, became active in the anti-war effort, and served as the first student speaker at commencement in Wellesley's history. At Yale Law School, she met and later married Bill Clinton. When Hillary returned to active churchgoing in Little Rock, she chose to worship at First United Methodist Church, where the Clintons' daughter, Chelsea, was baptized.

The Clintons' move from Arkansas to the White House in 1993 was filled with religious symbolism. In the days surrounding the inauguration, they attended Culpeper Baptist Church in Virginia and a late-night prayer service at the First Baptist Church in Washington. At Bill Clinton's request, the service scheduled for the morning of the inauguration was held at the Metropolitan African Methodist Episcopal Church in Washington, marking the first time an African-American church had been used for such a service. At the inauguration, Billy Graham gave the benediction.

After visiting several churches in Washington, the Clintons decided to attend Foundry United Methodist Church, a mile from the White House. During the eight years of his presidency, Clinton regularly attended church and participated in interfaith prayer breakfasts. On a visit to China, he worshiped in the same church in Beijing the Bushes had attended. The Clinton White House tended to ignore the increasingly conservative Southern Baptist Convention, but the president kept contacts open with a wide variety of religious groups. The overall effect of the Clinton administration was to broaden the religious spectrum represented in the nation's capital.[33] The contacts with religious leaders were especially beneficial when the scandal of Clinton's affair with Monica Lewinsky became known. In its aftermath he asked three ministers—two evangelicals and one mainline Protestant—to counsel him regularly.[34]

As a boy, Clinton seems to have found that Southern Baptist churches—places pervaded with goodwill and idealism—provided a sanctuary from the parental war continually going on in his home.[35] In later years, he was far more affected by African-American and Pentecostal Christianity than any previous president. He seems to have remained a Southern Baptist not only because it is the folk religion of the South but also because he remained at heart a southerner. Clinton tapped into the stream in the Baptist heritage that is concerned with such social sins as prejudice, segregation, and corporate greed—the tradition of Martin Luther King, Jr., Jimmy Carter, and Walter Rauschenbusch, the father of the Social Gospel.

Like many politicians, Clinton clearly used religion for political purposes. When the Southern Baptist Convention voted on a resolution calling for disfellowshiping Clinton following the Monica

Lewinsky scandal, the "messengers" came close to adopting the resolution. Clinton's apology on national television left many viewers unsatisfied. "I heard him say 'I lied,'" one Southern Baptist minister declared. "I heard him say 'I deceived.' But I did not hear what I believe to be a biblical confession or a biblical repentance."[36]

A long-time political associate wrote that two William Jefferson Clintons exist:

> The Sunday-morning President Clinton is . . . pious, optimistic, brilliant, principled, sincere, good-willed, empathetic, intellectual, learned, and caring. . . . But the Saturday-night Bill who cohabits within him is . . . willful, demanding, hedonistic, risk-taking, sybaritic, headstrong, unfeeling, callous, unprincipled, and undisciplined. . . . Each side of Clinton seems unaware of the other. This division of Clinton's personality makes him hard to comprehend.[37]

A biographer describes the Saturday night-Sunday morning Bill Clinton as "one of the most complex figures in contemporary American politics," and goes on to say, "No single world could keep him content for long." One thing is certain: the American people may not soon again get a president whose autobiography recommends, "If you ever get a chance to go to a Pentecostal service, don't miss it."[38]

The churches *George Walker Bush* has attended throughout his life chiefly belong to Protestant mainline culture. He has been an acolyte in St. Martin's Episcopal Church in Houston, a member of First Presbyterian Church in Midland, and, since 1982, a member of his wife Laura's First United Methodist Church of Midland. Probably for reasons of security, he and Laura now frequently attend St. John's Episcopal Church, adjacent to the White House. When they spend weekends at Camp David, they worship in the chapel there.

Like many children of influential families, Bush encountered difficulty living up to the expectations he believed incumbent upon him. Alcohol, wise-cracking, irreverence, disengagement, and a general party orientation were some of the ways he dealt with this tension until his thirties. He attended both public and private schools in Texas and Phillips Academy in Andover, Massachusetts, where his father was an alumnus. In spite of mediocre grades, Bush was accepted in

1964 to Yale University, where his grandfather and father had also attended.

Popular at Yale, Bush was active in the social aspects of campus life. Although some classes and professors interested him, Bush found Yale's faculty on the whole to be what he considered left-wing, intellectual snobs. During the unrest of the Vietnam period, he avoided campus protests, lectures, and teach-ins. A single meeting with Yale's noted anti-war chaplain, the Reverend William Sloane Coffin—whom Bush felt insulted his father during the conversation—may have soured his view of social activism in the mainline Protestant churches. Bush later told members of his family that he really didn't learn "a damn thing at Yale."[39]

Returning to Texas, Bush served part-time in the Air National Guard, attended Harvard Business School, ran for Congress, married, and worked in the oil industry. The mid-1980s were a turning point in Bush's life. Troubled by alcohol and by an overall lack of purpose, he had a long conversation with Billy Graham. Subsequently, Bush began to read the Bible frequently, to attend church more often, to read evangelical devotional books, and to stop drinking. Believing that Jesus Christ had entered his life, Bush, like many converts, tended to be rigid about his new faith. When he began to assert that only those persons who believed in Jesus Christ would go to heaven, his mother argued with him. Ultimately, she called Billy Graham, who urged both the Bushes not to "play God."

From 1986 on, such conservative evangelicals as James Robison of Texas and James Dobson of Colorado Springs have influenced Bush through books and meetings. He has also been influenced by the writings of neoconservatives, some (like Marvin Olasky) secular Jews who have converted to evangelical Christianity.

For better or worse, Bush seems to have no one at his right shoulder who represents moderate Judeo-Christian values—no Bill Moyers, for example, who advised Lyndon Johnson, and none of the Protestant Social Gospel figures who advised Roosevelt and Truman. He also seems to have no religious mentors who were active in the civil rights movement or who held a negative view of the Vietnam War. Thus with conservative evangelical advisors and with no mainline religious advisors other than his Methodist pastor in Midland, Bush's positions are unlikely to change. His opponents seem to realize that. Today, Bush largely identifies with what is often termed the Religious Right. His vision of what is amiss in America is akin to their vision; both argue that secular humanism threatens America's moral and Christian heritage. Like religious reformers, he desires a return to morality. Like conservative Roman Catholics and most evangelicals, he wants alternatives to abortion, the avoidance of euthanasia, the freedom to pray in schools, and the practice of sexual abstinence until marriage. In addition, he supports the assurance of racial equality for Hispanics and blacks, the supplementing of government programs with community or faith-based programs that provide the same services, and the increased influence of traditional religious values in American life. In every gubernatorial and presidential contest in which Bush has been involved, he has had the support of the Religious Right.

Yet Bush—like his father—appears not to be fundamentally comfortable with the Religious Right. The gap of social class, of inherited wealth, and of prep school and Ivy League background seems difficult to bridge between Bush and such leaders of the Religious Right as Dobson, Robison, T. D. Jakes, Pat Robertson, and Jerry Falwell. No reason exists to doubt his commitment to evangelical positions. But, significantly, when Sunday comes along, America's forty-third president does not attend megachurches or other churches in the conservative evangelical tradition. Rather, he attends the mainline Protestant churches of his youth.

In this one respect, George W. Bush seems not a conservative evangelical, but rather his mother and father's son as well as his wife's husband. He walks the evangelical walk, in that evangelicals define "walk" as an ongoing personal relationship with Jesus Christ. But he can appear uncomfortable talking the evangelical talk in public unless it is part of a prepared speech. Unlike Jimmy Carter, he does not regularly "witness." Unlike the public faith of evangelicals, his public faith—and particularly that of his wife—is neither demonstrative nor emotional.

Nevertheless, virtually all who know Bush well say his evangelical belief is not a marketing stunt for political gain. He is properly classified as an evangelical and a member of America's religious right. When his evangelical advisor, Doug Wead, was asked what distinguishes a "born-again" Christian, he answered: "A personal faith in Christ, Bible is the Word of God, accepting Christ as Savior being a turning point in their life." Bush then said that, according to that definition, he qualified as "born-again." Every sign indicates that his faith is sincere. Bush's cousin, John Ellis, once remarked: "I always laugh when people say George W is saying this or that to appease the religious right. He *is* the religious right."[40]

Notes

Abbreviations

DMDE   *Dolley Madison Digital Edition*, ed. Holly C. Shulman
(Charlottesville: University of Virginia Press, 2004). [Online]
Available: http://rotunda.upress.virginia.edu/dmde/DPM

Chapter 1: Religion in the American Colonies in 1770

1. Alexis de Tocqueville, *Democracy in America* (New York: Classics of Liberty Library, 1992), 308.
2. John Adams, *Diary and Autobiography*, eds. L. H. Butterfield et al., *The Adams Papers*, 4 vols. (Cambridge, MA : Belknap Press, 1961), 2: 150. See also David McCullough, *John Adams* (New York: Simon and Schuster, 2001), 84.
3. John Adams, *Adams Family Correspondence*, eds. L. H. Butterfield et al., *The Adams Papers*, 6 vols. (Cambridge, MA: Belknap Press, 1963), 1: 167. See also McCullough, 84.
4. Quoted in Edwin Scott Gaustad, *A Religious History of America*, new rev. ed. (San Francisco: Harper and Row, 1990), 70.
5. Non-predestinarian theologians take such claims seriously but try to reconcile biblical teachings on predestination with the concept that humans are free to accept or to reject salvation. Calvin and other predestinarians cited such episodes and passages as the calling of Abraham, the selection of Israel as the Chosen People, the selection of Jacob over Esau and similar divine selections,

and such New Testament passages as Matthew 20:23, Romans 8:28–30, Ephesians 1:3–14, 2 Timothy 1:9, and chapters 9 through 11 of Romans.

6. The text even of traditional hymns can change over the years. All quotations in this study are taken from *The Hymnal, 1982* (New York: Church Hymnal Corp., 1985), the official hymnal of the Episcopal Church.

7. More than ten American colleges claim colonial founding. But in all cases these claims stem from an institution's decision that a parson's school or classical academy in their area—what Americans would today call a primary or secondary school—was the direct ancestor of their college. In the twentieth century, as colleges adopted new institutional ancestors, some changed their founding date several times. Thus one four-year college in Maryland now lists its date of founding as 1696, though a history of the college published in 1890 "by the Alumni Association" is titled *1789–1889: Commemoration of the One Hundredth Anniversary of* (the college's name follows). On this subject the overriding question has to be, Did a college exist at this place in the year claimed? Uniformly applied, this criterion would change the dates of founding of some of the ten colonial colleges named in this study, for many started their first students at a pre-college level to prepare them for study at a level intended to equal that of Oxford and Cambridge or Calvin's Genevan Academy. But all ten institutions would still have genuine founding dates in the colonial period.

8. Edwin S. Gaustad, *Sworn on the Altar of God: A Religious Biography of Thomas Jefferson* (Grand Rapids, MI: Wm. B. Eerdmans, 1995), 164. Adams's list includes three kinds of Unitarians.

9. Winthrop S. Hudson and John Corrigan, *Religion in America*, 5th ed. (New York: Macmillan, 1992), 30.

10. Maryland Toleration Act of 1649. [Online] Available: www.mdarchives. state.md.us/msa/speccol/sc2200/sc2221/000025/html/titlepage.html.

11. Maryland Toleration Act of 1649, ibid.

12. Edward C. Papenfuse, Jr., *An Act Concerning Religion: April 21, 1649: an Interpretation and Tribute to the Citizen Legislators of Maryland: with an Appendix Containing an Act Concerning Religion, passed April 21, 1649, by the Maryland General Assembly, and an Act for the Relief of the Jews in Maryland, passed February [sic] 26, 1825, by the Maryland General Assembly* (Annapolis: Maryland State Archives, 1999). [Online] Available: www.mdarchives.state.md.us/msa/speccol/sc2200/sc2221/000025/html/titlepage.html.

13. A practicing Anglican, Byrd meant by "superstition" that the North Carolinians seemed to lack a sense of the supernatural. Hugh F. Lefler, ed., *North Carolina History Told by Contemporaries* (Chapel Hill: University of North Carolina Press, 1934), 56.

14. *Colonial Records of North Carolina*, ed. William L. Saunders, 10 vols. (Raleigh: P. M. Hale State Printer, 1887), 1: 601–602.

15. "The Spiritual Travels of Nathan Cole," *William and Mary Quarterly* 33, no. 1 (1976): 2–3, paragraphing added.

16. This discussion of George Whitefield's oratorical ability is found in chapter 8 of Benjamin Franklin's autobiography. Paragraphing has been added.

17. Walter Isaacson, *Benjamin Franklin: An American Life* (New York: Simon and Schuster, 2003), 110.
18. The quotation is from Paul Johnson, *A History of the American People* (New York: HarperCollins, 1997), 109.
19. Daniel Preston, ed., *The Papers of James Monroe: A Documentary History of the Presidential Tours of James Monroe* (Westport, CT: Greenwood Press, 2003), 1: 123.

Chapter 3: The Enlightenment Religion of Deism

1. Moncure C. Conway, ed., *The Writings of Thomas Paine*, 4 vols. (New York: G. P. Putnam's Sons, 1894–96), 4: 322.
2. L. W. Gibson, "Deism," in A. A. Benson, ed., *The Church Cyclopedia* (New York: M. H. Mallory, 1883), 224, italics added.
3. Quoted in Robert T. Handy, *A Christian America: Protestant Hopes and Historical Realities* (New York: Oxford University Press, 1984), 15–16.
4. *Paine versus religion, or, Christianity triumphant: containing the interesting letters of Sam. Adams, Tho. Paine, and John Gemmil: to which is added, Mr. Erskine's celebrated speech at the trial of the age of reason* (Baltimore: G. Douglas, 1803), 6–7, paragraphing added.
5. Thomas Paine, *The Age of Reason*, ed. Philip S. Foner (Secaucus, NJ: Citadel Press, 1974), 55, 162–163.
6. *Pain versus religion . . .*, 8.
7. Paine, *The Age of Reason*, 68.
8. Gaustad, *Sworn on the Altar*, 34–41. The descriptions come from Anthony Ashley Cooper, Third Earl of Shaftesbury, and Elihu Palmer.
9. The poet was Philip Freneau (1752–1832). For the poem, see [Online] Available: www.americanpoems.com/poets/philipfreneau/ onthe.shtml.
10. *Paine versus religion . . .*, 6.
11. Paine, *The Age of Reason*, 50.
12. The quotation can be found in Part I of Paine's *The Rights of Man*. See, for instance, Thomas Paine, *The Complete Writings of Thomas Paine*, ed. Philip S. Foner, 2 vols. (New York: Citadel Press, 1945), 1: 293.
13. Denis Diderot. The phrase appears in his posthumous "Dithyramb on the Festival of Kings."

Chapter 4: The Founding Fathers and Deism

1. William Meade, *Old Churches, Ministers and Families of Virginia*, 2 vols. (Baltimore: Genealogical Publishing, 1966), 1: 175.
2. Meade, *Old Churches*, 2: 99.

Chapter 5: The Religious Views of Benjamin Franklin

1. Isaacson, *Benjamin Franklin*, 19.
2. A. Owen Aldridge, "The Alleged Puritanism of Benjamin Franklin," in *Reappraising Benjamin Franklin: A Bicentennial Perspective*, ed. J. A. Leo Lemay (Newark: University of Delaware Press, 1993), 370.
3. Benjamin Franklin, "On the Providence of God in the Government of the World," in *The Papers of Benjamin Franklin*, eds. Leonard W. Labaree, et al. (New Haven: Yale University Press, 1959–), 1: 264.
4. Franklin, *The Papers of Benjamin Franklin*, ed. Labaree, 9: 121.
5. Franklin B. Dexter, ed., *The Literary Diary of Ezra Stiles*, 3 vols. (New York: C. Scribner's Sons, 1901), 3: 387.
6. Isaacson, *Benjamin Franklin*, 470.

Chapter 6: The Religious Views of George Washington

1. James Abercrombie, quoted in Paul Boller, *George Washington and Religion* (Dallas: Southern Methodist University Press, 1963), 18.
2. John Jay, *The Correspondence and Public Papers of John Jay,* ed. Henry P. Johnston, 4 vols. (New York: Burt Franklin, 1970), 3: 381.
3. Meade, *Old Churches*, 2: 92.
4. Nelly Custis Lewis to Jared Sparks, 26 February 1833, in Frank Grizzard, *The Ways of Providence: Religion and George Washington* (Buena Vista, VA: Mariner, 2005), 49.
5. For an assessment of Washington's religion by an evangelical author that mingles scholarly methodology with an occasional lack of caution with regard to sources, see John Eidsmoe, *Christianity and the Constitution: The Faith of Our Founding Fathers* (Grand Rapids, MI: Baker Books, 1987), 113–143, especially 113–115 and 132–134.
6. Nelly Custis (Mrs. Eleanor Parke Custis Lewis) lived for twenty years with her adoptive parents at Mount Vernon. In 1833, at the request of the first editor of Washington's papers—Jared Sparks—she wrote down her memories of Washington's religious practices. Sparks reprinted her letter in George Washington, *Writings of George Washington*, ed. Jared Sparks, 12 vols. (Boston: American Stationers, 1834–37), 12: 406.
7. Bird Wilson, *Memoir of the Life of the Right Reverend William White, D.D., Bishop of the Protestant Episcopal Church in the State of Pennsylvania* (Philadelphia: James Kay, 1839), 197.
8. James Abercrombie to Origen Bacheler, 29 November 1831, in *Magazine of American History*, 13 (June 1885), 597. See also Boller, *George Washington*, 33–34. The phrase about "repetitive patterns" comes from C. P. Snow, *In Their Wisdom* (New York: Scribner, 1974), 144.

9. Alf J. Mapp, Jr., *The Faiths of Our Fathers: What America's Founders Really Believed* (Lanham, MD: Rowman and Littlefield, 2003), 69.
10. See the highly useful list of such terms in Grizzard, *The Ways,* 4–5.
11. Quoted in Grizzard, *The Ways,* 28–47.
12. For Washington's description of "the miraculous care of Providence, that protected me beyond all human expectation" during the French and Indian War, see Grizzard, *The Ways,* 6. Grizzard, 29–47, also reprints a series of letters sent by Washington to diverse religious groups in the new republic.
13. James Madison, *A Nation Mourns: Bishop James Madison's Memorial Eulogy on the Death of George Washington,* ed. David L. Holmes (Mount Vernon, VA: Mount Vernon Ladies' Association, 1999).
14. Woodrow Wilson, *George Washington* (New York: Harper and Brothers, 1896), 227.
15. See such works as Peter Marshall and David Manuel, *The Light and the Glory* (Grand Rapids, MI: Revell, 1977); Tim LaHaye, *Faith of Our Founding Fathers* (Green Forest, AR: Master Books, 1994); John Eidsmoe, *Christianity and the Constitution* (Grand Rapids, MI: Baker Books, 1987); William Federer, *America's God and Country: Encyclopedia of Quotations* (Coppell, TX: Fame, 1994); Verna Hall, *The Christian History of the American Revolution: Consider and Ponder* (San Francisco: Foundation for American Christian Education, 1976); Benjamin Hart, *Faith and Freedom: The Christian Roots of American Liberty* (Dallas, TX: Lewis and Stanley, 1988); and the various publications of the Providence Foundation of Charlottesville, Virginia. Evangelical leaders such as Pat Robertson and Jerry Falwell also preach and publish on the subject.
16. *New York Herald Tribune,* 26 May 1902.
17. For a good analysis of the discrepancies in the story about Washington's praying at Valley Forge, see Grizzard, *The Ways,* 19–24.
18. Grizzard, *The Ways,* 19–24.
19. Nelly Custis Lewis to Jared Sparks, 26 February 1833, in Grizzard, *The Ways,* 48–49.
20. For a thorough analysis of the reliability of the stories of Weems and other early writers on Washington's religion, see Boller, 3–44.
21. Herbert Baxter Adams, *The Life and Writings of Jared Sparks: Comprising Selections from His Journals and Correspondence,* 2 vols. (Boston: Houghton Mifflin, 1893), 1: 565.

Chapter 7: The Religious Views of John Adams

1. The Council of Nicea (325, in modern-day Turkey) and the First Council of Constantinople (381, in modern-day Istanbul).

2. The founding fathers who were Anglican would have been familiar with the Nicene Creed from the 1662 Book of Common Prayer, where it appears in the service entitled "The Order of the Administration of the Lord's Supper, or Holy Communion."
3. The Athanasian Creed appears in the service for Morning Prayer in the English Book of Common Prayer, sometimes under the title *Quicunque Vult*.
4. From the First Parish Church in Quincy, MA. [Online] Available: www.ufpc.org/history/ministers.htm [18 July 2005].
5. John Adams to Benjamin Rush, 21 January 1810, in *Microfilms of the Adams Papers*, 608 reels (Boston: Massachusetts Historical Society, 1954–1959), reel 118.
6. Adams, *Diary*, 1: 42–44.
7. John Adams to Thomas Jefferson, 19 April 1817, in *Microfilms of the Adams Papers*, reel 123.
8. John Adams to John Quincy Adams, 15 November 1816, in *Microfilms of the Adams Papers*, reel 123.

Chapter 8: The Religious Views of Thomas Jefferson

1. Gaustad, *Sworn on the Altar*, xiii–xiv.
2. The quotations can be found in Query XVII, "religion," in any edition of *Notes on the State of Virginia*. See, for example, Thomas Jefferson, *Notes on the State of Virginia*, ed. Frank Shuffelton (New York: Penguin Books, 1999), 163–167.
3. Gaustad, *Sworn on the Altar*, 92.
4. Paine, *The Age of Reason*, 55, 66.
5. Thomas Jefferson to John Adams, 22 August 1813.
6. See, for example, Thomas Jefferson to Benjamin Waterhouse, 28 June 1822; Thomas Jefferson to William Short, 13 April 1820; Thomas Jefferson to Salma Hale, 28 July 1818. All are in Thomas Jefferson, *The Writings of Thomas Jefferson*, ed. Albert E. Bergh, 20 vols. (Washington, DC: Issued under the auspices of the Thomas Jefferson Memorial Association of the United States, 1907).
7. Thomas Jefferson to Benjamin Rush, 21 April 1803, in *The Writings of Thomas Jefferson*, ed. Bergh, 10: 379–380.
8. Thomas Jefferson to William Short, 13 April 1820, in *The Writings of Thomas Jefferson*, ed. Bergh, 15: 244–245.
9. Thomas Jefferson, "Jesus, Socrates, and Others—Letter to Dr. Joseph Priestley, April 9, 1803," in Thomas Jefferson, *The Library of America: Jefferson: Writings*, ed. Merrill D. Peterson (New York: Literary Classics of the U.S., 1984), 1120.

10. Thomas Jefferson to William Short, 13 April 1820, in *The Writings of Thomas Jefferson,* ed. Bergh, 15: 243–248. By Presbyterian, Jefferson meant Calvinist clergy of British origin, especially the New England Congregationalists.

11. Meade, *Old Churches,* 2: 52.

12. Meade, *Old Churches,* 2: 48–51, 61.

13. Thomas Jefferson to Jared Sparks, 4 November 1820, in *Thomas Jefferson: A Chronology of His Thoughts,* ed. Jerry Holmes (Lanham, MD: Rowman and Littlefield, 2002), 285.

14. William Meade, *Sermon, delivered in the Rotunda of the University of Virginia, on Sunday, May 24, 1829. On the occasion of the deaths of nine young men . . .* (Charlottesville: F. Carr, 1829). See also Meade, *Old Churches,* 2: 53–56.

15. Meade, *Old Churches,* 2: 55.

16. Jefferson's descriptions may be found in Thomas Jefferson to Jared Sparks, 4 November 1820; Thomas Jefferson to James Smith, 8 December 1822; Thomas Jefferson to Benjamin Waterhouse, 26 June 1822; Thomas Jefferson to Benjamin Waterhouse, 19 July 1822. All are in *The Writings of Thomas Jefferson,* ed. Bergh. See 15: 287–288, 408–410, 383–385, 390–392.

17. Thomas Jefferson to Benjamin Waterhouse, 19 July 1822, in *The Writings of Thomas Jefferson,* ed. Bergh, 15: 390–392.

18. Thomas Jefferson to John Adams, 22 August 1813, in *The Writings of Thomas Jefferson,* ed. Bergh.

19. Thomas Jefferson to Justin Pierre Plumard Derieux, 25 July 1788, in *The Papers of Thomas Jefferson,* ed. Julian P. Boyd et al., 30 vols. (Princeton, NJ: Princeton University Press, 1950–), 13: 418.

20. Thomas Jefferson to Benjamin Waterhouse, 26 June 1822, in *The Writings of Thomas Jefferson,* ed. Bergh, 13: 350.

21. Thomas Jefferson Coolidge, "Jefferson in His Family," in *The Writings of Thomas Jefferson,* ed. Bergh, 15: iv.

22. Thomas Jefferson to Ezra Stiles Ely, 25 June 1819, in Dickinson W. Adams, ed., *Jefferson's Extracts from the Gospels* (Princeton: Princeton University Press, 1983), 386–387.

Chapter 9: The Religious Views of James Madison

1. Meade, *Old Churches,* 2: 99–100.

2. Dorothy A. Boyd-Rush, "Molding a Founding Father," *Montpelier* (Spring 2003). [Online] Available: www.jmu.edu/montpelier/2003Spring/MoldingA FoundingFather.shtml [16 July 2005]; Meade, *Old Churches,* 2: 99–100.

3. Meade, *Old Churches,* 2: 89; cf. 100.

4. Meade, *Old Churches,* 2: 91–92.

5. George Ticknor, *Life, Letters, and Journals of George Ticknor,* ed. George Stillman Hillard, 2 vols. (Boston; Houghton Mifflin, 1909), 1: 29–30.

6. Gaustad, *Sworn on the Altar*, 139.
7. William Stevens Perry, ed., *Journals of General Conventions of the Protestant Episcopal Church in the United States, 1785–1835* (Claremont, NH: The Claremont Manufacturing Company, 1874), 1: 60.
8. James Madison to Frederick Beasley, 20 November 1825, in James Madison, *The Writings of James Madison*, ed. Gaillard Hunt (New York: G .P. Putnam's Sons, 1910), 9: 229–231.
9. Sarah ("Sally") Coles Stevenson to Dolley Payne Madison, December 1835, in *DMDE*.
10. For information on Sally Coles Stevenson's religious views, see Edward Boykin, ed., *Victoria, Albert, and Mrs. Stevenson* (New York: Rinehart, 1957), and Francis F. Wayland, *Andrew Stevenson: Democrat and Diplomat* (Philadelphia: University of Pennsylvania Press, 1949).
11. Meade's information about Madison's religious faith is found in his *Old Churches*, 2: 100.
12. David Mattern, senior associate editor of the James Madison Papers, to David L. Holmes, 20 July 2005, letter in my possession.
13. Madison to Beasley, 20 November 1825, in *Writings of James Madison*, ed., Hunt, 9: 229–231.
14. Meade, *Old Churches*, 2: 100.

Chapter 10: The Religious Views of James Monroe

1. James Monroe to Peter Duponceau, 11 April 1778, in Duponceau Papers, J. R. Tyson Transcripts, Historical Society of Pennsylvania. The original of this letter has disappeared. Only the transcript made in earlier decades by a researcher remains.
2. Thomas Jefferson to Peter Carr, 10 August 1787, in *The Writings of Thomas Jefferson*, ed. Paul Leicester Ford, 10 vols. (New York: G. P. Putnam's Sons, 1892–99), 4: 429–432.
3. A convenient source for the correspondence between Jefferson and Adams upon Abigail's death is James B. Peabody, ed., *John Adams: A Biography in His Own Words* (New York: Harper and Row, 1973), 404–405.
4. Meade, *Old Churches*, 2: 50–52.
5. Monroe, *The Papers of James Monroe*, ed. Preston, 1: 123.
6. Bliss Isely, *The Presidents: Men of Faith* (Boston: W. A. Wilde, 1953), 38.
7. I am indebted to David Voelkel, former curator/assistant director of the James Monroe Museum in Fredericksburg, Virginia, for this information.
8. I am indebted for many observations about Monroe and his correspondence to Daniel Preston, editor of *The Papers of James Monroe* at University of Mary Washington.

9. John Quincy Adams, *The Lives of James Madison and James Monroe: Fourth and Fifth Presidents of the United States* (Buffalo: G. H. Derby, 1850), 293–295.

Chapter 11: The Wives and Daughters of the Founding Fathers

1. I am indebted to the independent-study papers done at the College of William and Mary during the spring semester of 2005 by Ms. Jennie A. Davy and Mr. Robert G. Menna for some of the ideas expressed in the next three chapters.

2. Three recent and well-regarded studies of the role of women in American religion cover a wide range of topics but do not discuss Deism: Susan Hill Lindley's *You Have Stept Out of Your Place: A History of Women and Religion in America* (Louisville: Westminster John Knox Press, 1996); Catherine A. Brekus's *Strangers and Pilgrims: Female Preaching in America, 1740–1845* (Chapel Hill: University of North Carolina Press, 1998); and Joan R. Gundersen's *To Be Useful to the World: Women in Revolutionary America, 1740–1790* (New York: Simon and Schuster, 1996).

3. Catherine L. Albanese, *America, Religions and Religion*, 3rd ed. (Belmont, CA: Wadsworth, 1999), 440. Cf. 410, 441–442.

4. John Toland, *Christianity Not Mysterious* (New York: Garland Press, 1978). Initially published in 1696.

5. Martha Washington, *Worthy Partner: The Papers of Martha Washington*, ed. Joseph E. Fields (Westport, CT: Greenwood Press, 1994), 127, 224, 229.

6. Washington, *Worthy Partner*, 291.

7. Quoted in Grizzard, *The Ways*, 49.

8. Wilson, *Memoir of the Life*, 189.

9. Grizzard, *The Ways*, 48.

10. Margaret Conkling, *Memoirs of the Mother and Wife of Washington* (New York: Derby, Miller, 1980), 246–248.

11. Grizzard, *The Ways*, 49.

12. See Patricia Brady, ed., *George Washington's Beautiful Nelly: The Letters of Eleanor Parke Custis Lewis to Elizabeth Bordley Gibson, 1794–1851* (Columbia: University of South Carolina Press, 1991), 3–4, 16, and E. P. Lewis [hereafter "Lewis"] to Elizabeth Bordley Gibson [hereafter "Gibson"], 3 January 1822, in Brady, *George Washington's Beautiful Nelly*, 118.

13. Lewis to Gibson, 10 August [1824], in Brady, *George Washington's Beautiful Nelly*, 152.

14. Lewis to Gibson, 9 February 1834, in Brady, *George Washington's Beautiful Nelly*, 214–215.

15. Lewis to Gibson, 17 December 1848, in Brady, *George Washington's Beautiful Nelly*, 252.

16. See, for example, Brady, *George Washington's Beautiful Nelly*, 89, 190.

17. Brady, *George Washington's Beautiful Nelly,* 78, 190, 79, 105, 106, 231.
18. Lewis to Gibson, 1 March 1815, in Brady, *George Washington's Beautiful Nelly,* 78.
19. Lewis to Gibson, 27 November 1820, in Brady, *George Washington's Beautiful Nelly,* 93–94.
20. Lewis to Gibson, 3 October 1847, in Brady, *George Washington's Beautiful Nelly,* 250.
21. Lewis to Gibson, 27 July 1850, in Brady, *George Washington's Beautiful Nelly,* 254.
22. Lewis to Gibson, 22 March 1821, in Brady, *George Washington's Beautiful Nelly,* 107.
23. Brady, *George Washington's Beautiful Nelly,* 16.
24. Laurie Carter Noble, "Abigail Adams," The Unitarian Universalist Historical Society, 1999. [Online] Available: www.uua.org/uuhs/duub/aricles/abigail adams.html. In his two-volume compendium of biographies of Congregationalist clergy, *Annals of the American Pulpit: Volumes I, II: Trinitarian Congregationalism* (New York: Arno Press and the New York Times, 1969), William B. Sprague gives Smith (1: 67n.) only a brief footnote.
25. Cokie Roberts, *Founding Mothers: The Women Who Raised Our Nation* (New York: HarperCollins, 2004), 61.
26. Edith B. Gelles, *Portia: The World of Abigail Adams* (Bloomington: Indiana University Press, 1992), 21–22.
27. Abigail Smith Adams to John Quincy Adams, 20 March 1780, *The Letters of Mrs. Adams,* ed. Charles Francis Adams, 2 vols. (Boston: Charles C. Little and James Brown, 1840), 1: 147–148
28. Abigail Smith Adams to Mrs. Shaw, 21 November 1786, in *The Letters of Mrs. Adams* 2: 160–161.
29. Abigail Smith Adams, letter to John Quincy Adams, 5 May 1816, *Adams Papers,* Massachusetts Historical Society, Boston.
30. Quoted in Galles, *Portia,* 168. "So convulsive was the blow of her daughter's death," Gelles mistakenly declares, "that Abigail reverted to Trinitarian doctrine." Although Abigail's words in no way exclude belief in the Trinity, the passage is not Trinitarian in itself. Rather, the quotation is representative of the high Christology held by so many New England Unitarians of the time. Nowhere does it equate Jesus and the Holy Spirit with God.
31. Abigail Smith Adams to Abigail Adams Smith, 10 March 1794, *Letters of Mrs. Adams,* 2: 229.
32. Thomas Jefferson to the Marquis de Chastellux, 26 November 1782. [Online] Available: www.yale.edu/lawweb/avalon/jefflett/let19.htm.
33. Quoted in Merrill D. Peterson, *Thomas Jefferson and the New Nation: A Biography* (London: Oxford University Press, 1970), 295.
34. Sarah N. Randolph, *The Domestic Life of Thomas Jefferson* (Cambridge, MA: University Press, 1939), 114–115. Paragraphing added.
35. Randolph, *Domestic Life,* 114–115. Paragraphing added.

36. Joseph J. Ellis, *American Sphinx: The Character of Thomas Jefferson* (New York: Alfred A. Knopf, 1997), 91, 116.
37. Randolph, *Domestic Life,* 250. In the letter, Jefferson declares that he is sending her Priestley's history of the corruptions of Christianity, which he declares has had an important influence on his religious views. "My family by possessing this," he writes, "should be enabled to estimate the libels published against me on this . . . subject."
38. Thomas Jefferson to Martha Jefferson, 11 December 1783, in Randolph, *Domestic Life*, 45.
39. This story is repeated often. The example quoted is taken from www.fee.org/vnews/php?nid=3382.
40. Dolley Payne Todd Madison to Margaret Bayard Smith, 31 August 1834, in *DMDE*.
41. Conover Hunt-Jones, *Dolley and the "Great Little Madison"* (Washington, DC: American Institute of Architects Foundation, 1977), 7–8.
42. Quoted in Hunt-Jones, *Dolley and the "Great Little Madison,"* 12.
43. Dolley Payne Todd Madison to Elizabeth Brooke Ellicott, [December 1788], in *DMDE*.
44. Dolley Payne Todd Madison to Elizabeth (Eliza) Collins Lee, 16 September [1794], in *DMDE*.
45. Katharine Susan Anthony, *Dolley Madison* (Garden City, NY: Doubleday, 1949), 92.
46. Quoted in Virginia Moore, *The Madisons: A Biography* (New York: McGraw-Hill, 1979), 354.
47. Lucia B. Cutts, ed., *Memoirs and Letters of Dolley Madison: Wife of James Madison, President of the United States* (Boston: Houghton Mifflin, 1887), 72.
48. Dolley Payne Todd Madison to Edward Coles, 13 May 1813, in *DMDE*.
49. Dolley Payne Todd Madison to Anna Payne Cutts, 23 April 1827, in *DMDE*. The preacher was Harriet Livermore, an evangelical who taught the imminent Second Coming of Jesus. She was invited to speak before the House of Representatives four times.
50. Dolley Payne Todd Madison to Anna Payne Cutts, 19 August [1805], in *DMDE*.
51. Anthony, *Dolley Madison,* 381–382.
52. Dolley Payne Todd Madison to Richard D. Cutts, 16 July 1845, in *The Letters of Dolley Payne Madison*, 380–381.
53. Meade, *Old Churches, 2*: 99–100.
54. Dolley Payne Todd Madison to Eliza Vail Longueville, 24 August 1832, in *DMDE*. See, for example, Dolley Payne Todd Madison to Walter Coles Cutts, 21 November 1823, in *DMDE*.
55. Mason Locke Weems to Dolley Payne Todd Madison, 22 July 1813, in *DMDE*.
56. Dolley Madison to Frances Dandridge Henley Lear, 6 October 1832, in *DMDE*.
57. Dolley Madison to Mary Elizabeth Cutts, 1 August 1833, in *DMDE*.

58. Roberts, *Founding Mothers*, 269.
59. Hunt-Jones, *Dolley and the "Great Little Madison,"* 13.
60. Mary Ormsbee Whitton, quoted in Hunt-Jones, *Dolley and the "Great Little Madison,"* 11.

Chapter 12: A Layperson's Guide to Distinguishing a Deist from an Orthodox Christian

1. Steven Morris, excerpt from *Free Inquiry*. [Online] Available: www.sullivancounty.com/news/ffnc/ [20 August 2005].
2. Gordon C. Wood, *The Radicalism of the American Revolution* (New York: Vintage Books, 1991), 330.
3. LaHaye, *Faith*, 6.
4. LaHaye, *Faith*, 12.
5. These titles are all from LaHaye, *Faith*.
6. LaHaye, *Faith*, 15.
7. All denominations except the Quakers held services of Holy Communion.
8. Romans 5:8.

Chapter 13: Three Orthodox Christians

1. Samuel Adams, *The Life and Public Services of Samuel Adams*, ed. William B. Wells, 3 vols., 2nd ed. (Freeport, NY: Books for Libraries Press, 1969), 3: 427–429. Wells was Adams's great-grandson.
2. Adams, *Life and Public Services of Adams*, 1: 3.
3. Paul Lewis, *The Grand Incendiary: A Biography of Samuel Adams* (New York: The Daily Press, 1973), 7.
4. Lewis, *The Grand Incendiary*, x.
5. John Adams's Diary 11, 23 December 1765 [electronic edition], *Adams Family Papers: An Electronic Archive*, Massachusetts Historical Society. [Online] Available: www.masshist.org/digitaladams/.
6. Total depravity, unconditional election, limited atonement, irresistible grace, and perseverance of the saints. Taken together, they describe the workings of a God who predestines humans to heaven and to hell.
7. Adams, *Life and Public Services of Adams*, 1: 87; John Adams's Diary 11, 23 December 1765 [electronic edition], *Adams Family Papers: An Electronic Archive*, Massachusetts Historical Society. [Online] Available: www.masshist.org/digitaladams/.
8. Samuel Adams, *The Writings of Samuel Adams*, ed. Harry Alonzo Cushing, 4 vols. (New York: Octagon Books, 1968), 4: 52, 4: 385, 4: 201, 4: 52, 4: 407.

9. "Last Will and Testament of Samuel Adams," in Adams, *Life and Public Services of Adams*, 3: 379; "Will of Mrs. Elizabeth Adams," in Adams, *Life and Public Services of Adams*, 3: 399.
10. Mark A. Noll, *A History of Christianity in the United States and Canada* (Grand Rapids, MI: Wm. B. Eerdmans, 1992), 34.
11. K. L. Sprunger, "Covenant Theology," in *Dictionary of Christianity in America*, ed. Daniel G. Reed (Downers Grove, IL: InterVarsity Press, 1990), 322–324.
12. John Winthrop, "A Modell of Christian Charity," in Hanover Historical Texts Project. [Online] Available http://history.hanover.edu/texts/winthmod.html [15 July 2005].
13. John K. Alexander, *Samuel Adams: America's Revolutionary Politician* (Lanham, MD: Rowman and Littlefield, 2002), 146.
14. Samuel Adams to Elizabeth Adams, 11 December 1776, in Adams, *Writings*, 3: 326.
15. Samuel Adams to John Scollay, 30 December 1780, in Adams, *Writings*, 4: 238
16. "Proclamation," 19 February 1794, in Adams, *Writings*, 4: 361.
17. Alexander, *Samuel Adams*, 231.
18. Thomas Paine, *Paine versus religion, or, Christianity triumphant* (Baltimore: G. Douglas, 1803), 6.
19. Ibid.
20. Adams, *Life and Public Services of Adams*, 2: 429–430.
21. Quoted in Alexander, *Samuel Adams*, 220.
22. William Tennent officiated at the wedding ceremony of Elias Boudinot and Hannah Stockton, demonstrating the religious sentiments that the couple shared.
23. Donald W. Whisenhunt, "Elias Boudinot," New Jersey State Library: New Jersey's Revolutionary Experience, 1975. [Online] Available: www.njstatelib. org/NJ_Information/Digital_Collections/Revolution/Boudinot.pdf. [12 July 2005].
24. George Hills Morgan, *History of the Church in Burlington, New Jersey* (Trenton: W. S. Sharp, 1885), 384, 388, 465.
25. See George Adams Boyd, *Elias Boudinot: Patriot and Statesman, 1740–1821* (Princeton: Princeton University Press, 1952), 279 and *passim;* Elias Boudinot, *The Life, Public Services, Addresses and Letters of Elias Boudinot, LL.D., President of the Continental Congress*, ed. J. J. Boudinot (Boston: Houghton Mifflin, 1896), 2: 31 and *passim*; Boudinot, *Life,* 124; Boyd, 286; Boudinot, *Life,* 357; Boyd, 252, 255, 261, 286, 278. Boudinot's capitalization is inconsistent.
26. Elias Boudinot, *The Age of Revelation or The Age of Reason Shewn to be An Age of Infidelity*, reprinted at The Belcher Foundation, n.d. [Online] Available: www.belcherfoundation.org/boudinot.htm [12 July 2005].
27. Elias Boudinot, *The Age of Revelation* [Online].

28. Elias Boudinot, *The Age of Revelation* [Online].
29. Elias Boudinot, *Memoirs of the Rev. William Tennent* (Kingston, NY: Zenas Covel, 1813).
30. "The Remarkable Trance of William Tennent (1705–1777)," *Theology Today*, 34. Rev. July 1977. [Online] Available: http://theologytoday.ptsem.edu/jul1977/v34-2-article6.htm. [12 July 2005].
31. See Elias Boudinot, *The Second Advent, or coming of the Messiah in glory* (Trenton, NJ: D. Fenton and S. Hutchinson, 1815).
32. William Rehnquist, dissenting opinion in *Wallace v. Jaffrey*, argued 1984, decided 1985.
33. Quoted in Walter Stahr, *John Jay: Founding Father* (New York: Hambledon and London, 2005), 378.
34. John Jay, *The Correspondence and Public Papers of John Jay*, ed. Henry P. Johnston, 4 vols. (New York: Burt Franklin, 1970), 4: 504.
35. Timothy Dwight, *Travels in New England and New York*, ed. Barbara Miller Solomon (Cambridge, MA: Harvard University Press, 1969), 3: 148.
36. Jay, *Correspondence*, 1: 102–120; quoted in Stahr, *John Jay*, 342. The lengthy letter to Murray is useful for an overall view of Jay's religious beliefs. See Jay, *Correspondence*, 4: 403–419.
37. John Jay, *John Jay: The Winning of the Peace: Unpublished Papers, 1780–1784*, ed. Richard B. Morris, 2 vols. (New York: Harper and Row, 1980), 2: 531.
38. "Address to Trinity Church Corporation," in Jay, *Correspondence*, 4: 511.
39. Jay, *Correspondence*, 4: 502.
40. Stahr, *John Jay*, 384.
41. Jay, *Correspondence*, 4: 515; Stahr, 388; Jay, *Correspondence*, 3: 516.

Chapter 14: The Past Is a Foreign Country

1. Bird Wilson, *Untitled Sermon Reported in the Albany Daily Advertiser* on 29 October 1831.
2. To see the variety of arguments about Washington's religion, readers need only search the web for the words "Founding Fathers religion" or "George Washington religion." The quotation comes from an interview in the summer of 2000 with Mark Beliles of the Providence Foundation.
3. Wilson, *Memoir of . . . White*, 193.
4. This rich description is found in "Benjamin Franklin," *Concise Dictionary of American Biography* (New York: Scribner, 1964), 312. Later editions of the work continue to use it.
5. L. P. Hartley, *The Go-Between* (New York: Penguin Books, 1997), prologue.

Epilogue

1. Marjorie Hyer, "Episcopalian Ford Serious on Religion," *Washington Post*, 7 December 1973.

2. James T. Baker, *A Southern Baptist in the White House* (Philadelphia: Westminster Press, 1977), 36; paragraphing added.

3. E. Brooks Holifield, "The Three Strands of Jimmy Carter's Religion," *The New Republic* (5 June 1976), 16.

4. Jimmy Carter, *Sharing Good Times* (New York: Simon and Schuster, 2004), 45–47.

5. Kiron K. Skinner et al., *Reagan: A Life in Letters* (New York: Simon and Schuster, 2003), 276.

6. Mary Beth Brown, *Hand of Providence* (Nashville: Nelson Current, 2004), 88.

7. Garry Wills, *Reagan's America* (New York: Doubleday, 1987), 25.

8. Wills, 25.

9. Ronald Reagan, *An American Life* (New York: Simon and Schuster, 1990), 56.

10. Wills, 12ff; Richard V. Pierard and Robert D. Linder, *Civil Religion and the Presidency* (Grand Rapids: Academie Books, 1988), 18.

11. Anne Edwards, *Early Reagan* (New York: William Morrow, 1987), 145–146.

12. Following her divorce, Jane Wyman converted to Roman Catholicism, a religious change that required her to secure annulments of her two previous marriages. She insisted that Maureen and Michael be raised as Roman Catholics, though they later followed diverse paths religiously. For a time the church publicized her as a convert, but her subsequent marital history dimmed her appeal.

13. Rob Moll, "Pastoring a Wounded President," interview with Louis Evans, in *Christianity Today*, 22 June 2004. [Online] Available: www.christianity today.com/ct/2004/125/22.0.html (8 June 2005).

14. Dinesh D'Souza, *Ronald Reagan: How an Ordinary Man Became an Extraordinary Leader* (New York: The Free Press, 1997), 213.

15. William E. Pemberton, *Exit with Honor: The Life and Presidency of Ronald Reagan* (Armonk, NY: M. E. Sharpe, 1997), 10.

16. Moll, "Pastoring a Wounded President."

17. Interview with Sam Donaldson, quoted in Adriana Bosch, *Reagan: An American Story* (New York: TV Books, 1998), 187; capitalization changed.

18. Paul Kengor, "Robin and Growing Up," Catholic Educator's Resource Center. [Online] Rev. 2004 Available: http://catholiceducation.org/articles/catholic_stories/cs0123.html [June 17, 2005].

19. George H. W. Bush, "Peking China Diary," 281; Barbara Bush, *Barbara Bush: A Memoir* (New York: Charles Scribner's Sons, 1994), 114. Available online: http://bushlibrary.tamu.edu/research/chinadiary.html.

20. George Bush, *All the Best, George Bush: My Life in Letters and Other Writings* (New York: Scribner, 1999), 501.
21. Bush, *All the Best*, 504.
22. Bill Clinton, *My Life* (New York: Alfred A. Knopf, 2004), 27.
23. Clinton, *My Life*, 27.
24. Quoted in David Maraniss, *First in His Class: A Biography of Bill Clinton* (New York: Simon and Schuster, 1995), 35.
25. Clinton, *My Life, 25.* Nigel Hamilton, *Bill Clinton: An American Journey* (New York: Random House, 2003), 102, places the baptism on 17 October 1956, when Clinton was ten.
26. Clinton, *My Life*, 239–240.
27. Clinton, *My Life,* 40, 47.
28. Clinton, *My Life*, 39.
29. Maraniss, *First in His Class,* 50, 52; Clinton, *My Life*, 71.
30. Maraniss, *First in His Class,* 58; Clinton, *My Life*, 76.
31. Hillary Rodham Clinton, *Living History* (New York: Simon and Schuster, 2003), 22. A Lutheran pastor, Bonhoeffer was executed in Nazi Germany in 1945. Reinhold Niebuhr was one of the leading voices in twentieth-century American Protestantism.
32. Hillary Clinton, *Living History,* 22–23.
33. James M. Wall, "A Visit to the White House," *The Christian Century* 110 (April 7, 1993), 355.
34. The three were J. Philip Wogaman, an ethicist, former seminary dean, and senior minister at Foundry Methodist Church; Tony Campolo, a minister, professor, and author identified with the progressive wing of evangelicalism; and Gordon MacDonald, a Massachusetts evangelical who had once lost both his pastorate and the presidency of an influential evangelical organization when he admitted to an adulterous affair.
35. Hamilton, 72.
36. David M. Bresnahan, "Clinton's Trouble in the Pulpit: Another Southern Baptist Pastor Turns on Him," World Net Daily, 4 September 1998. [Online] Available: http://ads.wnd.com/news/article.asp?ARTICLE_ID=16701.
37. Dick Morris, *Behind the Oval Office* (Los Angeles: Renaissance Books, 1999), xiv.
38. Clinton, *My Life,* 252.
39. Peter Schweizer and Rochelle Schweizer, *The Bushes: Portrait of a Dynasty* (New York: Doubleday, 2004), 166.
40. Schweizer and Schweizer, *The Bushes,* 465.

Bibliography

General Works—Religion, the Revolution, and the Founding Fathers

Albanese, Catherine L. *Sons of the Fathers: The Civil Religion of the American Revolution*. Philadelphia: Temple University Press, 1976.

Bonomi, Patricia U. *Under the Cope of Heaven: Religion, Society, and Politics in Colonial America*. New York: Oxford University Press, 1986.

Butler, Jon. *Religion in Colonial America*. New York: Oxford University Press, 2000.

———. *Awash in a Sea of Faith: Christianizing the American People, Studies in Cultural History*. Cambridge: Harvard University Press, 1990.

Cousins, Norman. *The Republic of Reason: The Personal Philosophies of the Founding Fathers*. San Francisco: Harper & Row, 1988.

———. *"In God We Trust"; the Religious Beliefs and Ideas of the American Founding Fathers*. New York: Harper, 1958.

Davis, Derek. *Religion and the Continental Congress, 1774–1789: Contributions to Original Intent*. Oxford: Oxford University Press, 2000.

Eidsmoe, John. *Christianity and the Constitution: The Faith of Our Founding Fathers*. Grand Rapids, MI: Baker Book House, 1987.

Gaustad, Edwin S. *Faith of Our Fathers: Religion and the New Nation*. San Francisco: Harper & Row, 1987.

———. *Neither King nor Prelate: Religion and the New Nation, 1776–1826*. Revised and corrected ed. Grand Rapids, MI: Wm. B. Eerdmans, 1993.

Griffin, Keith L. *Revolution and Religion: American Revolutionary War and the Reformed Clergy*. New York: Paragon House, 1994.

Heimert, Alan. *Religion and the American Mind, from the Great Awakening to the Revolution.* Cambridge: Harvard University Press, 1966.

Hoffman, Ronald, and Peter J. Albert. *Religion in a Revolutionary Age, Perspectives on the American Revolution.* Charlottesville: Published for the United States Capitol Historical Society by the University Press of Virginia, 1994.

Hutson, James H. *Forgotten Features of the Founding: The Recovery of Religious Themes in the Early American Republic.* Lanham, MD: Lexington Books, 2003.

_____. *Religion and the New Republic: Faith in the Founding of America.* Lanham, MD: Rowman & Littlefield, 2000.

Lambert, Frank. *The Founding Fathers and the Place of Religion in America.* Princeton: Princeton University Press, 2003.

Mapp, Alf J. *The Faiths of Our Fathers: What America's Founders Really Believed.* Lanham, MD: Rowman & Littlefield, 2003.

Miller, William Lee. *The First Liberty: America's Foundation in Religious Freedom.* Expanded and updated ed. Washington, D.C.: Georgetown University Press, 2003.

Sheldon, Garrett Ward, and Daniel L. Dreisbach. *Religion and Political Culture in Jefferson's Virginia.* Lanham, MD: Rowman & Littlefield, 2000.

Staloff, Darren. *Hamilton, Adams, Jefferson: The Politics of Enlightenment and the American Founding.* New York: Hill and Wang, 2005.

The Religion of the Enlightenment: Deism

Aldridge, Alfred Owen. *Man of Reason: The Life of Thomas Paine.* Philadelphia: Lippincott, 1959.

Davidson, Edward H., and William J. Scheick. *Paine, Scripture, and Authority: The Age of Reason as Religious and Political Idea.* Bethlehem, PA: Lehigh University Press, 1994.

Foner, Eric. *Tom Paine and Revolutionary America.* New York: Oxford University Press, 1976.

Fruchtman, Jack. *Thomas Paine and the Religion of Nature.* Baltimore: Johns Hopkins University Press, 1993.

Grean, Stanley. *Shaftesbury's Philosophy of Religion and Ethics: A Study in Enthusiasm.* Athens: Ohio University Press, 1967.

Marshall, John. *John Locke: Resistance, Religion, and Responsibility.* Cambridge: Cambridge University Press, 1994.

Morais, Herbert M. *Deism in Eighteenth Century America.* New York: Columbia University Press, 1934.

Nuovo, Victor. *John Locke: Writings on Religion.* New York: Oxford University Press, 2002.

Kaminski, John P. *Citizen Paine: Thomas Paine's Thoughts on Man, Government, Society, and Religion.* Lanham, MD: Rowman & Littlefield, 2002.

Pollock, John Charles. *Shaftesbury: The Poor Man's Earl.* London: Hodder and Stoughton, 1985.

Sell, Alan P. F. *John Locke and the Eighteenth-Century Divines.* Cardiff: University of Wales Press, 1997.
Voitle, Robert. *The Third Earl of Shaftesbury, 1671–1713.* Baton Rouge: Louisiana State University Press, 1984.
Walters, Kerry S. *The American Deists: Voices of Reason and Dissent in the Early Republic.* Lawrence: University Press of Kansas, 1992.
_____. *Rational Infidels: The American Deists.* Durango, CO: Longwood Academic, 1992.
Wolterstorff, Nicholas. *John Locke and the Ethics of Belief.* Cambridge: Cambridge University Press, 1996.

Benjamin Franklin

Aldridge, Alfred Owen. *Benjamin Franklin and Nature's God.* Durham, N.C.: Duke University Press, 1967.
Anderson, Douglas. *The Radical Enlightenment of Benjamin Franklin.* Baltimore: Johns Hopkins University Press, 1997.
Isaacson, Walter. *Benjamin Franklin and the Invention of America: An American Life.* New York: Simon & Schuster, 2003.
Morgan, Edmund Sears. *Benjamin Franklin.* New Haven: Yale University Press, 2002.
Walters, Kerry S. *Benjamin Franklin and His Gods.* Urbana: University of Illinois Press, 1999.
Wood, Gordon S. *The Americanization of Benjamin Franklin.* New York: Penguin Press, 2004.
Wright, Esmond. *Franklin of Philadelphia.* Cambridge: Belknap Press of Harvard University Press, 1986.

George Washington

Alden, John Richard. *George Washington: A Biography.* Baton Rouge: Louisiana State University Press, 1984.
Boller, Paul F. *George Washington and Religion.* Dallas: Southern Methodist University Press, 1963.
Brookhiser, Richard. *Founding Father: Rediscovering George Washington.* New York: Free Press, 1996.
Ferling, John E. *The First of Men: A Life of George Washington.* Knoxville: University of Tennessee Press, 1988.
Flexner, James Thomas. *Washington, the Indispensable Man.* Boston: Little, Brown, 1974.
Higginbotham, Don. *George Washington Reconsidered.* Charlottesville: University Press of Virginia, 2001.
Longmore, Paul K. *The Invention of George Washington.* Berkeley: University of California Press, 1988.

John Adams

Chinard, Gilbert. *Honest John Adams*. Boston: Little, Brown, 1933.

Ellis, Joseph J. *Passionate Sage: The Character and Legacy of John Adams*. New York: Norton, 1993.

Ferling, John E. *John Adams: A Life*. Knoxville: University of Tennessee Press, 1992.

McCullough, David G. *John Adams*. New York: Simon & Schuster, 2001.

Shaw, Peter. *The Character of John Adams*. Chapel Hill: Published for the Institute of Early American History and Culture, Williamsburg VA, by the University of North Carolina Press, 1976.

Thomas Jefferson

Burstein, Andrew. *The Inner Jefferson: Portrait of a Grieving Optimist*. Charlottesville: University Press of Virginia, 1995.

Cunningham, Noble E. *In Pursuit of Reason: The Life of Thomas Jefferson*. Baton Rouge: Louisiana State University Press, 1987.

Ellis, Joseph J. *American Sphinx: The Character of Thomas Jefferson*. New York: Knopf, 1997.

Gaustad, Edwin S. *Sworn on the Altar of God: A Religious Biography of Thomas Jefferson*. Grand Rapids, MI: Wm. B. Eerdmans, 1996.

Peterson, Merrill D. *Thomas Jefferson and the New Nation: A Biography*. New York: Oxford University Press, 1970.

Sanford, Charles B. *The Religious Life of Thomas Jefferson*. Charlottesville: University Press of Virginia, 1984.

James Madison

Alley, Robert S. *James Madison on Religious Liberty*. Buffalo: Prometheus Books, 1985.

Banning, Lance. *The Sacred Fire of Liberty: James Madison and the Founding of the Federal Republic*. Ithaca: Cornell University Press, 1995.

Ketcham, Ralph Louis. *James Madison: A Biography*. New York: Macmillan, 1971.

McCoy, Drew R. *The Last of the Fathers: James Madison and the Republican Legacy*. New York: Cambridge University Press, 1989

Miller, William Lee. *The Business of May Next: James Madison and the Founding*. Charlottesville: University Press of Virginia, 1992.

Rakove, Jack N., and Oscar Handlin. *James Madison and the Creation of the American Republic*. Glenview, IL: Scott Foresman and Little, Brown, 1990.

Wills, Garry. *James Madison*. ed. Arthur Meier Schlesinger, *The American Presidents Series*. New York: Times Books, 2002.

James Monroe

Ammon, Harry. *James Monroe: The Quest for National Identity.* Charlottesville: University Press of Virginia, 1990.

Cresson, W. P. *James Monroe.* Hamden, CT: Archon Books, 1971.

Cunningham, Noble E., Jr. *The Presidency of James Monroe.* Lawrence: University of Kansas Press, 1996.

Hart, Gary. *James Monroe, The American Presidents Series.* New York: Times Books, 2005.

Morgan, George. *The Life of James Monroe,* New York: AMS, 1969.

Preston, Daniel. *A Narrative of the Life of James Monroe with a Chronology.* Charlottesville and Fredericksburg, VA: Ash Lawn-Highland and the James Monroe Museum and Memorial Library, 2001.

Preston, Daniel, and Marlena C. DeLong, eds. *The Papers of James Monroe: A Documentary History of the Presidential Tours of James Monroe, 1817, 1818, 1819.* Vol. 1. Westport, CT: Greenwood Press, 2003.

Women and Children of the Founding Fathers

Adams, Charles Francis, ed., *Letters of Mrs. Adams, The Wife of John Adams.* 2nd ed., vols. 1, 2. Boston: Charles C. Little and James Brown, 1840.

Brady, Patricia, ed., *George Washington's Beautiful Nelly: The Letters of Eleanor Park Custis Lewis to Elizabeth Bordley Gibson, 1794–1851.* Columbia, SC: University of South Carolina Press, 1991.

Conkling, Margaret, *Memoirs of the Mother and Wife of Washington.* New York: Derby, Miller, 1980.

Cutts, Lucia B., ed., *Memoirs and Letters of Dolly Madison.* Boston: Houghton Mifflin, 1887.

Gelles, Edith B., *Portia: The World of Abigail Adams.* Bloomington: Indiana University Press, 1992.

Moore, Virginia, *The Madisons: A Biography.* New York: McGraw-Hill, 1979.

Roberts, Cokie, *Founding Mothers: The Women Who Raised Our Nation.* New York: HarperCollins, 2004.

Gerald Ford

Cannon, James. *Time and Chance: Gerald Ford's Appointment with History.* Ann Arbor: University of Michigan Press, 1998.

Ford, Betty. *The Times of My Life.* New York: Harper & Row, 1978.

Ford, Gerald. *A Time to Heal: The Autobiography of Gerald R. Ford.* New York: Harper & Row, 1979.

Greene, John Robert. *The Presidency of Gerald R. Ford.* Lawrence: University Press of Kansas, 1995.

Mieczkowski, Yank. *Gerald Ford and the Challenges of the 1970s.* Lexington: University Press of Kentucky, 2005.

Jimmy Carter

Baker, James T. *A Southern Baptist in the White House.* Philadelphia: Westminster Press, 1977.

Bourne, Peter G. *Jimmy Carter: A Comprehensive Biography from Plains to Post-Presidency.* New York: Scribner, 1997.

Carter, Jimmy. *Keeping Faith: Memoirs of a President.* Fayetteville: University of Arkansas Press, 1995.

_____. *The Personal Beliefs of Jimmy Carter.* New York: Three Rivers Press, 2002.

Ronald Reagan

Brown, Mary Beth. *Hand of Providence.* Nashville: Nelson Current, 2004.

Cannon, Lou. *President Reagan: The Role of a Lifetime.* New York: Simon & Schuster, 1991.

Edwards, Anne. *Early Reagan.* New York: William Morrow, 1987.

_____. *The Reagans: Portrait of a Marriage.* New York: St. Martin's Press, 2003.

Reagan, Ronald. *An American Life.* New York: Simon & Schuster, 1990.

Strober, Deborah Hart, and Gerald S. Strober. *The Reagan Presidency: An Oral History of the Era.* Washington, D.C.: Brassey's, 2003.

Wills, Gary. *Reagan's America: Innocents at Home.* Garden City, NY: Doubleday, 1987.

George H. W. Bush

Bush, Barbara. *Reflections: Life after the White House.* New York: Scribner, 2003.

_____. *Barbara Bush: A Memoir.* New York: Scribner's Sons, 1994.

Bush, George. *All the Best, George Bush: My Life in Letters and Other Writings.* New York: Scribner, 1999.

Parmet, Herbert S. *George Bush: The Life of a Lone Star Yankee.* New York: Scribner, 1997.

Radcliffe, Donnie. *Barbara Bush: A Portrait of America's Candid First Lady.* NewYork: Warner Books, Inc., 1989.

Schweizer, Peter, and Schweizer, Rochelle. *The Bushes: Portrait of a Dynasty.* New York: Doubleday, 2004.

Bill Clinton

Clinton, Bill. *My Life.* New York: Knopf, 2004.

Clinton, Hillary Rodham, *Living History.* New York: Simon & Schuster, 2003.

Hamliton, Nigel. *Bill Clinton: An American Journey: Great Expectations.* New York: Random House, 2003.

Harris, John F. *The Survivor: Bill Clinton in the White House.* New York: Random House, 2005.

Klein, Joe. *The Natural: The Misunderstood Presidency of Bill Clinton.* New York: Doubleday, 2002.

Maraniss, David. *First in His Class: A Biography of Bill Clinton.* New York: Simon & Schuster, 1995.

Morris, Roger. *Partners in Power: The Clintons and Their America.* New York: Henry Holt, 1996.

Radcliffe, Donnie, *Hillary Rodham Clinton: A First Lady for Our Time.* New York: Warner Books, 1993.

George W. Bush

Black, Amy E. *Of Little Faith: The Politics of George W. Bush's Faith-Based Initiatives.* Washington, D.C.: Georgetown University Press, 2004.

Bush, George W. *Bush on God and Country: The President Speaks Out about Faith, Principle, and Patriotism.* Fairfax, VA: Allegiance Press, 2004.

———. *A Charge to Keep.* New York: Morrow, 1999.

Kengor, Paul. *God and George W. Bush: A Spiritual Life.* New York: Regan Books, 2004.

Mansfield, Stephen. *The Faith of George W. Bush.* New York: Jeremy P. Tarcher/ Penguin, 2003.

Illustration Credits

Page

2   **Touro Synagogue, Newport, Rhode Island.**
Courtesy of Touro Synagogue.

8   **Ephrata Solitary Sister in Habit**
From Julius Friedrich Sachse, *The German Sectaries of Pennsylvania: 1742–1800* (Philadelphia, 1900).

10   **First Baptist Church, Providence, Rhode Island.**
From Peter T. Mallary, *New England Churches & Meetinghouses: 1680–1830* (New York, 1985).

14   **Yale College and Chapel**
From Reuben A. Holden, *Yale: A Pictorial History* (New Haven, 1967).

19   **Jesuit Father Andrew White**
Reprinted with permission of the Special Collections Division, Georgetown University Library, Washington, DC

22   **Charles Calvert, third Lord Baltimore and second proprietor of Maryland, by Sir Godfrey Kneller**
Courtesy of Enoch Pratt Free Library, Baltimore, MD

25   **George Whitefield**
From Mark A. Noll, *A History of Christianity in the United States and Canada* (Grand Rapids, MI, 1992).

29 **Francis Asbury**
From Elmer T. Clark, ed., *The Journal and Letters of Francis Asbury: Volume I* (London, 1958).

34 **James Madison**
Courtesy of Virginia Historical Society, Richmond, VA.

43 **John Adams's copy of Thomas Paine's *Common Sense***
From James Bishop Peabody, ed., *John Adams: A Biography in His Own* Words (New York, 1973).

54 **Benjamin Franklin**
From Thomas Fleming, ed., *Benjamin Franklin: A Biography in His Own Words* (New York, 1972).

60 **The interior of St. Peter's Church, Philadelphia**
Courtesy of Cornwall Collection, Archives of the Episcopal Church, U.S.A.

67 ***The Apotheosis of George Washington***
Courtesy of Mount Vernon Ladies' Association, Gift of Mr. Stanley Deforest Scott.

74 **John Adams**
Library of Congress, Prints & Photographs Division, Reproduction #LC –USZ62-119056. Boston: published by N. Dearborn, between 1814 and 1852.

80 **Thomas Jefferson**
Library of Congress, Prints & Photographs Division, Reproduction #LC –USZ62-3795.

92 **James Madison, circa 1830, by Asher B. Durand**
Courtesy of The Century Association, New York City.

100 **James Monroe**
Library of Congress, Prints & Photographs Division, Reproduction #LC –USZ62-87925.

110 **Elizabeth Kortright Monroe**
Miniature portrait painted by Louis Sene, circa 1795, depicting Elizabeth Monroe at the age of twenty-four. Courtesy of Ash Lawn-Highland.

113 **Martha Washington**
Library of Congress, Prints & Photographs Division, Reproduction #LC –USZ62-3833. Boston: published by L. Prang & Co., circa 1864.

117   **Abigail Adams at Age 22**
        Courtesy of Massachusetts Historical Society, Boston/Bridgeman Art
        Library.

121   **Martha "Patsy" Jefferson Randolph**
        Courtesy of Monticello/Thomas Jefferson Foundation. Portrait by
        Thomas Sully.

126   **Dolley Madison**
        Library of Congress, Prints & Photographs Division, Reproduction
        #LC –USZ62-68175. From an original picture by Gilbert Stuart,
        created between 1804 and 1855, in possession of Richard Cutts, Esq.
        MD, Washington.

136   **Bishop John England**
        Reprinted with permission of the Diocese of Charleston Archives.

144   **Samuel Adams**
        Library of Congress, Prints & Photographs Division, Reproduction
        #LC –USZ62-102271. Painted by Copley, engraved by C. Goodman
        & R. Piggot, between 1810 and 1835.

155   **John Jay**
        Library of Congress, Prints & Photographs Division, Reproduction
        #LC –USZ62-50375. Photo by A.W. Elson, circa 1905.

Index

Numbers in boldface indicate illustrations.

Abbaye Royal de Panthemont, France, 122–124
Abercrombie, James, 63
"Act Concerning Religion" (Maryland Toleration Act), 20–21
Act for Establishing Religious Freedom, 86, 93
Adams, Abigail ("Nabby"), 120
Adams, Abigail Smith, 2–3, 77, 78, 83, 88, 95, 103, *117*, 117–121, 123, 141
Adams, John, *Chapter 7*; and 2–3, 7, 17, 30, 31, 36, 41, 43, 50, 51, 66, *74*, 76, 77, 81, 82, 83, 87, 88, 95, 100, 103, 107, 120, 133, 137, 146, 154, 157
Adams, John Quincy, 107, 118, 119, 128
Adams, Mary Fifield, 143–144
Adams, Samuel, xi, 42, 143–150, *144*
Adams, Samuel (the elder), 143–144
Addison, Joseph, 54
African-American religion and life, 30, 156, 157, 179, 181, 184;

churches: "Invisible Institution," 30
African Methodist Episcopal Church, 30, 181; Metropolitan A.M.E. (Washington, DC), 181
Age of Reason, The, 42, 44–46, 48, 149, 151, 152
Agnew, Spiro T., 165, 166
Allen, Ethan, 44, 46, 82, 110, 140
American Unitarian Association, 119, 141
Anabaptism, 6, 9, 17, 21
Anglican and Episcopal parishes, churches, and chapels: Annunciation (New York, NY), 101; Bruton (Williamsburg, VA), 99, 101; Christ (Alexandria, VA), 60, 61, 114, 115; Christ (Philadelphia, PA), 55, 57, 60, 61, 63–64, 114, 115, 161; Christ (Greenwich, CT), 175; College of William and Mary (Williamsburg, VA), 99; Forge

Anglican and Episcopal parishes
(*continued*)
(Albemarle County, VA), 104, 122;
Henrico (Richmond and Henrico
County, VA), 101; Immanuel on-
the-Hill (Alexandria, VA), 165;
Pohick (Fairfax County, VA), 59,
60, 61, 114; Shelburne (Loudoun
County, VA), 101; St. Anne's
(Albemarle County, VA), 80, 85,
101, 122; St. Ann's by the Sea
(Kennebunkport, ME), 175; St.
George's (Fredericksburg, VA),
101; St. John's, Lafayette Square
(Washington, DC), 94, 101, 129,
130, 131, 166, 173, 182; St. John's
(Richmond, VA), 103; St. Martin's
(Houston, TX), 176, 182; St.
Mary's (Burlington, NJ), 151; St.
Matthew's (Bedford, NY), 158,
159; St. Paul's (New York, NY),
60, 114, 115; St. Peter's (Philadelphia, PA), *60*, 63, 114; St.
Thomas's (Orange, VA), 92, 94,
130; Trinity (New York, NY), 60,
100, 114, 155, 158, 159; Truro
(Fairfax County, VA), 59; Washington (Westmoreland County, VA),
99, 101
Anglican (Church of England) and
Episcopal (Protestant Episcopal
Church) tradition, *Chapters 2, 4, 6,
8, 9, 10*; and 6, 9, 10, 11, 12, 13, 15,
16, 17, 18, 20, 21, 22–25, 28, 30, 31,
40, 41, 55, 74, 109, 110, 112, 114–
117, 120, 121–122, 125, 126, 129–
131, 135–138, 139, 140, 141, 151,
154–162, 165–167, 168, 175–177
Anointing with oil, revived by
Christian sects in America, 7
Anti-Trinitarianism, 74, 76. *See also*
Unitarianism

Arkansas, 177–181; Hope, 178; Hot
Springs, 178; Little Rock, 179, 180
Arianism, 17, 74
Arius of Alexandria, 74
Arminianism, 17
Articles of Confederation, 145
Asbury, Francis, *29*
Ash Lawn-Highland. *See* Highland
(home of James Monroe)
Athanasius of Alexandria, 35, 74, 82
Atheism, 9, 17, 42, 46, 50, 81
Augustine of Hippo, 12, 82

Bacon, Francis, 40, 79
Baltimore, 18, 88
Baptism, 87, 112; adult ("believer's"),
3, 6, 7, 9, 10, 11, 23, 47, 75, 76, 168,
172, 179; infant, 6, 9, 10, 11, 23, 47,
75, 76, 79, 92, 99, 121, 122, 135
Baptist churches: Culpeper (Culpeper,
VA), 181; First (Dallas, TX), 167;
First (Hope, AR), 178; First
(Providence, RI), *10*; First (Wash-
ington, DC), 170, 181; Maranatha
(Plains, GA), 169; Immanuel (Little
Rock, AR), 180; Park Place (Hot
Springs, AR), 178, 179; Plains
(Plains, GA), 168, 169, 170
Baptists, 9, 10, 14, 15, 17, 22, 23, 24,
28, 30, 65, 81, 84, 85, 168; social
teachings of, 168–169, 181. *See
also* Cooperative Baptist Fellow-
ship, Separate Baptists, and
Southern Baptist Convention
Baker, James A., III, 177
Baltimore, Lord. *See* Calvert
Battles: Brandywine, 7; Trenton, 102;
Yorktown, 115
Beasley, Frederick, 96
Beijing, China, 176, 181
Bible societies, 150, 154, 157
Black religion. *See* African-American
religion

Blythe, William Jefferson, III, 178
Book of Common Prayer, 34, 35, 36, 65, 74–75, 79, 80, 95, 100, 122, 135, 175
Bonaparte, Napoleon, 49, 153
Bonhoeffer, Dietrich, 180
Boston, 10, 53–54, 76, 95, 105, 120, 143–145, 147, 148, 177
Boudinot, Elias, 83, 150–154, 155, 157
Boudinot, Hannah, 151
Boudinot, Elias (the elder), 150
Brethren, Church of the, 7
Briant, Lemuel, 77
Brinton, Crane, 40
Brown University. *See* College of Rhode Island
Browning, Edmond L., 177
Burlington, NJ, 151
Burr, Aaron, 126, 127, 128
Bush, Barbara Pierce, 175–177, 181, 183, 184
Bush, Dorothy Walker, 175
Bush, Dorothy W. ("Doro"), 176, 177, 181
Bush, George H. W., 173, 175–177, 181, 184
Bush, George W., 177, 182–185
Bush, John E. ("Jeb"), 177
Bush, Laura Welch, 182, 184
Bush, Pauline Robinson ("Robin"), 176
Bush, Prescott S., 175
Byrd, William, 23

California, 173
Calvert, Charles (third Lord Baltimore), *22*
Calvert, George (first Lord Baltimore), 18, 21, 22
Calvin, John, 10–12, 35; and Calvinism, 5, 6, 9–13, 17, 21, 27, 35, 53–55, 76, 77, 82, 84, 88, 118, 140, 143–150, 150–154, 155, 156, 159
Camp David (near Thurmont, MD), 173, 182

Campbell, Archibald, 99
Carr, Peter, 103
Carroll, Charles and Daniel, 20
Carter, James Earl ("Jimmy"), 166, 167–171, 174, 181, 184
Carter, Lillian, 169
Carter, Rosalynn Smith, 170
Carter, Ruth Stapleton, 169
Charles I and II (kings of England), 21, 148
Charleston, 1, 24, 136
Chastellux, Marquis de (François Jean de Beauvoir), 122
Checkley, Elizabeth, 144
Checkley, Samuel, 144
Cheney, Richard B., 177
Cherbury, Lord Herbert of. *See* Herbert, Edward
China, People's Republic of, 176, 180, 181
Christian Church (Disciples of Christ), 172–175; churches: Dixon (Dixon, IL), 172; Hollywood-Beverley (Los Angeles, CA), 173
Church and state, union or separation of, 3–4, 6–7, 13, 48, 49, 56, 86, 107, 148, 149, 154. *See also* Established (state) churches
Churches of Christ, 81
Church of England. *See* Anglican (Church of England) and Episcopal (Protestant Episcopal Church) tradition
Church of the New Jerusalem, 66
Clay, Charles, 85, 87, 122
Cleaver, Ben and Margaret, 172
Clinton, Chelsea, 180
Clinton, Hillary Rodham, 180
Clinton, Roger, 178
Clinton, Virginia, 177–178
Clinton, William Jefferson, 173, 177–182
Coffin, William Sloane, 183
College of New Jersey. *See* Princeton University

College of Philadelphia (University of
    Pennsylvania), 17, 96
College of Rhode Island (Brown
    University), 14, 15, 17
College of William and Mary, 23, 34,
    50, 53, 79–80, 85, 87, 91, 92, 99,
    101, 104, 110, 116, 117, 121, 136
Colleges, American, dates of found-
    ing, 188n.7
Collins, Anthony, 41, 54
Colorado, 183
Columbia University. *See* King's
    College
Common Prayer, Book of. *See* Book
    of Common Prayer
Common Sense, 41, *43*, 149
Communalism, revived by Christian
    sects in America, 4
Confirmation, 62, 94, 129, 130, 135–
    136, 138–139; avoidance of by
    Anglican founding fathers, 62, 94,
    104, 136, 138–139, 140
Congregationalism, *Chapter 7*; and 9,
    10, 11, 14, 16, 17, 28, 31, 34, 53,
    55, 56, 81, 116, 117–121, 141,
    143–150. *See also* Calvinism
Congregationalist churches: Brattle
    Street (Boston, MA), 120; Center
    (New Haven, CT), 105; First
    (Kennebunkport, ME), 175; New
    South (Boston, MA), 143–144; Old
    South (Boston, MA), 144
Connecticut, 9, 15, 26, 34, 175, 183
Constitutional Convention, 20, 133,
    161
Continental Congresses, 2, 65, 117,
    145, 150, 151, 154, 156, 160, 161,
    162
Cooper, Anthony Ashley (third earl of
    Shaftesbury), 54
Cooper, Myles, 156
Cooperative Baptist Fellowship, 169
Cotton, John, 150

Craik, James, 68
Creeds, Christian: Apostle's, 35;
    Athanasian, 35, 75, 87, 95–96;
    Nicene, 35, 74–75
Crisis, The, 41
Criswell, Wally A. ("W. A."), 167
Custis, Daniel Parke, 114
Custis [Lewis], Eleanor Parke
    ("Nelly"), 61, 62, 63, 70, 111, 114,
    115–117
Cutts, Anna, 129

Dartmouth College, 14
Deism, *Chapters 3, 4, 5, 6, 7, 8, 9, 10,
    11, 12*; and 17, 31, 36–37, 144, 145,
    146, 148, 150, 151, 152, 153, 156,
    158, 159, 160, 162–164; social
    teachings of, 44, 46, 48, 55, 66, 68
Declaration of Independence, 20, 47,
    93, 145, 150, 155, 161
Delaware, 8, 96
Desk and Pulpit service, 62, 63
Dewees, William, 70
Diderot, Denis, 40, 48
Disciples of Christ. *See* Christian
    Church
Doane, George Washington, 129
Dobson, James, 183, 184
Donaldson, Samuel A., 174–175
Duane, James, 96, 158
Dunkers. *See* Brethren, Church of the
Duponceau, Peter S., 101, 102
Dutch Reformed Church. *See*
    Reformed Churches
Dwight, Timothy, 157

Eastern Orthodoxy, 6, 12, 34, 35, 164,
    178
Edwards, Jonathan, 28, 145
Eisenhower, Dwight D., 165
Elizabeth I (queen of England), 35
Ellis, John, 185

England, 5, 9, 18, 21, 28, 33, 35, 40–
41, 44, 48, 53, 54, 99, 106, 145,
155. *See also* London
England, John, *136*, 145
English Toleration Act, 15
Enlightenment, the, *Chapters, 3, 4*;
and 22, 55, 76, 77, 78, 79, 80, 89,
92, 95, 141
Ephrata Community, 7, *8*
Episcopal Church. *See also* Anglican
(Church of England) and Episcopal
(Protestant Episcopal Church)
tradition
Eppes, John Wayles, 124
Eppes, Maria Jefferson, 122–125
Established (state) churches, *Chapter
2*; and 8–9, 18, 22, 24, 25, 31, 59,
76, 99, 118, 143, 155, 158
Ethical Culture movement, 48
Eureka College, 172
Evangelical tradition, *Epilogue*; and
23–24, 25–31, 85, 117, 141, 145,
146, 150, 152, 154–160, 164;
reassessment of religion of
founding fathers by, 68–71, 97,
105, 133–134, 141, 161–164
Evans, Louis, 173, 174

Falwell, Jerry, 179, 184
Federalist Papers, 154
Federalist Party, 81, 148, 149, 157
Finland, colonists from, 16
Florida, 24, 100
Foot washing, 139; revived by
Christian sects in America, 4, 7
Ford, Gerald R., 165–167, 170
France, 8, 23, 41–42, 44, 80, 99, 106,
164. *See also* Paris
Franklin, Benjamin, *Chapter 5*; and 7,
17, 27–28, 30, 34, 36, 37, 41, 47,
51, *54*, 106, 107, 145, 150, 154,
159, 163, 174
Franklin, Sarah, 55

Frederick II ("the Great"), king of
Prussia, 40
Freemasonry, 48, 68, 105–106, 110, 146
Freneau, Philip, 45

Gelles, Edith, 121
General Theological Seminary, New
York, NY, 161
George III (king of England), 145,
147, 148
Georgetown, 88
Georgetown, College and University,
20, 179
Georgia, 5, 24–25, 26, 27, 34, 167–
171; Atlanta, 170, 171; Plains,
167–169; Savannah, 1
Germany, 5, 7, 8, 17, 18, 23, 40, 44,
101, 106
Gouverneur, Maria Hester Monroe,
100, 101, 107, 109, 110
Graham, Ruth, 176
Graham, William F. ("Billy"), 165,
167, 176–177, 179, 181, 183
Grand Rapids, Michigan, 165
Great Awakening, 28, 30, 31, 56, 76,
118, 141, 145, 146, 150; Second,
104
Greece, 8
Grizzard, Frank E., Jr., 70
Guilford College, 126

Habitat for Humanity, 171
Hamilton, Alexander, 81, 133, 151, 154
Hampden-Sydney College, 23
Hartley, L.P., vi, 164
Harvard Business School, 183
Harvard College and University, 14,
49, 50, 76, 110, 144, 145
Hay, Eliza Monroe, 100, 101, 107, 109
Henry, Patrick, 36, 126, 141
Herbert, Edward (Lord Herbert of
Cherbury), 46
Highland (home of James Monroe),
100, 101, 104

Hispanic Americans, 184
Holley, Horace, 105
Holy Communion services, 4, 47, 62–
65, 68, 91, 114, 135–136, 137–140,
159, 166; avoidance of by
founding fathers, 62–65, 114, 137–
141. See also Lord's Supper
Huguenot tradition. See Reformed
Churches, French
Huss, John, 5
Hussein, Saddam, 177

Illinois, Chicago, 180; Park Ridge, 180
Indians (American). See Native
Americans
Iowa, 173
Iran, 170
Iraq, 177
Ireland, 16
Islam, 46, 106, 119
Italy, 8, 106

Jakes, Thomas D. ("T.D."), 184
Jay, John, 61, 83, 154–160, 155;
Jay, John Jr., 156, 160
Jay, Mary Van Cortlandt, 155
Jay, Peter (the elder), 155
Jay, Peter, 156, 160
Jay, Sarah Van Burgh Livingston, 156,
157, 159, 160
Jay, William, 156, 160
Jefferson, Jane Randolph, 79
Jefferson, Lucy Elizabeth, 122
Jefferson, Maria Wayles, 122
Jefferson, Martha "Patsy" (TJ's
daughter). See Randolph, Martha
"Patsy" Jefferson
Jefferson, Martha Skelton Wayles
(TJ's wife), 80, 111, 121, 122
Jefferson, Peter, 79
Jefferson, Thomas, Chapter 8; and 30,
33, 34, 36, 41, 45, 50, 51, 66, 69,
78, 80, 93, 99, 100, 103, 104, 105,
107, 121–125, 133, 137, 139, 145,
149, 151, 154, 163, 174; Anglican
and Episcopal heritage of, 80–81;
Memorial Church, 86–87; Unitarianism of, 80, 86–89
Jesuits (Society of Jesus), 19, 20, 21,
179
Jesus of Nazareth, atonement of, 40,
47, 137–138, 146, 158; divinity
of, 21, 39, 44, 46, 47, 56, 57, 65,
69, 74, 78, 83, 88, 95, 109, 118,
119, 120, 133, 138, 140, 141, 146,
151, 152, 158, 163, 171, 172, 183,
184, 185; resurrection from the
grave, 44, 47, 56, 77, 88, 109, 120,
137, 140, 141, 160, 163; second
coming of, 4, 109, 120, 125, 150,
153; virgin birth of, 47, 75, 88,
104, 120, 163
John Paul II (Pope), 177
Johnson, Lyndon Baines, 183
Johnson, Samuel, 156
Jones, Don, 180
Jones, William, 97
Joseph II (Holy Roman Emperor), 40
Judaism, 1, 4, 16, 17, 24, 25, 42, 44,
46, 47, 48, 62, 63, 66, 96, 106, 112,
119, 140, 164, 178, 179; social
teachings of, 174

Kennebunkport, ME, 175
Kentucky, 36
King, Martin Luther, Jr., 170, 180, 181
King's College (Columbia University),
15, 156

Lafayette, Marquis de, 106, 123
Laurens, Henry, 155
Lear, Tobias, 113, 114
Lee, Charles Carter, 116
Lee, Henry, 116
Lewinsky, Monica, 181–182

Lewis, Eleanor Parke ("Nelly") Custis, 61, 62, 63, 70, 111, 114, 115–117

Lewis, Lawrence, 115

Life and Morals of Jesus (The Jefferson Bible), 83, 139

Livingston, Robert R., 156, 158, 159

Livingston, William, 156

Locke, John, 40, 54, 79, 144

Lodge, Henry Cabot, 69

London, England, 16, 26, 54, 155

Lord's Supper, 4, 63, 64, 94, 137, 139, 159. *See also* Holy Communion service; Mass

Los Angeles, CA, 173

Louis XVI (king of France), 124

Louisiana, 115–116, 156

Love feasts, revived by Christian sects in America, 4, 5, 7

Lowell, James Russell, 177

Luther, Martin, 3, 6, 11; and Lutheranism, 5, 6, 11, 16, 17, 18, 21, 22, 23, 24, 25, 35, 137, 164

Madison, Dorthea "Dolley" Payne Todd, 94, 95, 96, 125–131, *126*, 141

Madison, Eleanor Rose Conway, 94

Madison, James (Episcopal bishop and President of William and Mary), *34*, 80, 87, 104, 136

Madison, James (President of United States), *Chapter 9*; and 33, 34, 36, 50, 51, 62, 69, 70–71, 86, *92*, 104, 105, 107, 128, 130, 131, 136, 138, 161

Maine, 175

Marion, Francis, 155

Marshall, John, 99

Martin, Thomas, 92

Maryland, 2, 5, 7, 18–22, 34, 44, 135. *See also* Baltimore

Maryland Toleration Act ("Act Concerning Religion"), 21–22

Mason, George, 36

Masonic Order. *See* Freemasonry

Mass, 1–3, 20, 21, 22, 34, 35, 135, 137, 139, 172

Massachusetts, 9, 15, 34, 76, 117, 141, 143–150, 182, 183. *See also* Boston

Mather, Cotton, 150; Increase, 54

Maury, James, 79

McGuire, Edward C., 68

Meade, William, 85, 91–92, 94, 97, 104, 105

Medeiros, Humberto S., 177

Mennonites, 6, 7, 16

Methodism, 17, 22, 26, 29, 30, 172. *See also* United Methodist Church

Michigan. *See* Grand Rapids

Monroe, Eliza. *See* Hay, Eliza Monroe

Monroe, Elizabeth Kortright, 41, 100, 103, 104, 107, 109, *110*, 111, 128

Monroe, James, *Chapter 10*; and 31, 33, 36, 41–42, 50, 51, 86, *100*, 138, 141, 160, 161, 177

Monroe, James Jr., 103

Monroe, James Spence, 103, 107, 111

Monroe, Joseph Jones, 103

Monroe, Maria Hester. *See* Gouverneur, Maria Hester Monroe

Monroe, Spence, 99

Monticello (home of Thomas Jefferson), 79, 80, 83, 85, 88, 100, 121, 122, 124, 125

Montpelier (home of James Madison), 92, 94, 128, 130, 131, 136

Moore, Richard Channing, 80, 94, 100

Moral Majority, 179

Moravianism, 5, 6, 17, 23, 25

Morris, Anthony, 127

Morris, Richard, 182

Mount St. Mary's College, 20

Mount Vernon (home of George Washington), 59, 61, 63, 70, 113, 114

Moyers, William D., 183

Native Americans, 19, 65, 100, 150, 153–154
Neoconservative political thought, 183
Netherlands, The, 9
New England, *Chapter 7*; and 4, 9, 10, 13, 14, 15, 17, 23, 36, 53, 95, 104, 118, 119, 120, 140, 143, 147
New Hampshire, 4, 9, 34
New Jersey, 5, 16, 61, 96, 150–151, 156; Burlington, 151
New Netherland, 15, 16, 155. *See also* Reformed Churches, Dutch
New York, 4, 5, 10, 15, 16, 34, 68, 69, 96, 103, 135, 136, 154–160; Albany, 15, 161–162; Bedford, 157, 158, 159; New Rochelle, 16, 156; New York City, 1, 60, 61, 69, 100–101, 105, 115, 155, 171; Rye, 155, 159
Newton, Isaac, 40, 79
Niebuhr, Reinhold, 180
Nixon, Richard M., 165–166, 173
Noll, Mark, 146–147
Nonresistance. *See* Pacifism
North Carolina, 5, 17, 23–24, 25, 34, 126; Greensboro, 126

Oak Hill (home of James Monroe), 100, 101
Ohio, 104
Olasky, Marvin N., 183
"Old Swedes" churches, 16, 18
Orthodoxy (Protestant), *Chapters 11, 12, 13*; and 15, 41, 42, 49, 50, 55, 56, 66, 69, 70, 76, 77, 85, 88, 92, 93, 96, 97, 98, 102, 107, 145, 161, 162–164
Orthodoxy (Roman Catholic), *Chapter 12*; and 42, 48, 51, 107, 136

Pacifism (nonresistance), taught by Christian sects, 3, 4, 5, 6
Paine, Thomas, *Chapter 3*; and 49, 56, 77, 82, 102, 110, 125, 149, 151–152, 174

Palmer, Elihu, 46, 110
Papacy, 3, 12, 35, 106, 177
Paris, 122–124, 126, 151, 154
Payne, John, 126
Payne, Lucy, 127
Payne, Mary ("Molly") Coles, 126
Penn, William, 5, 17, 18, 22
Pennsylvania, 2, 5, 6, 7, 8, 15, 17–18, 23, 27, 63, 96, 114, 135, 136, 161 *See also* Philadelphia; Pittsburgh
Pentecostalism, 4, 31, 181, 182
Philadelphia, 1, 2, 6, 8, 17–18, 27, 28, 55–57, 60, 61, 63, 66, 88, 95, 110, 114, 115, 126, 127, 128, 129, 133, 150, 155, 161, 162
Phillips Academy, Andover, MA, 182
Pittsburgh, 17, 104
Potts, Isaac, 70
Powell, Colin L., 177
Predestination, Calvinist doctrine of, 12, 27, 78, 118, 187n.5
Presbyterian churches: Bel Air (Los Angeles, CA), 173; First (Midland, TX), 176, 182, 184; National (Washington, DC), 173, 174
Presbyterianism, 9, 10, 11, 16, 21, 22, 23, 24, 25, 46, 55, 65, 82, 84, 85, 92, 93, 101, 150, 151, 154, 155, 158, 175, 177. *See also* Calvinism
Priestley, Joseph, 82, 88
Princeton Theological Seminary, 150, 154
Princeton University (College of New Jersey), 15, 16, 50, 91, 92, 93, 136, 150, 154
Protestant Reformation, teachings of, 3, 5, 12, 34
Providence, references to by founding fathers and others, 47, 56, 66, 86, 102, 113, 133, 139–140, 141, 151, 158, 163
Puritanism, 2, 9, 10, 12, 13, 15, 21, 34, 35, 36, 53–54, 143–150, 168. *See*

also Baptists, Calvinism, Congregationalism, and Presbyterianism
Pyne, Smith, 129, 131

Quakerism, 4, 5, 9, 11, 16, 17, 18, 22, 23, 24, 25, 41, 48, 66, 70, 84, 95, 125–129, 131
Queen's College (Rutgers University), 16

Randolph, Martha "Patsy" Jefferson, *121*, 122–125
Randolph, Sarah, 124
Randolph, Thomas Mann, 124
Rauschenbusch, Walter, 181
Reagan, John ("Jack"), 172, 173
Reagan, Nancy Davis, 173, 175
Reagan, Maureen, 173
Reagan, Michael, 173
Reagan, Neil, 172
Reagan, Ronald Wilson, 171, 172–175
Reformed Churches, 10, 11; Dutch, 15, 16, 155; French (Huguenot), 16, 150, 155, 156; German, 17, 18, 23, 65. *See also* Calvinism
Regan, Nelle Wilson, 172, 173, 174, 175
Rehnquist, William, 154, 161
Religious freedom, belief of founding fathers in, 20, 21, 22, 93, 102, 163
Religious Right, 133–134, 170–171, 184–185, 191n.15
Religious Society of Friends. *See* Quakerism
Restorationist thought, in Christianity, 3–7, 76, 81–82; Jefferson as a restorationist, 81–84, 88
Revolution, American, 5, 11, 16, 7, 21, 25, 33, 36, 41, 46, 49, 59, 61, 62, 65, 68, 69, 70, 82, 99, 101, 102, 105, 106, 109, 110, 112, 126, 135, 139, 140, 143, 145, 147–148, 151, 154, 155, 156, 162

Revolution, French, 41, 46, 49, 82, 153
Rhode Island, 5, 9, 14, 15, 17, 118; New Port, 1
Ringgold, Tench, 101
Robertson, Donald, 92
Robertson, Marion G. ("Pat"), 184
Robison, James, 183, 184
Roman Catholic churches: St. Ignatius (St. Mary's City, MD), 22; St. Mary's (Philadelphia, PA), 2; Mass station (Stafford County, VA), 22
Roman Catholicism, 1–3, 6, 9, 10, 11, 16, 18–22, 30–31, 34, 35, 44, 51, 66, 76, 84, 102, 104, 106, 116, 120, 123, 135, 136, 137, 139, 164, 172, 177, 178, 179; social teachings of, 174, 184
Roosevelt, Franklin D., 183
Roosevelt, Theodore, 46
Rousseau, Jean-Jacques, 40, 110
Rush, Benjamin, 77, 82
Russia, 8
Rutgers University. *See* Queen's College

Sandemanians (Glasites), 4
Schwenkfelders, 6
Scots and Scots-Irish, 4, 9, 16, 17, 18, 23, 35, 125, 172
Sects, Christian, definition and characteristics of, 3–8. *See also individual Christian sects*
Separate Baptists, 23, 24, 25
Shakers (United Society of Believers in Christ's Second Appearing), 4
Short, William, 83, 84
Skelton, Bathurst, 121
Skelton, John, 121
Small, William, 79
Smith, Ethan, 154
Smith, Joseph, 154
Smith, William, Sr., 117–118
Snowden, Nathaniel Randolph, 70
Social Gospel, 174, 181, 183

Society for the Propagation of the
Gospel in Foreign Parts (S.P.G.),
16, 25
South Carolina, 10, 17, 24, 34, 96. *See
also* Charleston
Southern Baptist Convention, 166,
167–171, 172, 177–182
Spain, 8, 24, 99, 154, 156
Stevenson, Sarah Coles, 96–97
Stockton, Richard, 150–151
Sweden, colonists from, 16, 18
Synagogues, 1, 4, 16, 17, 24, 25, 47,
56, 62, 66; Touro (Newport, RI), *2*

Taylor, Nathaniel, 105
Tennent, Gilbert, 152–153
Tennent, William, 150, 152–153
Texas, 176, 182, 183; Houston, 176,
182; Midland, 176, 182, 184
Ticknor, George, 86, 95
Tocqueville, Alexis de, 1
Todd, John Jr., 127; [John] Payne,
127, 128; William Temple, 127
Treaty of Paris, 126, 151, 154
Trinity, doctrine of, and
Trinitarianism, *Chapter 7*; and 4, 7,
21, 46, 56, 66, 87, 95, 119–120,
140, 141, 152, 163
Truman, Harry S, 183

Unitarian-Universalist churches: First
Parish (Quincy, MA), 76, 77, 120,
121, 141; Thomas Jefferson
Memorial (Charlottesville, VA),
86–87
Unitarianism, *Chapter 7*; and 9, 14,
31, 48, 50, 51, 80, 82, 86, 87, 95,
105, 109, 117–121, 133, 141, 162;
in first five centuries of Christianity, 73–76. *See also* Anti-
Trinitarianism
Unitas Fratrum. *See* Moravianism
United Methodist Church, 180, 181

churches: First (Little Rock, AR),
180; First (Midland, TX), 182;
First (Park Ridge, IL), 180;
Foundry (Washington, DC), 181;
social teachings of, 180
United Society of Believers in Christ's
Second Appearing. *See* Shakers
United States Congress, 65, 94, 99,
124, 165, 183
United States Military Academy at
West Point, 103
United States Naval Academy
(Annapolis), 168
United States Supreme Court, 154,
157, 161
Universalism, 4, 17, 45, 48, 66
University of Virginia, 85–86, 89, 93

Vermont, 46
Virginia, *Chapters 2, 6, 8, 9, 10*; and
5, 7, 17, 22–23, 24, 121, 123, 126,
135, 136, 164
Virginia cities and counties:
Albemarle, 85, 104 ; Alexandria,
60, 115, 165; Charles City, 121;
Charlottesville, 86, 104; Culpeper,
93; Fairfax, 115; Fredericksburg,
99, 106; Hanover, 126, 127;
Henrico, 101; King and Queen, 92;
King George, 92; New Kent, 114;
Loudoun, 100; Richmond, 1, 99,
101, 105, 112, 122; Stafford, 22;
Williamsburg, 50, 121
Voltaire (Francois-Marie Arouët), 40,
41, 42, 110
Von Steuben, Frederick Wilhelm
Augustus, 101

Wars: 1812, 93, 100; First Iraq (Gulf),
177; Vietnam, 183; World War II,
175. *See also* Revolution, American
Washington, George, *Chapter 6*; 2, 7,
33, 36, 41, 50, 51, *67*, 73, 97, 99,
105, 107, 112, 114, 115, 127, 136,

137, 138, 140–141, 145, 154, 155,
160, 161, 162, 163, 175, 177
Washington, Martha Custis, 59, 62,
63, 68, 112–115, *113*, 117
Waterhouse, Benjamin, 87
Wead, Doug, 185
Weems, Mason Locke, 68–70, 130
Wellesley College, 180
Wells, Elizabeth, 144, 146
Wesley, Charles, 25–26
Wesley, John, 25–26, 28
Wheaton College, 167
White, Andrew, *19*
White, William, 63, 69, 96, 115, 116,
161, 162, 163
Whitefield, George, *25*, 26–28, 55–
56, 150
Whittingham, William R., 129

William and Mary, College of. *See*
College of William and Mary
Williams, Roger, 9
Wilmer, William Holland, 117
Wilson, Bird, 161–163
Wilson, James, 161–162
Wilson, Woodrow, 69
Winthrop, John, 147, 150
Witherspoon, John, 93
Wollaston, William, 48
Wyman, Jane, 173
Wythe, George, 36

Yale College and University, *14*, 49,
56, 116, 157, 176, 180, 183
Yale Law School, 180

Zeoli, William ("Billy"), 166